T0044336

THE
IMPOSSIBLE
ART

THE
IMPOSSIBLE
ART

Adventures in Opera

MATTHEW AUCOIN

FARRAR, STRAUS AND GIROUX

NEW YORK

Farrar, Straus and Giroux
120 Broadway, New York 10271

Owing to limitations of space, all acknowledgments for permission
to reprint previously published material can be found on page 299.

Library of Congress Cataloging-in-Publication Data
Names: Aucoin, Matthew, 1990– author.
Title: The impossible art : Adventures in opera / Matthew Aucoin.
Other titles: Adventures in opera
Description: First edition. | New York : Farrar, Straus and Giroux, 2021. |
    Includes bibliographical references.
Identifiers: LCCN 2021032228 | ISBN 9780374175382 (hardcover)
Subjects: LCSH: Opera. | Operas—Analysis, appreciation. | Aucoin, Matthew,
    1990– . Eurydice.
Classification: LCC ML1700 .A9 2021 | DDC 782.1—dc23
LC record available at https://lccn.loc.gov/2021032228

Designed by Gretchen Achilles

Our books may be purchased in bulk for promotional, educational,
or business use. Please contact your local bookseller or the Macmillan
Corporate and Premium Sales Department at 1-800-221-7945, extension 5442,
or by email at MacmillanSpecialMarkets@macmillan.com.

www.fsgbooks.com
www.twitter.com/fsgbooks • www.facebook.com/fsgbooks

3   5   7   9   10   8   6   4

This book is for my family:
my parents, Carol and Don, who taught me
to read and to listen,

and my sister, Christine, who doesn't like opera,
but who makes an exception for Mozart.

Contents

CONTENTS

Preface

Opera is impossible and always has been. Impossibility is baked into the art form's foundations. The operatic ideal, an imagined union of all the human senses and all art forms—music, drama, dance, poetry, painting—is itself an impossibility. But this impossibility is productive and even liberating: all of opera's bizarre and beautiful fruits, its cathartic embodiments of the extremes of human psychology, its carnivalesque excesses, its improbable moments of intimate revelation, stem from artists' ongoing search for this permanently elusive alchemy. The art form's first practitioners, in seventeenth-century Italy, strove to re-create the effect of ancient Greek drama, which of course they had never *heard*, and which no one can be sure was sung in the first place. Nearly four centuries later, Karlheinz Stockhausen wrote a twenty-nine-hour operatic cycle titled *Licht* (*Light*), which he called an "eternal spiral" with "neither a beginning nor an end."

These are not merely ambitious endeavors. They are impossible ones. And this impossibility, this perpetual sense that the real thing is just out of reach, is opera's lifeblood. If its essence weren't unrealizable, the art form wouldn't exist at all.

But never in living memory has opera felt impossible in the way it does now.

I'm writing this from the farmhouse where I live with my

husband, Clay, in southern Vermont. We are deep into the barren doldrums of the winter of 2020–21. A foot of snow fell here the other night, heightening the sense that the world is stuck in an eerie, enforced hibernation. The composer in me feels lucky to live in a place where such stillness is possible: on the country roads where I go for my daily run, I'm as likely to encounter a herd of deer as another human being. But I have also never felt so distant from live music, from the nourishing symbiosis of performing and appreciating the performances of others. Around here, I couldn't tell you where the nearest—no doubt shuttered—music venue is, even a coffee shop with an open-mic night, never mind a concert hall or an opera house.

A year ago, I was relishing the sublime desert clarity of winter in Southern California as I conducted the world premiere of my opera *Eurydice* at the Los Angeles Opera. I wrote *Eurydice* in collaboration with the playwright Sarah Ruhl between 2016 and 2019, and the LA production was the long-awaited first chance to bring our efforts to life; as of this writing, the opera is also slated for production at New York's Metropolitan Opera in the fall of 2021. I was proud of every note of *Eurydice*—I wouldn't have said that of my previous operas—and throughout the two months I spent in LA, I woke up every day eager to share it with as many people as possible.

Eurydice's first production was not entirely free of behind-the-scenes drama: practically every member of our stellar cast fell mysteriously ill at some point during the process, and as a result, nearly every performance was preceded by hours of nail-biting about whether this or that principal singer would feel well enough to take the stage. Danielle de Niese, our star soprano, suffered from a persistent cough; Barry Banks, our stratospherically agile principal tenor, had a bad bout of laryngitis; and Rod Gilfry, a veteran baritone who's usually sturdy and imperturbable as a redwood, was plagued by a cold that lingered for weeks. Nobody thought much of it at the time. Opera singers are notoriously prone to colds and the flu, and since their careers depend on the faultless functioning of two temperamental bands of muscle tissue within the larynx, they can be forgiven for their hypersensitivity (even if it does, at times, verge on hypochondria). Though this barrage of inexplicable maladies was stressful, it didn't feel so far outside the norm for a midwinter production of a grand opera. And hey, we made it through every performance, even if it was by the skin of our teeth.

But from my current vantage point—the snowbound, black-and-white hush of the Green Mountains—the whole experience of *Eurydice*'s first production seems like a dream that I keep mixing up with reality, a memory from a past life or parallel universe. It doesn't quite compute that throughout February 2020, even as news of a newly discovered, rapidly spreading coronavirus grew bleaker by the day, audiences of nearly three thousand people continued to gather night after night in the auditorium of the Dorothy Chandler Pavilion for the singular communion that is live opera. In the pit, the orchestra and I crammed together to form one sweaty, subliminal sound machine. Onstage, the soloists sang in each other's faces with spittle-spraying vehemence. The audience coughed cheerfully and continuously, as opera audiences do. The cast and I hugged at our curtain calls, and celebrated afterward at crowded bars. Now, after eleven months in a sepia-tone quarantine, every aspect of the *Eurydice* experience seems as fantastical, in its Technicolor vividness, as a memory of Oz.

After our last performance, I flew home to New York, where Clay and I shared an apartment with our friend, the director Zack Winokur. The virus was on everyone's mind, but in Trump's

America, it was hardly the only potential source of anxiety in our polluted informational ether, and the threat still felt pretty remote.

A couple of weeks later, however, the distant alarm bells got louder, and the halfhearted precautions we'd all been following—the elbow bumps, "don't touch your face," and so on—suddenly seemed hilariously ineffective. Abstract unease curdled overnight into panic, and the world creaked to an unpracticed halt. In such a moment, performing artists were anything but "essential," as nurses and grocery store workers were; we were, instead, suddenly a public health liability. I'm sure I was far from the only musician who detected the metallic whiff of some unknown anesthetic being released into the air. Our whole field was being lowered into a medically induced coma.

Even before the onset of the COVID-19 pandemic, I wanted to write a book celebrating opera's generative impossibilities. But I wasn't sure when, if ever, I'd manage to step off the merry-go-round of musical work—composing, performing, traveling—long enough to gather my thoughts. When the pandemic took hold, eighteen months' worth of performances evaporated from my calendar, and in-progress commissions were pushed back a year or more.

Though this exile from my usual practice was (and remains) intensely dispiriting, I realized it also afforded me a window like none other in my lifetime to write down why I love this maddening, outlandish, impossible art form, and what I think it's capable of at its best. To borrow the title of a great opera by Kaija Saariaho and Amin Maalouf, this book is full of *l'amour de loin*—love from afar.

There's something to be said for distance, for loving from afar: there's a reason that Jaufré, Saariaho's troubadour protagonist, perfects the art of longing only when he's worlds away from his imagined beloved, Clémence. (When Jaufré makes the mistake of trying to visit Clémence, he dies. Some love affairs, like some art forms, are meant to remain impossible.) In the same vein, if I may channel Jaufré's idealism, I think there's a strong argument to be made for getting to know opera "from afar," in a setting other than the opera house.

When I was growing up in the suburbs of Boston, I hardly ever attended live operatic performances. I got to know the art form mainly through scores and recordings, thanks in large part to a nearby public library that had an extensive collection. Throughout elementary and middle school, whenever my mom was willing to drive me, I'd ransack the library's shelves and stock up on as many scores and CDs as I could carry.

I immersed myself in opera the same way I immersed myself in books: operas, like the young-adult fiction I was reading at the time, felt to me like interior adventures rather than extravagant public spectacles. I didn't associate opera with overpriced tickets or ladies in fur coats or venomously picky aficionados. Opera was pure *sound*, wild and lush and improbably beautiful sound. And opera taught me that music, a medium that already obsessed me, could be channeled as a vivid means of storytelling.

We performing artists tend to insist on the primacy of the live experience. This is partly because live performances *do*, of course, have many unique properties, but it's also—let's face it—in part because our livelihoods depend on them. Putting aside the latter consideration for a moment, I'd argue that the in-person experience of opera is not always the ideal gateway drug to an appreciation of the art form. The atmosphere of the opera house, and its many rituals, can have a double-edged effect. If you're not already an opera fan, the opera-house experience might seem *impressive*, but being impressed is not the same thing as falling in love, and the theater's many trappings might also obscure the opera at hand. (Think of the thick frame of gilt that surrounds the Metropolitan Opera's stage. It seems almost engineered to swallow any opera that dares to wander into its gaping gullet.)

From outside, many opera houses look forbidding and ornate, part Masonic temple and part courthouse. Once you make it into the lobby, you might find the audience's more seasoned operagoers to be an intimidating bunch: at intermission, they're likely to hiss their devastating assessment of the performance by that evening's leading lady, who, if she keeps singing the way she's singing now, will have *ruined herself* within a few years, *just you wait.* If you're sitting in a cheap seat, the orchestra might sound distant and muted. How could such an experience possibly compare to hearing Frank Ocean croon in your ears on your headphones back home?

I sympathize with people who feel this way. It makes perfect sense to me that the *social* experience of live opera might seem fun only the way an overpriced multicourse dinner or an elaborate themed dress-up party is fun. It's worth the expense and the effort maybe once a year, tops.

But if you're someone who savors the experience of reading books, or watching movies, or listening to music of whatever genre from the comfort of home, I want to invite you to think of opera as another art form that can be experienced this way. (And then, once you've established a basic familiarity with it, you're likely to develop a taste for hearing it live.) Think of this book as a portal into your own inner opera house.

Over the past year, distanced for the first time in a decade from the daily grind of rehearsing, performing, coaching, and casting, I've felt closer than ever to my original, innocent experience of opera, that early love from afar. I've been reminded that operas can be approached from many angles. They can be treated as musical texts, works of theater, works of literature, immersive at-home audio experiences, historical documents, drag pageants, horror movies, Freudian psychodramas, even as a complexly vicarious form of primal scream therapy.

In this book, I want to invite you *inside* a wide array of operas written across more than four centuries. My aim is to close-read these operas, to take a deep dive into what makes them tick and what they have to tell us. This book is, in a way, a musical autobiography: from Verdi to Monteverdi, Adès to Birtwistle to Czernowin, every composer considered here has nourished my own work in some way. (It's hardly comprehensive, though: Wagner's operas, for example, are close to my heart, but Wagner barely features here. That guy gets enough airtime elsewhere.)

I also want to offer a practitioner's view of the art form: these essays draw extensively on my experience as composer, conductor, pianist, and vocal coach. My hope is that you might gain a sense of how an opera's creators experience a piece as it comes to life, both as it's being written and as it's brought to the stage. To that end, I'll touch on the creative process for my operas *Crossing* and *Eurydice*, not because I want to make grand claims on behalf of either piece, but rather to offer a window into the many challenges of opera-making.

This isn't a book that needs to be read strictly from beginning to end. If you're interested in the nature of the working relationship between composer and librettist, you might jump to the chapter on Igor Stravinsky and W. H. Auden's collaboration on *The Rake's Progress*. If you're a Shakespeare buff, you might want to dive into the chapter on Giuseppe Verdi's fruitful lifelong Shakespeare fixation. If you're drawn to mythology and magic, you might check out the chapter on the long history of Orpheus and Eurydice operas.

The notion of a productive impossibility—a goal that is both foundational and unreachable—recurs throughout the book. In a moment when so much in our world feels impossible in the bad sense, it has been liberating for me to look again at an art form that will *always* be impossible, and whose intrinsic impossibility is somehow also an inextinguishable life force.

THE
IMPOSSIBLE
ART

ONE

A Field Guide to the Impossible

Opera is another planet, and if you haven't spent much time breathing its air, you might find it helpful, before visiting, to have a sense of its atmosphere and of the inscrutable natural laws that govern it. On this planet, apparent opposites—internal and external, sense and nonsense, pain and pleasure—tend to reverse themselves, and violent pressure systems have a habit of forming at a moment's notice. Before we look more closely at individual operas, let's get a feel for the art form's terrain.

COLLISION AND TRANSFORMATION

Opera's basic ingredients are among the most primal human needs: song and narrative. By combining the two, opera gives voice to sensations that are either too raw or too subliminal for words alone, and incarnates them in specific individuals—people with names and faces in concrete dramatic and historical situations—in a way that music on its own cannot. It is a fusion of the too-big and the too-small, the unnamable and the named.

At the core of the art form are the improbable feats of strength, stamina, and self-magnification that the voice is capable of achieving in the service of cathartic expression. The orchestral music that surrounds the voice and buoys it up is equally important: the atmosphere, in opera, is made not of air but of music. And since, in music, many voices speaking at once can be illuminating rather than chaotic, opera has the singular ability to manifest multiple individuals' inner states simultaneously, and to embrace and absorb the contradictions that this entails. As a result, I think opera can, at its best, spark a liberating uncertainty—call it negative capability—in the listener.

There's no such thing as a wholly reliable objective definition of opera, but my favorite is one that I've honed together with my colleagues in the American Modern Opera Company (AMOC, pronounced "a-muck," as in "to run amok"). I cofounded AMOC with Zack Winokur a few years ago in part to figure out what opera is and what it means to us; the idea was to gather some of our most inventive colleagues—singers, instrumentalists, dancers—into the petri dish of an artists' collective, and see what sort of strange, explosive work might result.

The AMOC definition of opera is this: opera is the medium in which art forms collide and transform one another.

Opera is a composite medium made of multiple constituent art forms, each of which undergoes a mysterious chemical transformation through contact with the others. In any given opera, the drama might seem blunt or absurd if it were divorced from the music; the musical logic, were it detached from the dramatic situation, would seem to be full of gaps; and the words, considered as poetry, would often be merely bad. Put these things together, however, and in a strong opera each element is capable of transcending itself.

Because of this complex interdependence, each ingredient needs to manifest a certain openness and volatility: each one must have the potential to be transformed through contact with other media. As a composer, you have to be able to intuit what kinds of stories would be enhanced by music, not deflated by it; to find a musical language dynamic and fluid enough to serve the drama; to know what kind of poetic text will function effectively as dry kindling that the music can set ablaze. The impossible Wagnerian dream is to combine all these elements into the Gesamtkunstwerk, the "total work of art." I've come to believe that it's not especially helpful—in fact, it risks feeling totalitarian—to treat all of opera's constituent elements as a single entity. It feels healthier, to me, to say that opera's elements should never quite *merge*, but they should aspire to transform one another through collision.

With collision-transformation in mind as opera's essential feature, plenty of apparent non-operas feel distinctly operatic to me (and vice versa). The pressurized silences of late Beckett plays, for instance, make for an intensely musical atmosphere: every word that is spoken must contend with the oppressive weight of the surrounding silence, and the resulting friction is quintessentially operatic. Counterintuitive as it might seem, certain silent films also resemble operas, since the music in such films functions not just as occasional seasoning or commentary but as a through-line, a kind of mirror of the visible action.

One of the most operatic non-operas I know is *A Study on Effort*, an hour-long duet between the dancer Bobbi Jene Smith and the violinist Keir GoGwilt (both AMOC members). As its title suggests, this piece is an inquiry into the extremes of physical effort, and it requires a consummate steadiness and stamina of dancer and musician alike. Both performers might be required to sustain a single gesture—Smith maintaining a strenuous and delicate physical pose, GoGwilt tracing a slowly rising violin tremolo—for many minutes, beyond what seems physically possible. Sometimes the two performers enact their "efforts" separately, sometimes together; sometimes they move on parallel tracks, and sometimes one artist will literally cradle the other in their arms. The differences between dance and music are visible at every moment, but the two art forms seem at various times to be pushing against and supporting each other. Even though there's no singing in *A Study on Effort*, this mutually transformative encounter between artistic media strikes me as the concentrated essence of what opera is capable of.

THE BODY AS MICROPHONE

Every operatic artist has probably been asked at some point what the difference is between opera and "musical theater," a term that I wish were a broad one but that, in American English, has come to mean just one thing: Broadway musicals.

The question is trickier than it appears. It's clear that opera and Broadway, in their mainstream incarnations, long ago evolved into distinct genres: if you compare familiar exemplars of each— say, *La bohème* and *Rent*—the differences between them are probably more obvious than their similarities. But is there a clear, readily definable distinction? If so, what is it?

Bad answers abound.

Answer #1: on Broadway, the singers are amplified, and in opera, they're not.

Two decades into the twenty-first century, this is plainly untrue. Plenty of opera composers, working across a wide spectrum of musical idioms, require their performers to be amplified—including composers as unlike one another as John Adams, Kaija Saariaho, Chaya Czernowin, and David T. Little.

Answer #2: Broadway is "pop music," and opera is "classical music."

Definitions of "pop" and "classical" music are notoriously elusive, and rarely worth the effort of pursuing them. One of the more consistent features of classical music is the presence of a notated score, and that distinction doesn't apply here, since Broadway musicals use scores too. Opera has also, at many times in its history, functioned as a popular art form; and there are numerous American operas whose musical vocabulary overlaps heavily with Broadway's. So the presumed pop-classical binary, however concrete it might seem in many individual cases, isn't universally helpful.

Answer #3: Broadway makes money, and opera loses money.

Well . . . it's actually pretty hard to argue with this one.

My own admittedly imperfect answer is this: opera focuses attention on the innate power of the human body, whereas in contemporary Broadway musicals, every sound is created with the *assumption* that it will be electronically processed. Opera's materials are organic; Broadway's are deep-fried. This distinction is closely *linked* to the matter of amplification, but it can't be reduced to the question of whether microphones are or are not present in a given circumstance. The issue runs deeper than that, to the question of how the performers in each idiom have been trained to produce sound.

The musical techniques required to perform most operas implicitly assume that electronic amplification doesn't exist. These techniques, which predate the invention of the microphone by many centuries, originated in the desire to amplify the body's expressive power. The assumption, in opera, is that each performer is personally responsible for filling the performance space with sound. Every apprentice opera singer is required to learn how to use her own skull as an amplifying device; she has to be able to manipulate muscles in her mouth and throat that most of us never even notice are there. She will learn that the sound of her voice as *she* hears it, ricocheting around her skull, will be very different from the sound that reaches the listener a hundred feet away. It's a mysterious and maddening crucible.

If she knows she'll be singing into a microphone, on the other hand, she is likely to sing very differently. The microphone is not just a means of making the voice louder; it's also a sophisticated instrument in its own right, a tool that among other things invites the singer to sing *softer*. She won't have to give her sound nearly as much physical support, or to focus on projecting outward into the performance space. The microphone takes care of all that, and invites the singer to focus her energy elsewhere.

For more than a hundred years, the microphone's possibilities have proven irresistible, and the many singing techniques that emerged over the course of the twentieth century are all fundamentally predicated on the existence of amplification. Tom Waits's gravelly confidences, Ella Fitzgerald's crooning, Animal Collective's ecstatic, reverb-drenched shouts—all these vocal idioms would be inconceivable without the artist's direct engagement with technologies of amplification. The methods of singing that you're likely to hear on Broadway—speak-singing, belting, etc.—are more closely related to these recently developed techniques than to pre-electronic ones.

The opera scholar and conductor Will Crutchfield has spoken perceptively about this difference, comparing it to the way public speaking changed with the advent of radio and TV. To paraphrase Crutchfield's analogy, in the pre-TV age, a would-be public figure—someone running for political office, for example—had to learn how to speak with sufficient power and resonance to fill a large hall: you had to be sure the voter sitting in the last row heard every word. On TV, none of that is necessary: the effective politician is not the one with the most powerful voice but rather the one who sounds relaxed and conversational, who might as well be having a beer with you. In the early days of TV, viewers might have noticed a glaring contrast between older politicians, who were accustomed to thundering their way through their speeches, and younger, savvier ones, who were native to this new medium. Put a TV-illiterate politician in front of a camera, and the audience will wonder why they're being shouted at. As Crutchfield notes, even though supporting the voice so that it projects in an operatic way is "essentially an act of physical control," if you do so on TV, "you sound like you're out of control. You sound like you're getting inappropriately emotional. Your listeners are likelier to be embarrassed than persuaded." (Anyone who has ever seen an opera singer in the wrong context, broadly gesticulating into a too-close camera or steamrolling a jazz standard with high-decibel schmaltz, will know exactly what this looks like.)

These differences don't constitute a hierarchy: one kind of singing, or speaking, isn't automatically better or capable of greater nuance than the other. But many opera lovers, both professionals and aficionados, viscerally fear the incursion of amplification into opera's turf. The understandable concern is that since *anyone* can sound powerful if they sing into a microphone, young would-be singers might lose the desire to undergo the rigorous training that is required to single-handedly project the voice into a four-thousand-seat auditorium.

It's a manifestation of a familiar contemporary anxiety: technological improvements will make us forget our most treasured, hardest-won skills; we will grow weaker as a species; the inevitable outcome is rot, decline, destruction. The great mezzo-soprano Marilyn Horne, in a 1992 interview with the *Chicago Tribune*, described the issue in apocalyptic terms: "The microphones are coming, I can feel it in my bones . . . When they come, that will be the beginning of the end. Who will really learn to sing? There will be no need to." (Horne was admittedly speaking from a privileged position, as the possessor of a voice so potent she wouldn't have needed amplification if she were guesting at a Motörhead concert.)

I sympathize with this concern, but I can't say I share it. The invention of cars did not bring about the end of walking, never mind running. The human impulses both to test the body's limits and to master virtuosic means of creative expression are deep-seated ones, and the decline that Horne predicted thirty years ago has not come to pass. There are many things wrong with the field of opera in the early 2020s, but a lack of dedicated young singers is not one of them. Plenty of young artists still sense how empowering it can be to train the body to achieve superhuman feats of projection and resonance.

And I don't think there's a contradiction between wanting to nurture the pedagogical tradition of teaching people to sing *as if* amplification didn't exist, and also wanting to make use of all the possibilities that are available to us through electronic manipulation of sound. (How could we not make use of them? The genie won't go back in the bottle.) Opera composers who amplify their singers take a lot of flak from self-proclaimed purists, but such composers rarely use electronics just to make the music louder. They do so because such methods can yield their own rich, orchestra-like palette of possibilities.

In fact, some composers use electronic means to further *focus* attention on the body, to allow the listener to more clearly perceive intimate and infinitesimally virtuosic acts of vocalization. Sometimes, as in the music of Chaya Czernowin (whose work I'll consider in detail later in this book), this takes the form of unconventional vocal and instrumental techniques that range from extreme delicacy to extreme ferocity. Sometimes, as in John Adams's operas, the performers are gently amplified so that the composer can make use of the orchestra's full range of coloristic possibilities without drowning out the singers. In both cases, the essential act of channeling the body's energy into organically produced sound is, it seems to me, in good health.

LAWS OF GRAVITY

Opera is governed by strict, unwritten, irrational laws. These laws are diabolically hard to predict or pin down, but they enforce themselves implacably, like the edicts of the Queen of Hearts in *Alice in Wonderland*. I think these laws are best articulated as reversals: reversals between what works in life and what works onstage, between communication through speech and through song.

Opera's first law of gravity: the external is the internal. Opera is a highly extroverted art form—sometimes grotesquely so—but what we perceive as abundant exteriority is always the manifestation of an inner state, whether individual or collective. There is no such thing as objectivity in opera; we are always inside someone's head, either an individual's or a crowd's.

There's an important distinction here between opera and spoken theater. In plays, as in everyday life, the actors' lines emerge from silence, and are surrounded by it. In opera, however, the surrounding atmosphere is made not of silence but of music, and music is puppyishly incapable of remaining objective. (Cinema emerges directly from opera in this sense: films' interstitial spaces are almost always filled with music.) Even the sections of operas during which no one sings—overtures, interludes, etc.— give voice to interior states, even if we are not sure exactly *whose*. The intermezzo in Pietro Mascagni's *Cavalleria rusticana* (1890) is the boiling-over of an entire community's grief and frustration. The overture to Mozart's *Le nozze di Figaro* (1786) captures both the giddy, bubbling energy of the characters' conflicting desires and the sense that a playful spirit is hovering just overhead, a mischievous Ariel- or Puck-like presence that makes itself felt, in flashes, through the orchestra.

Total objectivity is surely impossible in other media, too. But opera composers—unlike, say, documentary filmmakers—never had a prayer of creating the illusion of objectivity in the first place. This is both a constraint and a liberation.

Opera's second law of gravity: in opera, all speech is dream speech, whether it wants to be or not. The dreamlike and the surreal are opera's daily bread, whereas everyday speech acts, like making small talk or ordering takeout, have a strong tendency to go wonky. The more normal a speech act would be in real life, the more likely it is to sound absurd, or unintentionally funny, in opera. A world whose atmosphere is made of music is automatically a dreamworld, and within this world, what is communicated tends to have the unguardedness, the childlike directness, of dream speech. It makes perfect sense, in opera, to lucidly reveal long-buried traumas, to confess to shameful desires, to utter curses, prayers, prophecies, wordless primal cries. If they're done right, a listener can take all these things very seriously.

An earnest, in-depth debate about health care, on the other hand, would make no sense at all. There is a thriving YouTube subgenre of musicians setting speeches by public figures (often politicians) to music, in some cases simply playing an instrument along with the unfortunate orator's speech patterns, a note for every syllable, carefully tracing the voice's implied pitches as it rises and falls. This is usually more than sufficient to make the speaker sound ridiculous. Why? Because in music's parallel universe, to talk about tax policy or congressional gridlock is to spew incomprehensible nonsense. Since these utterances are unlikely to have inspired music in the first place, they sound ridiculous when *set* to music.

John Adams and Peter Sellars's opera *Doctor Atomic* (2005) provides an illuminating example of this gravitational law, because of the strong contrast between the piece's dreamlike elements and its more prosaic ones. The opera is a complex, collage-like critique of the history of the Manhattan Project; its action takes place in the days leading up to the "Trinity" test of the atomic bomb, and long stretches of the libretto consist of direct transcripts of conversations among scientists at the Los Alamos

National Laboratory. (I had the memorable experience of conducting *Atomic* in the Santa Fe Opera's stunning outdoor theater in 2018, in a new Sellars production that was built specifically for Santa Fe. Sellars wisely left the back of the stage wide-open so the audience could see the lights of Los Alamos glimmering on the horizon.)

As is often the case in Sellars's work, the men in *Doctor Atomic* are notably less empathetic, and less in touch with the world around them, than the women are. The women—Kitty Oppenheimer and Pasqualita, a Pueblo woman working as the Oppenheimers' maid—communicate exclusively through poems: Charles Baudelaire, Muriel Rukeyser, a Pueblo lullaby. The men, by contrast, spout scientific jargon, bicker about military policy, and fret about how much weight they're gaining. Only J. Robert Oppenheimer, Doctor Atomic himself, moves freely between these two registers. Among the scientists, he is capable of perversely antipoetic language ("the extreme pressures and temperatures reached in the interior of our explosion will not be high enough to fuse the hydrogen with either nitrogen or helium"), but when he's finally left alone with the bomb, his monstrous masterpiece, he recites one of John Donne's Holy Sonnets in a moving act of prayer and self-flagellation.

In the second act, during the tense countdown before the bomb's test, the contrast between the men and the women becomes extreme. The two women, Cassandra-like in their prophetic skepticism about the coming detonation, sing excerpts of Rukeyser's poetry to music that seethes with a hallucinatory intensity. It's potent stuff; I remember going into a kind of trance as we performed these passages.

But the trance dissipated whenever we returned to the male-dominated world of the scientists. The men in *Doctor Atomic* are myopic, self-important, dangerously capable of self-deception. One wonders, from the beginning, why exactly they are *singing* their lines, which so clearly belong to the register of spoken conversation. The answer is that, for the purposes of *Atomic's* creators, it's helpfully unflattering to force these technocrats to sing. *Okay*, Sellars seems to be saying, *you can* talk *about letting millions of people die by pressing a button, but try* singing *it*. A statement's singability, for Sellars, is a test of its spiritual veracity. And as he knows, these lab transcripts fail the test. To sing them is in part to parody them: Adams's music inflates the scientists' utterances, which makes them more readily deflatable. (Remember those YouTube satirists.)

After a while, it seems almost cruel to force these poor schmucks to keep singing. We could tell from the outset that they're fundamentally unmusical souls.

This dynamic is a constant in opera's dreamworld: some speech acts disintegrate and lose all possibility of being taken seriously; others, which would sound absurd if spoken, take on a life-and-death urgency. So, in creating an operatic libretto, the question that should underlie every word is not "Would a person *really* say this?" but rather "Does this *need to be sung*?"

The third law of gravity: opera transforms pain into pleasure. In opera, happiness is not only a sad song but also frequently a song of madness or blind, bloodthirsty rage. The whole art form depends on music's power to make pain bearable, or even pleasurable, both to the listener and the participating artists: as W. H. Auden put it, "The singer may be playing the part of a deserted bride who is about to kill herself, but we feel quite certain as we listen that not only we but the singer herself is having a wonderful time."

The ramifications of this power are complex and ethically murky. The line between empathy and mere voyeurism is an unstable one, and part of the uneasy pleasure of listening to opera arises from a pervasive, subliminal uncertainty: Am I empathizing with my fellow human beings, or am I just voyeuristically relishing someone else's pain?

This ambiguity is a salient feature of opera's foundational story, the myth of Orpheus and Eurydice. As we'll explore in the next chapter, music's power to transform pain into pleasure is the Orpheus myth's central subject. But it's not clear whether Orpheus wields this power for good or evil. Orpheus's backward look is opera's original sin: by looking back, he subconsciously chooses the pleasures of lamentation over the possibility of saving his wife. And though this dynamic is at its most mercilessly distilled in the Orpheus story, it's present to some degree in every opera.

OPERA IN OUR WORLD

Since I'm a composer, the aspect of opera that feels most real to me is the inner work of writing music: the labor of crafting a vocal line or lovingly coloring in a scene's orchestration is tangible to me in a way that even live performances aren't. But I want to take a moment to zoom the camera out from the composer's studio to consider the confusing, contradictory position that opera occupies in twenty-first-century America.

America has never quite trusted opera. It was brought over from *Europe*, after all, by Americans who had the gall to find homegrown entertainments inadequate. Opera in America is a kind of imported cheese, an especially pungent and funky one; the fact of its provenance marks it off as unforgivably highfalutin. No matter that the poor cheese, in itself, has little to do with these connotations; no matter that it isn't viewed with the same suspicion where it was first produced (in German cities, even small ones, the local opera house is usually a civic landmark, barely distinguishable from their libraries or fire stations); and no matter that opera is now cultivated all over the world, so that it doesn't really make sense anymore to think of it as a foreign agent. None of this makes a difference in the American imagination. The word "opera" still automatically summons the mental image of its supposed patrons: mustachioed Gilded Age financiers and ladies in pearls with opera glasses, like Margaret Dumont in the Marx Brothers' *A Night at the Opera*.

These stubborn associations surround the art form with a toxic cloud of paradox. Opera is somehow both elitist and enfeebled, an over-the-top spectacle and a quaint curiosity, forbiddingly inaccessible and plainly ridiculous. Looked at one way, opera is the clearest possible manifestation of material waste and excess, a kind of circus for the superrich. From another perspective, it's a humble old classical art form on life support, staggering on its last legs from one dwindling NEA grant to the next.

The first of these two ideas is clearly in need of an update: it's been well over a century since opera was the medium capable of delivering the showiest, most gratifyingly excessive public pageants. Cinema, Broadway, professional sports, stadium-scale pop concerts, the more-operatic-than-opera phenomenon that is the American megachurch—all these have long since replaced opera as prime appeasers of the human need for gladiatorial spectacle. The notion of opera as a central gathering place for society's movers and shakers is a dated one, too. Megacorporations looking to show off their buying power or reward top earners are far likelier to buy a box at a Bruce Springsteen concert or the Super Bowl than at their local opera house; and Silicon Valley, the locus of latter-day robber barons, has displayed a notable lack of interest in any form of classical music.

The latter idea—that opera is either about to expire or already has, and persists only in a kind of zombie state—is puzzling to me. When I started out as an opera-house pianist and vocal coach, I remember feeling a cognitive dissonance between the pessimistic diagnoses of many older colleagues (to hear them tell it, we were surely living in opera's end-times) and the reality I saw around me. In my first few years as a professional musician, I met and worked with hundreds of formidably gifted young singers, some of whom were fellow students and some of whom are a generation older: Lawrence Brownlee, Lisette Oropesa, Paul Appleby, Julia Bullock, Anthony Roth Costanzo, Erin Morley, Angela Meade, Russell Thomas, Joshua Hopkins, Davóne Tines, J'Nai Bridges, Michael Fabiano, John Holiday, Ying Fang, and many others. And it's not just singers: an incomplete, off-the-cuff list of fellow youngish American composers with an opera fixation would have to include Missy Mazzoli, David Hertzberg, Dylan Mattingly, Kate Soper, Ellen Reid, and Nico Muhly; gifted composers like Jessie Montgomery are now setting their sights on the art form. Why does an ecosystem that's brimming with such an abundance of talent have such a sickly self-image?

I don't have an all-purpose cure for opera's cultural dysmorphia. But I've come to believe that opera has the potential to be a strong countercultural force rather than a feeble mainstream one. And I think the art form is healthier when its practitioners think of it in the former sense, as a field of resistance and experimentation.

To be sure, this wasn't always opera's function. At various

points in its history, opera *was* a mainstream, commercially viable endeavor, and opera fans who lament the art form's supposed fallenness are really, I think, mourning the disappearance of the days when New York reporters would gather on the docks to greet the steamship carrying Puccini. These days, new operas are unlikely to unite the hearts of a weary nation, as legend tells us Verdi's *Nabucco* (1842) did; we composers are no longer regularly carried home from the opera house on the shoulders of a cheering, torch-bearing throng.

As tempting as these glamorous perks might seem, I think opera should embrace its apparent marginality, its ability to fly under the cultural radar. To operate within the cultural mainstream is also to accept a set of sometimes-suffocating pressures and restrictions, and in periods when opera *has* been primarily a popular art form, new operas tended to follow tried-and-true formulas, as Broadway shows do today; revolutionaries like Wagner were surpassingly rare. Back in the supposed glory days of opera in America, a shockingly small handful of operas—most of them by Verdi or Puccini—counted as surefire hits, and these select few tended to crowd out other repertoire and stifle the appetite for new work.

Today, by contrast, I think opera is best thought of as a vast, capacious category, like "fiction." A two-page short story, a pulpy page-turner, a three-thousand-page epic—the umbrella term "fiction" embraces all three. In the same way, the field of opera, taken broadly, now encompasses luminous, playful chamber works by Kate Soper and sprawling epics by Dylan Mattingly; Du Yun's avant-garde thrash metal and Salvatore Sciarrino's gossamer shadow plays. Opera's position just under the radar of the cultural mainstream has made it messier, weirder, more polyphonic, and more diverse.

Any genuine diversity of creative voices within the field, however, is still a long way off. For too long, diversity in American opera's mainstream meant diversity only of *performers*, not composers, conductors, stage directors, or influential administrators. Throughout the history of opera in this country, a disproportionately vast percentage of our greatest singers have been Black, but until recently, Black artists could become stars almost exclusively by serving as mouthpieces of the same nineteenth-century chestnuts everyone else was singing. Just a few decades ago, a major singer like Jessye Norman bluntly defined success as the power to sing the music of European men: in an interview, Norman expressed her gratitude to pioneering artists like Marian Anderson and Leontyne Price, whose work "made it possible for me to say, 'I will sing French opera' or 'I will sing German opera,' instead of being told 'You will sing *Porgy and Bess*.'"

Norman's attitude does, thank goodness, feel dated today. The most urgent question currently facing the art form is surely not "How do we expand access to the German Romantics so that people from all backgrounds have the chance to sing Wagner?" but rather "What creators haven't we heard from, and what might they have to tell us?"

The refusal to ask the latter question—a disastrous failure of imagination on the part of opera's movers and shakers—had a deadening, emaciating effect on American opera for many years. Those dreary decades of the mid-twentieth century, when so many new American operas were either bloated neo-Romantic pageants or studiously spiky twelve-tone dissertations! How much richer the century would have been for the art form if more opera companies had taken an interest in the sectors of American musical life where stuff was *really happening*! Can you imagine the operas Duke Ellington or (even more enticingly) his consummately gifted arranger Billy Strayhorn might have written, or, a couple of decades later, the operas that might have emerged from the creative ferment of the composers of the Chicago-based Association for the Advancement of Creative Musicians (AACM)?

If we treat opera in its broadest, most welcoming sense—as the medium where art forms collide and transform one another—I think we'll find that this strangest of art forms, a mere infant at four centuries old, is just getting started.

TWO

Primal Loss

Orpheus and Eurydice
in Opera

The stories we call myths are those that have rung true for so long that they've transcended the divide between history and fiction. Of course the events recounted in these tales of gods and monsters didn't "really happen"; rather, as the poet Jorie Graham put it, "they are, at all times, happening." These stories repeat themselves within us.

For musicians, the most inescapable myth of all is the story of Orpheus and Eurydice, a tale that serves as music's foundational legend, its primal self-justification and self-glorification. The story's basic events, for anyone who needs a refresher, are as follows: Orpheus, a singer of superhuman beauty and power, is in love with Eurydice. On their wedding day, Eurydice is bitten by a snake, and dies. The grief-stricken Orpheus goes to the underworld, where he sings a plea to Hades, the god of death, to give Eurydice a second chance at life. Hades is so moved by Orpheus's music that he agrees. But there's one condition: as

Eurydice follows Orpheus back to the land of the living, he must not look back to make sure she's there. If he does, Eurydice will die a second death. As they walk toward the sunlight, of course Orpheus can't resist. He looks back. Eurydice vanishes. Orpheus returns alone to the world above.

This story continues to resonate because, I think, of its brutally honest admixture of hope and despair. Music can conquer death itself—of course it can—but not for *us*, not for human beings. We aren't worthy of it. We'll always find a way to screw things up.

But the standard reading of the myth as a parable of human frailty, of our inability to control even our most destructive momentary impulses, misses some of the story's darker implications. Even its basic narrative structure betrays that there's more to it than meets the eye. Dramatizations of the story typically begin with Eurydice's death; this is usually followed by a lot of voluptuous lamentation from Orpheus. Then Orpheus goes down to the underworld, where he mourns still more ostentatiously. When Eurydice dies a second time, Orpheus's response is, of course, to sing even more beautiful music. The story's primary events are death → lamentation → failed rescue → death → lamentation. In opera, loss is, almost automatically, an excuse for the catharsis of music-making, but in the Orpheus story, this is the case in an egregiously literal way. This myth has something distressing to tell us about the relationship between life and art, and the perils of narcissism and aestheticism: Orpheus seems more at home singing elegies for Eurydice than he is actually living with her. You can't help but wonder if there is something calculated in that backward glance.

And the figure of Orpheus grows more mysterious the harder you look at him. Is he a mortal or a god, or something in between? In Apollodorus's *Library of Greek Mythology*, Orpheus's mother is identified as the muse Calliope, and his father is, nominally, the Thracian king Oiagros, but this is no sooner stated than it is called into question: "Calliope bore to Oiagros—or really, it is said, to Apollo— . . . Orpheus, who practised the art of singing to the lyre." Orpheus might be at least half-human, but he might also be the son of the sun god. The uncertainty surrounding his parentage captures an ambiguity about the nature of music itself, an art that continues to mystify even its most committed practitioners: What *is* music anyway, and where does it come from? Like Orpheus himself, music often seems, to its devotees, to be both human and more-than-human, in permanently unknowable proportions.

Orpheus's legendary musical prowess, and the aura of mystery that surrounds him, have long made him catnip for musicians. We composers have precious few superheroes, and Orpheus is chief among them; as a colleague of mine put it, he is "our boss." This persistent Orphic fixation has yielded so many Orpheus operas that they practically constitute a genre of their own. These works, from Monteverdi to Glass to Birtwistle, are kaleidoscopically different from one another, but every one of them is forced to confront a few core challenges that are inherent in the myth.

The central challenge—or rather, impossibility—is that Orpheus is required to sing the most beautiful music ever heard, music so sublime that it triumphs over death. This makes a daunting ask of composer and performer alike. There is surely no other story in which a composer, studying the libretto they are about to set to music, will find the stage direction, "And then we hear the most beautiful music ever written."

The depiction of Orpheus and Eurydice's relationship is another crux. We all know who Orpheus is, but Eurydice is a wild card; she can be practically anyone. Some artists treat Eurydice as little more than a ghostly cipher, while others, like the playwright Sarah Ruhl, invent a rich interior world for her. But whoever Eurydice is in a given piece, the nature of her relationship with Orpheus is inevitably laid bare in the scene of Orpheus's backward look. The possible motivations for that gesture are endless, and the composer and librettist must decide what, out of a complex and delicate web of possibilities, ultimately pushes Orpheus over the edge and makes him turn around.

Anyone who adapts this myth must also wrestle with the unsettling way that it blurs the line between pain and pleasure, grief and aesthetic ecstasy. The way a composer engages (or refuses to engage) with this issue can reveal a lot about their priorities. Do they put pressure on this dynamic? Do they give in to it? Or do they simply pretend it's not there?

A Guide to Four Hundred
Years of Orphic Operas

The earliest opera that remains widely known and beloved today is Claudio Monteverdi's *L'Orfeo* (1607), a work of such breathtaking beauty that it has lodged itself in many listeners' minds as the first opera, the cornerstone of the genre. But before *L'Orfeo*, there was *L'Euridice*—or rather, there were two. The first surviving opera is a curious case, a kind of forked tree trunk: a single libretto was set to music almost simultaneously by two composers, and thus ended up as two distinct pieces.

Around 1600, the extraordinary concentration of artistic activity in Florence made the city a fertile ground for interdisciplinary experiments, including new modes of collaboration between poets and musicians. A number of these artists had a quixotic fixation on rediscovering the performance practices of ancient Greek drama—a productive impossibility if ever there was one, since it was no more achievable in late-Renaissance Italy than it is today to establish what performances from two millennia earlier could possibly have sounded like. But this illusory goal yielded real fruit. By pondering the question of how ancient Greek tragedy was performed, and by deciding, in the words of the musicologist John Walter Hill, that it probably "derived its effects from a rhythmically accurate and dramatically emphatic intoning of a poetic text," these artists were really asking themselves what their own values were. Whether they did so consciously or not, they constructed an imaginary ideal in order to effect actual changes.

One of the most successful partnerships forged at this juncture was that of the composer Jacopo Peri and the poet Ottavio Rinuccini, who first worked together on a dramatization of the myth of Apollo and Daphne in 1598. The music for Peri's *Dafne*, which has a strong claim to be the earliest work of art that we would recognize as an opera, is almost entirely lost, but Peri and Rinuccini's next collaboration, a setting of the story of Orpheus and Eurydice, has survived.

The intrigue and confusion surrounding the birth of *Euridice* in 1600 might be taken as an omen for the offstage dramas, the battles of diva contra diva, that would define the business of opera-making for centuries. The composer Giulio Caccini, a rival of Peri's in Florence, participated for a while in the same artistic salon as Peri and Rinuccini. But the salon's patron stopped supporting Caccini in 1595, and over the next few years, Caccini, evidently jealous of Peri and Rinuccini's partnership, tried to undermine Peri's work and claim credit for the development of opera as an art form.

Caccini seems to have been a singularly unsavory character, one whose influence in Florence was both musical and political. In 1576, he had informed Pietro de' Medici that his wife, Eleonora, was having an affair; both Eleonora and her lover were swiftly murdered as a result. Decades later, the first production of Peri's *Euridice* might have depended on Caccini's cooperation, since the latter's students, including his children, were among the most sought-after singers in the city. Caccini might have made it a condition of his entourage's participation that they sing *his* music rather than Peri's. The first performance of *Euridice* might thus have been a mash-up of music by the two composers. After this first production, Caccini seems to have rushed to set the rest of Rinuccini's libretto to music, and to publish his own full version of *Euridice* before Peri's appeared in print. The enduringly awkward result is that the first surviving opera, *Euridice*, is in fact two separate musical compositions set to the same words.

The skeletal nature of Peri and Caccini's scores makes it difficult to get a full sense of their music today. For one thing, these operas are not "orchestrated" in the modern sense of the term. The instrumental parts for both *Euridice* operas consist, at any given moment, only of a single bass note, with no instrumentation specified. The essential harmonic information is sketched above the bassline in Roman numerals, a form of notation that came to be known as "basso continuo." These scores resemble fully notated compositions less than they resemble jazz "lead sheets," which contain only the bare minimum of information—the melody line, the harmony—required for a musician trained in the idiom to flesh it out in performance.

Caccini, a lutenist himself, helped develop this stripped-down notation for performers who would both sing and accompany themselves; the point was to give the performer maximum rhythmic freedom and flexibility. What this actually sounded like—exactly *how* flexible was the tempo, how rich were the harmonic realizations, and how much improvisation was expected on top of the written vocal line?—is unknowable today. (Imagine a future civilization trying to reconstruct the sound of a Charlie Parker solo just from the chord changes to "A Night in Tunisia.")

Even so, there is a lot to admire, especially in Peri's version. Though Peri's music modestly defers at every moment to the clear articulation of the poetic text, it has a satisfying warmth and generosity. After Euridice's death, the chorus sings a manifold lament for her: individual singers step forward to offer personal expressions of grief, with a recurring choral refrain after each individual contribution. Near the end of each verse, the soloist invites the return of the choral refrain with a beguiling harmonic change on the word *sospirate* ("sigh"). It is a poignant ritual of mourning: the grief of each individual is subsumed in turn back into the chorus's comforting sonic fabric.

As for Caccini, I'm keenly aware that the historical evidence of his nefariousness may taint my appreciation of his artistry. It's difficult to forget that one is listening to music by a man who, had he lived a couple of centuries earlier, might easily have ended up in Dante's catalogue of Florentines condemned to grotesque eternal torments. But I think even an objective observer would find certain features of his music hopelessly anti-theatrical. As the conductor and lutenist Stephen Stubbs points out, Caccini cadences (that is, comes to a full stop) at the end of practically every phrase, a disastrous decision for a work of music-theater: the music's plodding, stop-and-start motion thwarts any possibility of accumulating dramatic tension even over the course of a single scene, never mind throughout the evening.

In both Peri's and Caccini's versions of *Euridice*, however, the star of the show is arguably not the music so much as Rinuccini's poetry. The balance of power between opera's constituent art forms is very different in the medium's earliest exemplars than it is in the Classical- and Romantic-era operas that are most familiar to modern-day audiences. These later pieces often privilege musical opulence over crisp enunciation of the text; even a native Italian speaker might have a hard time making out exactly what the soprano in a Puccini opera is saying when she ventures into her upper register. By contrast, the operas of Peri and Caccini unambiguously foreground the poetry. Rinuccini's verses are so elaborately wordy that, with the exception of a few choral numbers, listening to these operas is more like listening to a poetry recitation than it is like listening to a symphony. Because of this, even though the poetry is often beautiful, these operas might seem a little monotonous to listeners who don't speak Italian. Dense, allusive Italian Renaissance poetry, unlike music, is not exactly a "universal language."

Given that these two ur-operas are called *Euridice*, it's notable that Euridice herself is a relatively minor figure in them. The drama is organized around her absence; she is the void at its center. Euridice makes a brief appearance early in the opera, dies offstage, and does not return until its last scene. This set a precedent: for centuries, she would more often than not be a shadowy figure, a kind of chalk outline, an evanescent symbol of loss.

The story of Orpheus and Eurydice quickly grew ubiquitous as an operatic subject, and the strongest among the seventeenth century's many Orpheus operas take notably divergent approaches to the myth. We'll take a closer look at Monteverdi, who built on Peri's achievements to create, in his *L'Orfeo*, a work of heightened harmonic sophistication and textural specificity. (Monteverdi's librettist, Alessandro Striggio, was nowhere near the poet Rinuccini was, but the relative banality of Striggio's libretto allowed Monteverdi's music to step into the spotlight in a way that Rinuccini's poetry may not have permitted.) Stefano Landi's *La morte d'Orfeo* (1619) begins where most Orpheus operas end, after Eurydice's second death, and follows Orpheus through his own demise at the hands of the maenads and his ascent to join the gods on Olympus. Luigi Rossi's musically magnificent *Orfeo* (1647) has the unenviable distinction of having been so expensive to stage at its Paris premiere, which was organized by the powerful Cardinal Mazarin, that the lavish production was a contributing factor to the outbreak of the Fronde, the civil conflict that shook France between 1648 and 1653. (Opera may have a reputation for "elitism" today, but I don't think it's among the elements in contemporary society most likely to start a civil war.) Marc-Antoine Charpentier's seemingly unfinished *La descente d'Orphée aux enfers* (ca. 1686), which we'll also examine in greater depth, is among the most tantalizing of operatic torsos, a work whose mesmerizingly beautiful music trails off just before the crucial scene of Orpheus's backward look.

Dozens of Orpheus operas hit the stage in the eighteenth century, but only one has remained in the repertoire: Christoph Willibald Gluck's *Orfeo ed Euridice* (1762), whose many melodic earworms, as well as its relatively modest scope (it has the virtue, uncommon in opera, of being less than ninety minutes long), have made it the most frequently performed of all Orphic adaptations. It may seem surprising that Gluck's is practically the only eighteenth-century Orpheus opera to remain in circulation, since the Classical style that took root in European music in the latter half of the century might seem a natural fit for a story like this one. But I think there's a deep aesthetic mismatch here. The Classical style is founded on the Enlightenment virtues of cleanness, clarity, and logic, whereas Orpheus thrives in an atmosphere of Dionysian darkness and mystery. This myth tells a fundamentally pessimistic story about human nature: Orpheus's impulse to look back wins out over his awareness that Eurydice will be lost if he does so. There is little comfort to be found for listeners who want to believe in the inevitable triumph of rational thought.

This tension, between the clear geometry of the Classical idiom and the wildness and violence at the myth's heart, can be felt even in Gluck, but it is most palpable in Franz Joseph Haydn's

L'anima del filosofo (*The Soul of the Philosopher*, composed circa 1791 but premiered only in 1951). I'd wager that relatively few opera lovers are even aware that Haydn wrote an Orpheus opera, and it's not some fragmentary student piece: he wrote *L'anima* when he was nearly sixty, at the height of his powers, with more than ninety symphonies to his name.

How is it possible that a two-hour-long work by the mature Haydn is performed so infrequently today? There is the issue of its pedantic title: even without changing a note of the score, this opera would no doubt be better known if it were called *Orpheus and Eurydice* rather than *The Soul of the Philosopher*. But there are deeper reasons for its obscurity. Haydn's music is beloved for its wit, its clarity, the crispness of his textures, and the chiseled rightness of his melodies. These are rare and precious qualities, but they have almost no place in the Orpheus myth. The libretto, by Carlo Francesco Badini, tells an atavistically brutal version of the story—wild shepherds attempt to sacrifice Eurydice to the Furies in the opening scene, and the opera ends with Orpheus being poisoned by witchlike worshippers of Dionysus—but Haydn is rarely willing to channel, in his music, the feral energies that these scenarios demand. (Badini also frequently interrupts the action of the drama with tedious philosophical commentary.) Though *L'anima del filosofo* is full of masterful music, it somehow fails to be a genuine Orpheus piece. Orphic energy is elusive and hard to define, but Haydn's opera proves the necessity of such energy by its absence.

The nineteenth century proved to be a still more barren one for Orpheus operas. The Romantic era was the first time in opera's history that Greco-Roman source material, which had been a unifying force across linguistic and cultural borders for two centuries, went decisively out of fashion. As a result, Romantic opera composers made strikingly little use of Orpheus, who would seem to be the ideal Romantic archetype. The era's most influential operatic movements all engaged, one way or another, with the nationalism that had spread across Europe in the wake of the French Revolution: the German Romantics drew heavily on Germanic folklore; Verdi sought historical subjects that resonated with Italy's struggle for unification; Czech, Polish, and Russian composers all wrote works that aspired to be national epics. There wasn't much room for Orpheus in any of this. It's telling that the only nineteenth-century Orpheus opera that has kept a toehold in the repertoire is Jacques Offenbach's riotous *Orphée aux enfers* (1858), a kind of Olympic drag pageant that gleefully mocks the story it's telling.

If the seventeenth century was the first golden age for Orpheus operas, the twentieth century was the second, and arguably the richer of the two. Many early modernists returned to mythological source material, finding in these ancient stories a fruitful ambiguity and a susceptibility to abstract psychological interpretation. No myth proved more fertile than that of Orpheus, which served as a kind of Rorschach test, infallibly uncovering many a composer's obsessions, fetishes, and anxieties. In earlier centuries, the Orphic operas of a given time period tended to bear strong family resemblances: you can tell that Monteverdi, Peri, and Caccini were all drinking the same water. But the twentieth century's Orpheus operas tended to approach the myth from radically different angles; it's hard to find two pieces that even inhabit the same universe.

There is the Austrian composer Ernst Krenek's youthfully angst-ridden setting of Oskar Kokoschka's play *Orpheus und Eurydike* (1926), which was inspired by Kokoschka's turbulent affair with Alma Mahler. There is Darius Milhaud's charmingly mopey chamber opera *Les malheurs d'Orphée* (1926). The composers Pierre Schaeffer and Pierre Henry turned to Orpheus as the subject for *Orphée 53* (1953), an uncategorizable piece that fuses live performance with pre-recorded tape, using a technique that became known as "musique concrète." It is a hauntingly lovely work: fragments of past Orpheus operas, enigmatic spoken texts, and reverb-soaked ambient noises merge together to form a kind of echo chamber, as if Orpheus had returned to the tunnel that leads to the underworld to listen to its reverberations. The murky atmosphere of the underworld also inspired some of Igor Stravinsky's most luminously beautiful music, though his *Orpheus* (1948) is a ballet rather than an opera. Among more recent efforts, Philip Glass's *Orphée* (1993), based on Jean Cocteau's film, is gently magical and inexplicably hypnotic as is so much of Glass's music.

And then there is the phenomenon that is Harrison Birtwistle. This composer's lifelong Orpheus obsession has yielded three operas: *The Mask of Orpheus* (1986), which is a worthy contender, alongside Wagner's *Ring* cycle and Stockhausen's *Licht*, for the distinction of being the most preposterously ambitious opera ever written; the mythological mélange of *The Second Mrs. Kong* (1994); and the chamber-scale one-act *The Corridor* (2009). Birtwistle has also written an array of Orpheus-inspired vocal chamber music, and there is a case to be made that *all* of his music enacts a cyclically Orphic process of loss and attempted recovery. By making certain pieces openly "about" Orpheus, Birtwistle merely makes explicit a process that is fundamental to his musical DNA.

Each of the pieces referenced above is worth exploring, but in the remainder of this chapter I'll concentrate on three favorite composers: Monteverdi, Charpentier, and Birtwistle. The work of these three artists makes it clear that Orpheus has the power to push composers to outdo themselves, and to explore remote regions that they would never have dared to visit without the doomed, untrustworthy singer as their guide.

The Impossible Moment:
Claudio Monteverdi's L'Orfeo

Much to the annoyance of latecomers like myself, no composer to this day has done a better job with the Herculean challenge at the heart of the Orpheus myth—the scene in which Orpheus is required to sing the most beautiful music ever heard—than Monteverdi did in 1607. Monteverdi's *L'Orfeo* contains a gratifying bounty of gorgeous music: richly layered choruses, meltingly beautiful instrumental sinfonias, rousing dance music full of disarming rhythmic ambiguities. Its influence has been wide and deep, and has made its presence felt in the unlikeliest places: the conductor John Eliot Gardiner has even noted a striking similarity between Orfeo's light-footed "Vi ricorda, o boschi ombrosi" and Leonard Bernstein's "America," in *West Side Story*. The two pieces share a distinctive rhythmic footprint defined by alternating bars of 6/8 and 3/4, two time signatures that contain the same number of eighth notes per bar (six), but whose emphases fall at different points within each bar (broadly speaking, the eighth notes in a bar of 6/8 are divided into two groups of three, while in 3/4 they're divided into three groups of two). According to Gardiner, Bernstein acknowledged privately that "America," that indelible sonic snapshot of the streets of mid-twentieth-century Manhattan, may indeed owe something to the seventeenth-century maestro of Mantua.

I'll focus on Orfeo himself, since Monteverdi is careful to

infuse practically every note his protagonist sings with a specifically "Orphic" atmosphere. There is a burnished glow to his music;
he sometimes seems to be speaking to us through a dusky haze,
a cloud of incense. Monteverdi creates this atmosphere through
Orfeo's ritualistic gestural vocabulary (he is fond of beginning his
arias with incantatory, prayerlike flourishes), his harmonic world
(he is most at home in a deep-hued G minor), and a careful blend
of virtuosity and restraint. Though Orfeo does occasionally sing
long bursts of dazzling coloratura, such displays are the exception, not the rule: it is clear that his power is limitless, but he uses
it sparingly, saving his longer-than-humanly-possible phrases for
the climactic verses of his plea to gain entrance to the underworld. He and Euridice appear together only in public—even
in the scene of Orfeo's backward look, the guardians of Hell are
watching—and they invariably address each other with ceremonial formality. (Euridice's role is vanishingly brief.) On the whole,
this Orfeo is a pretty solemn creature; it is only occasionally that
his music bubbles over with an irrepressible passion. These moments of abandon are all the more potent for their scarcity.

In the language of modern voice types, Orfeo lies somewhere
between a tenor and a baritone. Like the role of Pelléas, in Claude
Debussy's *Pelléas et Mélisande* (1902), Orfeo can be sung either by
a tenor with a strong low range (and one who's willing to forgo the
crowd-pleasing "money notes" at the top of the tenorial compass)
or by a baritone who is able to sing long stretches of music with
delicacy and sensitivity in a physically demanding upper register.
Given that much of Orfeo's music is in G, it's worth mentioning
that he never sings the tenor's upper G, a note that many baritones can manage also. Orfeo's highest note is a half step lower,
the F-sharp above the piano's middle C. It's just not his style to

venture beyond the border of the male voice's plummy, warm-sounding central region.

Orfeo sings an aria in each of *L'Orfeo*'s five acts: the incantatory "Rosa del ciel" in Act One; the lament "Tu sei morta" in Act Two; the epic "Possente spirto," sung at the gates of Hell, in Act Three; "Qual onor di te sia degno," a cheerful (and overconfident) song in praise of his lyre, in Act Four; and "Questi i campi di Tracia," sung through a stupor of grief and rage, in Act Five. (This tally omits the songs "Ecco pur ch'a voi ritorno" and "Vi ricorda, o boschi ombrosi," because these are integrated into a larger sequence of celebratory musical numbers.)

There is a subtle symmetry to these five arias: they build in intensity toward Act Three's "Possente spirto," which stands almost at the opera's exact center and serves as its dramaturgical fulcrum, before diminishing again. By "Questi i campi di Tracia," which opens the fifth and final act, the desolate Orfeo is stuck in the basement of the tenor range, paralytically singing long, dull stretches of low Ds and Es. (Many tenors have a tough time projecting down there, so it's not hard for them to sound miserable, as the drama demands.) All five of these arias are in the key of G: the four melancholy or solemn ones are in G minor, and Orfeo's sunny song of gratitude to his lyre is in G major.

Orfeo's first solo is sung at his wedding: when a shepherd asks him to say a few words, Orfeo responds with "Rosa del ciel," a notably intense little aria for what is essentially a wedding toast. He begins by addressing not his wife but rather the sun itself, the "rose of heaven." Over an invocatory, repeatedly struck G minor chord, Orfeo praises the sun in its omnipotence, and asks if it has ever seen a happier lover than himself. This is perhaps a less austere ritual than it seems: in Monteverdi and Striggio's reading of the myth, Orfeo is the son of the sun god, Apollo, and in a sense he is simply acknowledging his dad's contributions to the festivities.*

It's only at the end of the aria that Orfeo's happiness, his youthful enthusiasm, finally shines through:

This phrase manifests a touching sense of impatience and irrepressible joy. Orfeo begins on D-natural, swoops downward, and returns to D; then he repeats the gesture, this time in an extended, embellished form. I recognize this impulse: it's a slightly tipsy and very Italian expression of affection, a statement that's repeated twice, intensified the second time, to drive home the depth of one's feeling. But this sense of passion and urgency does not last long: with his next words ("tutti colmi sarieno"), Orfeo returns to a more measured mode, steadily applying the brakes through the cadence that brings this brief aria to a close. But we

---

* Orfeo's solar lineage, his status as a kind of cult leader, and his brief hymn to the sun might remind some listeners of another legendary figure who became an operatic hero: the pharaoh Akhenaton, protagonist of Philip Glass's *Akhnaten* (1984).

have caught a glimpse of his impetuous side, a ray of light through the haze of ritual smoke.

Orfeo's next aria, "Tu sei morta," is a lament, sung after he learns of Euridice's death (though its essential atmosphere is not *so* far from that of the ostensibly celebratory "Rosa del ciel"). Within a similarly mysterious G-minor atmosphere, however, Monteverdi makes very different harmonic choices. The earlier aria consists mostly of a comforting series of harmonic resolutions, but in "Tu sei morta," Orfeo lingers masochistically on dissonance after dissonance. There is a lugubrious richness to the harmonic motion that is redolent of music from later centuries: one brief phrase, on the words "e intenerisce il cor," could almost have been written by Wagner. My favorite line brims with uncontainable energy:

At the thought of being forced to remain alive when Euridice is dead, Orfeo ruptures the stately harmonic rhythm that had prevailed till this point. He pushes desperately forward; the syncopations on the word "rimango" and the outburst "No, no!" create the sense that he's lashing out, thrashing around, trying to break free of the musical texture, as if to prove that none of this is real, that it's just a nightmare.

A phrase like this serves as a useful reminder that though

L'Orfeo predates by centuries the kind of Italian opera that we think of as red-blooded spectacle—Verdi, Puccini, and the verismo school—Monteverdi is nonetheless an important fountainhead of this tradition. The role of Orfeo benefits from a singer who can channel, at a few key moments, a certain Italianate fire—a quality that is not typically associated with the early-music movement, but that was surely no less plentiful in 1607 than it was in 1907.

Just as, in Orfeo's earlier arias, a single line sometimes surges up out of the texture, manifesting an unexpected passion, so "Possente spirto," Orfeo's aria at the gates of Hell, surges up out of the texture of the whole opera. Nothing in the opera's first two acts quite prepares us for this formidable feat of hypnotism.

From Orfeo's perspective, however, "Possente spirto" is really not the main event; it's more of a warm-up routine. He has been guided as far as the entrance to the underworld by the allegorical figure of Hope, who forsakes him in a groan-inducing moment of literary humor: Hope explains that the Dantean inscription on Hell's portal ("ABANDON ALL HOPE, YE WHO ENTER HERE") prohibits her from going farther. Orfeo then addresses not Plutone, the underworld's big boss, but Caronte (Charon), the ferryman whose job it is to shepherd the souls of the dead across the river Styx. Orfeo's immediate task is to convince Caronte to grant him passage across the river. If he succeeds, he'll face the still greater challenge of convincing Plutone and Proserpina to release Euridice.

"Possente spirto," Orfeo's plea to Caronte, is notable both for its scope (depending on the pacing, it can last anywhere from eight to ten minutes) and for its brilliantly canny musical structure. Striggio's text is in terza rima, the rhyme scheme invented by Dante in *The Divine Comedy*: the poetry is organized in three-line stanzas, each of whose first and third lines rhyme; the end rhyme of each stanza's middle line then becomes the end rhyme for the first and third lines of the following stanza. The stanzas thus rhyme *aba, bcb, cdc,* and so on. Like a Dantean canto, the text of "Possente spirto" concludes with a single four-line stanza, with alternating end rhymes. The basic effect of terza rima is a perpetual sense of deferred gratification, since each three-line stanza contains two rhyming lines and one that doesn't yet rhyme with anything. This "orphan" line then rhymes with two lines in the following stanza. After a long sequence of interleaved tercets, the solitary quatrain at the poem's end creates a satisfying sense of closure.

Monteverdi's music first hews closely to, then subtly diverges from, this poetic structure. The music is divided into verses, each of which maps onto a stanza of poetry. Each verse traces essentially the same labyrinthine harmonic sequence, but Orfeo's vocal melody differs substantially from verse to verse. In a striking sign of this aria's unique status, Monteverdi notates two distinct versions of the vocal line, a simple version and a highly embellished one, throughout the first four verses. The difference between the two versions is extreme. In one case, a single note in the unadorned version corresponds to *fifty-four* notes in the embellished version. (I have never heard a singer perform the simple, stripped-down version. To do so would strike many singers as a distinctly un-Orphic admission of weakness.)

In each of the first three verses, a different instrument, or pair of instruments, plays brief flourishes in between Orfeo's vocal phrases: two violins, which echo each other, in the first verse; two cornetti in the second; and a harp in the third. These instruments hover like sympathetic attendant spirits, and at the end of each verse, Orfeo seems to bow his head and invite them to take over, to extend his utterances into wordlessness. The alluring, dance-like instrumental ritornelli that follow each verse manifest an inscrutably Orphic affect: they are equal parts seduction and sup-plication, grace and grief.

I'm not an expert in Baroque performance practice, but I have always felt that the music's tempo, and indeed its whole character, radically shifts at the beginning of the fourth verse. (Monteverdi typically does not write specific indications of tempo or dynamics, so a great deal is left to the discretion and taste of the performers.) The previous verse ends with an extended ritornello for harp, an especially elaborate passage that falls down a rabbit hole into the instrument's sonorous depths. By the end of the harp solo, Orfeo seems newly energized. He sings the simple declaration "Orfeo son io" ("I am Orpheus"), but Monteverdi's text-setting is any-thing but simple: Orfeo sings a long coloratura run, a phrase that is especially challenging to sing because it is punctuated by bold, sharp-edged little two-note gestures. After three verses of persua-sion through sheer beauty, Orfeo is ready to show some muscle. Whenever I perform this piece—which I do as often as possible, including in my own (admittedly anachronistic) transcription for voice and piano—I keep the pacing quite flexible in the first three verses, but I make sure there's a deep, steady pulse in the fourth. There's almost a martial quality to it: Orfeo seems to be calling for reinforcements, asking the whole orchestra to join him in hopes of overwhelming Caronte.

At the end of the fourth verse, Monteverdi finally breaks the harmonic pattern that has held throughout the aria so far. The text's fifth stanza opens with the exclamation "O," and Monte-verdi uses this wordless cry (the first of its kind in the aria's text) as an opportunity to enter a new musical space. After a G minor chord, which would seem to signal the start of yet another verse, Monteverdi moves to E-flat major rather than the expected D minor, thus initiating a new harmonic progression. There's a thrilling sense of urgency and abandon to this section. When Orfeo sings of how a single glance from Euridice would restore him to life ("può tornarmi in vita"), the word "vita" prompts his highest note of the whole opera, a fleeting F-sharp.

After this climactic outburst, Orfeo reins himself in. He sings a gentle descending figure on the words "Ahi, chi niega il conforto à le mie pene?" ("Oh, who could refuse me comfort for my pains?"). For the first time in the aria, Monteverdi has Orfeo sing a single line of poetry twice. This sequence functions as an opportunity to cool down, to carefully descend from the previous section's passionate heights: the tempo can ease up slightly, and the ensemble should play more and more softly. Though he claims to be in agony, Orfeo seems to be smiling broadly as he approaches the long-awaited cadence to G major.

We've reached the final quatrain of poetry, for which Orfeo returns to the "verse" music, though this last verse feels more like a coda. Unlike in the earlier verses, Monteverdi does not notate two separate versions of the vocal line here. There is only one option, and it's quite spare. By now there's no need for embellishment: Orfeo has shown what he's capable of, and he seems to lay his cards on the table. You, he says to Caronte, are the only one who can help me. It would be easy to read this final gesture as further evidence of Orfeo's humility, but I've always heard something smugly triumphant in it. Orfeo knows what an amazing feat he's just pulled off. There's a quick flash of coloratura on his last word, "invan" ("in vain"), a gesture that's almost a sneer.

The irony is that "Possente spirto," the best imaginable proof of Orfeo's power, fails to achieve his goal. Caronte applauds politely, and tells Orfeo that he enjoyed the music very much. However, he says, it isn't really in his nature to feel pity, and it's certainly not in his job description. So he unfortunately can't let Orfeo across the river.

Orfeo is irritated. His music has never failed to work its charm before. Like any self-respecting diva, he is hell-bent on performing an encore, even though Caronte didn't ask for one. Orfeo repeats the sinfonia that preceded "Possente spirto," and Caronte, understandably enough, falls asleep. Orfeo is then able to commandeer his boat and row into the underworld. The lesson (which many opera composers learned all too well) seems to be that if you can't beat 'em, you can always put 'em to sleep.

Monteverdi and Striggio's reading of the myth does not seem to admit much ambiguity. Indeed, they arguably choose the bland-est possible version of the tale's denouement: after Euridice van-ishes, Orfeo returns to the world above and wallows in self-pitying grief. Eventually, for no discernible reason, his dejection morphs into misogynistic fury against all women other than Euridice. Just when Orfeo goes entirely off the rails—our noble hero sounds momentarily like a deranged, ranting incel—Apollo descends, sternly tells Orfeo to pull himself together, and carries him up to heaven, where he promises that Orfeo will see Euridice's image shining in the sun and the stars.

However, this version of the finale, with its blunt deus ex machina, is almost certainly an after-the-fact renovation rather than an original feature of the opera. We know this because of a discrepancy between the earliest edition of the libretto, which was printed around the time of the opera's premiere in 1607, and the earliest edition of the score, which was not printed until 1609. In the first edition of the libretto, the drama has a very different conclusion: Orfeo's chauvinistic rant attracts the attention of a menacing group of bacchantes, female followers of Bacchus (that is, Dionysus). When Orfeo notices them, he says, more or less, "Uh oh," and seems to run off in terror, leaving the bacchantes free to hijack the drama. They take center stage, condemning Orfeo ("our wicked adversary") before launching into an extended chorus in praise of their god. And so the opera ends. It's not clear if Orfeo has escaped, or if the bacchantes are about to slay him, as they do in Ovid's *Metamorphoses*.

These two versions of the opera's finale make for a rather on-the-nose example of the persistent tension, in the figure of Orfeo himself, between Apollonian and Dionysian energies: one version ends with Apollo triumphantly leading Orfeo to heaven, the other with a hymn to Dionysus. Orfeo embodies certain distinctly Apollonian qualities—physical beauty, youthfulness, radiance—but the effect of his music (sometimes he puts his listeners into a trance, sometimes he drives them into a frenzy) surely owes something to Dionysian dark magic as well.

It seems that Monteverdi himself was unsure about which god would win out in the end. We don't know if the composer simply decided that he wanted to write a happier ending, and one with a clearer sense of resolution, for the published version of the score, or if some external force—some voice of censorship or theatrical convention—pressured him to do so. But whatever its cause, this double ending, this fork at the end of the road, presents a fascinating case of extratextual ambiguity. The music for the "Dionysian" ending, if indeed Monteverdi ever wrote any, has not survived,* and a libretto whose music is missing is a blueprint for an unconstructed building. But the fact of that blueprint's existence presents us with the possibility of a tantalizing alternate reality, full of a different, wilder form of Orphic energy.

---

* That is, unless a fragment of it is hiding in plain sight: Stephen Stubbs, influenced by a theory proposed by the musicologist Silke Leopold, suggests that the instrumental dance that concludes the opera (a spirited "Moresca") might be the lone remnant of the original Dionysian ending.

Music as Consolation: Marc-Antoine Charpentier's
La descente d'Orphée aux enfers

An Orpheus opera that ends before the scene of Orpheus's backward look might seem almost a contradiction in terms. But Marc-Antoine Charpentier's *La descente d'Orphée aux enfers* triumphs in spite of this seemingly fatal omission. Charpentier's is the tenderest and most humane of Orpheus operas, a warm sonic bath of a piece that contains hardly a moment of dull or unmemorable music. If the salient feature of Monteverdi's score is the slightly unnerving power of Orfeo himself, Charpentier, by contrast, emphasizes music's powers of consolation, the way it can bring comfort to those who need it. The whole cast of *La descente d'Orphée* palpably yearns for the nourishment of Orphée's singing; even the Furies end up cheering him on from the sidelines.

We know little about this opera's genesis, just as we know frustratingly little about its composer's life. Charpentier was born in the environs of Paris in 1643, and though he spent his whole artistic career in the heart of that city's bustling music scene, we have almost no descriptions of his personality from friends or colleagues, and not a single contemporaneously painted portrait has survived. Though he was hardly unknown during his lifetime, Charpentier's professional life seems to have been marked by bad luck and questionable timing. He studied in Rome as a young man, and found upon his return to Paris that his music's perceived *italianità* made him suspect: the memory was still fresh of Cardinal Mazarin's attempts to dominate French musical life with Italian imports. A promising partnership with a dream librettist, Molière, was cut short within a year of its formation by Molière's death. But Charpentier's greatest misfortune was simply that his career coincided with the aesthetic dictatorship of the composer Jean-Baptiste Lully, music master to the royal family, whose influence was vast and stifling: any opera performed *anywhere in France* had to be personally approved by Lully, whose favorite composer was of course himself. The clearest sign of how Charpentier might have felt about his professional marginalization might lie in a cantata called *Epitaphium Carpentarii*, which portrays the ghost of the composer himself addressing two friends, like some spirit out of *A Christmas Carol*: "I was a musician," the phantasm explains wryly, "thought to be among the good ones by the good, and among the ignorant ones by the ignorant" (trans. H. Wiley Hitchcock).

Charpentier is far from the only great composer to have been underappreciated in his lifetime, but in his case, the neglect deepened after his death, and lasted for centuries: his music was almost forgotten until around 1900, and the score of *La descente d'Orphée* was rediscovered only by chance in Paris's Bibliothèque nationale in 1930. We do not know who wrote the work's libretto, nor do we know the details of its first performance, though it seems that the composer himself, who was also a tenor, sang in its ensemble. The surviving score consists of two acts, which total just under an hour of music; if Charpentier composed a third act, its music has not been found. The second act ends with Orphée setting out on his long ascent back to the land of the living, and the addition of a third act whose proportions resemble those of the first two would yield a satisfying ninety-minute triptych, comparable in scale and structure to Gluck's better-known adaptation of the myth.

The opera's title, which promises to tell the story of Orphée's descent into the underworld but says nothing of his subsequent return to the world above, might seem to imply that the surviving music constitutes the complete piece. As John S. Powell notes in his edition of the score, however, there are convincing signs that what we have of *La descente d'Orphée* is indeed fragmentary. For one thing, at the end of the surviving score, Charpentier writes "fin du Sd Acte" ("end of Act Two") rather than the standard, and more conclusive, "fin de l'opéra." For another, Pluton's final warning to Orphée, that he must not look back at Eurydice as he ascends, strongly hints at an approaching catastrophe: the music, as Powell notes, is full of foreboding, and Pluton underlines the import of his message by singing the last phrase ("or else I shall reclaim her in a second death") twice. It seems unlike Charpentier, whose sense of dramatic pacing is otherwise faultless, to end the opera abruptly after a moment that is so fraught with foreshadowing.

Charpentier's special achievement in *La descente d'Orphée* lies in his handling of the myth's vexed relationship between pain and pleasure. One of the challenges faced by any composer who engages with the Orpheus story is to make this tension palpable without being either heartless or sentimental; the most common misjudgment (I think even Gluck falls into this trap) is to try to avoid the question by presenting a po-faced, self-serious Orpheus. If Orpheus does nothing but insist, like a sullen teenager, that everything sucks and he's miserable, the audience may lose patience with him. If he's so unhappy, why does he seem to relish stewing in his own juices all evening long? An Orpheus who protests too much risks coming across as both disingenuous and dull.

Charpentier nimbly sidesteps this issue by making his depictions of suffering openly pleasurable, and exquisitely so. Orphée, the Furies, and the damned all seem unambiguously grateful to be able to sing their sorrows away. There is even a sense that they have a kind of shared mission, as if they had all gathered for a sing-along around some infernal campfire.

The contrast between the sorrowful libretto and the radiant good cheer of Charpentier's music is at its most extreme in the first scene of Act Two. We have just arrived in the underworld, where we meet a trio of iconic wrongdoers condemned to bespoke eternal punishments: Tantale (Tantalus) bends thirstily over the pool of water that perpetually retreats from his lips; Ixion lies bound to his flaming wheel; and Titye (Tityus) endures daily disembowelment by a pair of vultures. "Oh, dreadful torments!" they sing. "Cruel suffering!" But the music, a laid-back triple-time dance in F major, could hardly be sunnier. Sure, a couple of relatively spicy harmonies—an F dominant-seventh chord melting into a B-flat major-seventh chord, for instance—might have struck a seventeenth-century audience as twangingly dissonant, but to modern ears the whole thing sounds positively groovy. We seem to be listening to the Beach Boys of the shores of Hell.

Eurydice appears only in the opera's first scene, but Charpentier makes more of her role than Monteverdi does in the equivalent scene in *L'Orfeo*. After a brief, jaunty overture, *La descente d'Orphée* opens with a pastoral tableau of Eurydice and her friends preparing for her wedding. Eurydice's aria, in which she tells her friends to quit trampling flowers as they dance in the meadow, manifests a calm, smiling poise: the harmonies playfully walk in circles, and the end of the verse flows seamlessly into its repetition. Even in what is little more than a cameo, this Eurydice makes a beguiling impression of vitality and verve.

Charpentier perfectly judges the moment of the snakebite, which (unlike in Monteverdi) happens onstage. When Eurydice cries out, one of her friends, thinking she's just pricked her finger on a thorn, continues to sing in a mincing, dancelike rhythm. Since we know what has actually happened, the dance music suddenly sounds unbearably cloying. When Eurydice sings again, the change in harmony seems to drain all light out of the scene. From the overture through this moment, the music has been exclusively in A major or closely related keys: E major, D major, F-sharp minor. With a dramatist's cunning, Charpentier has so far almost entirely avoided C-natural, the note that marks the essential difference between A major and A minor. (The bassline in the overture contains only a fleeting pair of C-naturals during a harmonic transition.) When Eurydice sings again after having been bitten, her music is in A minor, and she begins on C-natural. The effect is breathtaking in its simplicity: the whole atmosphere seems to have slightly warped, gone sour.

The role of Orphée, who makes his first entrance as Eurydice dies, is written for *haute-contre*, an exceptionally high-lying subspecies of tenor voice. The *haute-contre* was a standard voice type in the French Baroque period, but it's far less common today. Because of this, Charpentier's Orphée poses the same kinds of challenges for contemporary tenors that Monteverdi's Orfeo does for baritones: the role requires uncommon sweetness and stamina in a high register where the singer might be tempted either to let all hell break loose or to switch to a white-toned falsetto.

Meltingly lovely as Orphée's music is, he doesn't radiate a special aura of his own, as Monteverdi's Orfeo does. This Orphée is a likable singer-songwriter type rather than a shamanic cult leader. The focus is less on the singular virtuosity of Orphée himself and more on the miracles that are made possible through communal music-making. Accordingly, Charpentier doesn't waste time keeping us in suspense about whether Orphée will get the denizens of the underworld on his side: Tantale, Ixion, and Titye fawn over him as soon as he opens his mouth, and the chorus of Furies soon follows suit.

In this opera full of spellbinding moments, the chorus might have the most sublime music of all. We initially encounter them in the pastoral first act, in the guise of friendly nymphs and shepherds. The first entrance of the full, mixed-voice chorus, just after Eurydice has suffered her fatal snakebite, features a jarring harmonic turn of the screw: a diminished chord is followed by a deliciously film-noirish dissonance, an E major chord skewered from below by the bass note, C-natural. In the scene that follows, Orphée and the chorus take turns singing an achingly beautiful lament ("Ah! Bergers, c'en est fait, / Il n'est plus d'Eurydice"). When Orphée and the chorus reach the word "Eurydice," they trail off, falling silent in the middle of the bar. Something seems to catch in the throat of the music. The ensemble resumes singing again only after a moment of silence and a collective deep breath.

I'm convinced that what we have of *La descente d'Orphée* is incomplete, but the chorus that ends Act Two is so satisfying that it *could* serve as an opera's finale. As Orphée prepares to return to the world above, the inhabitants of the underworld bid him a tearful farewell. They pray that they'll always remember this experience, the "charmante impression de cette voix touchante / qui nous ravit, qui nous enchante" ("lovely impression of this touching voice / that ravishes us, that enchants us"). Listen to the magical change of harmony on the word "ravit" ("ravishes"), E minor sliding sensually into an A minor seventh chord. If this opera had a third act, the *finale ultimo* would no doubt feature the death or apotheosis of Orphée, but as the piece stands, the last word belongs to the whole ensemble as they sing this poignant collective hymn of thanks.

After the chorus ends, there is a gentle instrumental postlude, a softly circling sarabande. As Orphée walks farther and farther away, we are left with the sense that everyone who remains on-stage yearns for his music to go on forever. You can hardly blame them.

Supersaturation: Harrison Birtwistle's
The Mask of Orpheus

The British composer Harrison Birtwistle (b. 1934) is a seemingly unlikely candidate for the Orphic spirit of our age. Birtwistle, the creator of a vast body of dense, dazzling music, is the ultimate composer's composer: never exactly beloved by multitudes of concertgoers but revered by generations of his composer colleagues, myself included. His oeuvre is full of fruitful paradoxes. Moment by moment, the texture of Birtwistle's music might seem rough or jagged, but over long stretches its effect is lushly hypnotic. Many Birtwistle pieces are epic in their scale, but one always has a sense that they are fragments of something still larger. He employs an arsenal of contemporary techniques to create an aura of ancientness.

Music lovers who don't frequent new-music circles may be most familiar with Birtwistle through the relatively infrequent controversies his work has generated over the years. Early in his career, Birtwistle gained a certain notoriety for his gleefully gory puppet opera *Punch and Judy* (1968); Benjamin Britten, whose Aldeburgh Festival hosted the piece's premiere, supposedly walked out of the first performance at intermission, unwilling to endure its stylized ultraviolence. Nearly thirty years later, Birtwistle's exhilarating piece *Panic* (1995), a kind of chamber concerto for saxophone and ensemble, had the misfortune of being premiered on the final night of the BBC Proms, London's epic classical-music summer festival. In the UK, the Last Night of the Proms is practically a national holiday, an event characterized by meat-and-potatoes patriotic fare like "Pomp and Circumstance" and "Rule, Britannia!" Featuring a Birtwistle piece on such an occasion makes about as much sense as inviting a death-metal band to sub for the Boston Pops on the Fourth of July. *Panic* wailed and writhed its way into existence before a live television and radio audience of millions, thousands of whom then complained to the BBC.

Birtwistle is, admittedly, not great at ingratiating himself to a general audience when he talks about his music; his monosyllabic description of his opera *The Last Supper* (2000)—"It's a tough grub"—is hilariously typical. On the rare occasions when he addresses such an audience, he seems to enjoy assuming the posture of the grizzled, unshakably grumpy avatar of high modernism. In 2006, as the lone classical-music awardee at the Ivor Novello Awards—a Grammys-like, pop-dominated affair—Birtwistle's "acceptance speech" was anything but accepting: from the stage, the composer trained a withering, beady-eyed gaze on the audience and suggested that, on the evidence of the music he'd heard that evening, "you must all be brain-dead."

When I was in college, I heard Birtwistle give a talk to a small group of student composers, and the experience almost dissuaded me from exploring his music further. I found his demeanor perplexing and off-putting. The great composer looked disheveled and bleary, and he sat slightly hunched, staring down at the table as he spoke. He sounded awfully glum for a composer whose new violin concerto was being premiered that week by Christian Tetzlaff and the Boston Symphony Orchestra. I remember him complaining at length about the way visiting composers are treated by orchestra players: as the solitary composer sits forlornly in the empty hall, Birtwistle said, members of the orchestra rarely even bother to come by and say hello. I was tempted to suggest that the Boston Symphony's musicians might well have mistaken him for a sleepy drunk guy who'd wandered into their rehearsal by mistake.

Now that I know Birtwistle's music more deeply, I find his prickliness endearing. He simply doesn't care about what little glitz or glamour can still be found in the world of classical music. His motives are pure; he is an artist you can trust.

THE GREEN MAN

There's a wonderful moment in *Harrison Birtwistle: Wild Tracks*, the journalist Fiona Maddocks's illuminating "conversation diary," in which Birtwistle and Maddocks flip through a book of photos of African and Haitian masks. "Many of the figures are in full-body disguise," Maddocks writes, "swathed in wood, material, dyes, transforming them into strange spirits of the forest." Birtwistle personally identifies with a certain recurring type: "At all the ones that look most buried, or forest-like, or like a walking tree, submerged beneath branches and leaves, Harry says: 'That's me. That one's me.'"

I find this unaccountably moving. Though the masks Birtwistle refers to are in this case not European, the figures with which he feels a kinship sound, from Maddocks's description, like cousins of the "Green Man," the image of a human face emerging from a sea of leaves, or itself sprouting shoots and vines, that is mysteriously ubiquitous in medieval European art and architecture. No one can quite pin down what the Green Man symbolizes—is he a pagan fertility god?—and yet I think everyone who sees him instinctively knows who he is, and why he's inescapable. The Green Man is an embodied emblem of regeneration, of life messily pushing its way through the soil in springtime. He is an image of humankind's relationship to nature, of our being simultaneously bound to, and also irreparably distinct from, the earth we stand on. He is the spirit emerging from the flesh, the gleam of consciousness twinkling through the dirt and the tangled greenery.

The Green Man is the best possible image for Birtwistle's music, which has an intoxicating quality of earthy overgrownness. His harmonies and rhythmic gestures, many of which would sound acerbic in isolation, are often layered with an extraordinary, pressurized density, like the earth's strata; this mass of details yields a pungent funkiness, a sharp smell of the soil. Birtwistle has also made his affinity with the Green Man more or less explicit in certain pieces: one of his strongest operas is his adaptation of the medieval romance *Sir Gawain and the Green Knight*, whose story could be interpreted as a confrontation between humankind and a particularly frightening incarnation of the Green Man; and during his time teaching at a high school early in his career, he evidently wrote music for a school production that was literally called *The Green Man*. (In recent years, the composer, with his tangled curls and his barely landscaped beard, has come to resemble the Green Man himself.)

As a number of commentators have noted, Birtwistle is also a perfect specimen of a "hedgehog," according to Isaiah Berlin's still-helpful fox/hedgehog dichotomy. Some artists are foxes, eclectic and varied in their interests, and some are hedgehogs: they know "one big thing." Birtwistle, who has said that all of his music could be thought of as one ever-expanding piece, is one-hundred-percent hedgehog. Every one of his works seems to be guided by the same inscrutable law.

I would suggest that this law, this guiding force, is essentially an insight into the way that time moves, above and outside the linear, goal-oriented temporal motion that human beings experience day to day. In Birtwistle's music, time moves cyclically, in eternally recurring patterns of loss, decay, rupture, and regeneration. We feel the motion of the seasons, the groaning and shifting of tectonic plates, the death and rebirth of generation after generation. Human beings appear only as all-but-helpless participants in vast planetary processes. The title of Birtwistle's most recent orchestral opus, *Deep Time* (2017), could apply to his whole body of work, just as Wallace Stevens named his first book of poems *Harmonium* but thought of his collected work as "the whole of *Harmonium*." Birtwistle's pieces are dispatches from "deep time," messages unearthed from the mysterious time-tunnel down which he has patiently burrowed throughout his seven-decade artistic life.

THE MASK'S IMPOSSIBILITIES

Each Birtwistle piece is its own little myth: an act of rupture and loss that implies eternal repetition. This recursive conception of time makes Birtwistle uniquely suited to adapt the Orpheus story, and it also means that his take on the myth—especially in his biggest Orphic piece, *The Mask of Orpheus*—is fundamentally different from that of any other composer. I would define this difference in two ways.

First, Birtwistle and *The Mask*'s librettist, Peter Zinovieff, engage as few other artists have with the myth's instability and ambiguity. They treat the story not as a linear fiction but as a tragic *process* that—to return to Jorie Graham's phrase—is "always happening" in the human psyche. In most Orphic operas, Eurydice dies, Orpheus finds her in the underworld, and Eurydice dies a second time. The narrative moves inexorably toward loss. In Birtwistle's hands, by contrast, the myth is a kind of recurring dream that contradicts itself with each new iteration. Every major character is portrayed by multiple performers, and most of the drama's signal events occur multiple times, viewed from multiple perspectives. In the world of *The Mask*, sometimes you dream that you're Orpheus. Sometimes you're Eurydice. Sometimes you stand outside the drama, watching helplessly as the tragedy unfolds. Sometimes the myth is just a memory, a momentary sense of déjà vu, of having lost something you can't quite put your finger on, something you're not sure was real in the first place.

The other quality that distinguishes *The Mask of Orpheus* is that it has nothing to do with the Romantic image of its protagonist—the sensitive, weepy singer, gorgeously pining away for his lover. Many composers have treated the myth as a welcome excuse to write self-indulgently dilatory music of lamentation, but Birtwistle's music is Orphic in a different sense. Much of the music in *The Mask* has the aura of an ancient ceremony, a ritual performed by members of some cult of Orpheus or Dionysus. (We might be reminded of Peri and Rinuccini's very different attempt to resurrect an unknowable ancient practice.) The energies that Birtwistle seeks to channel are largely pre-Romantic, pre-modern, even pre-Classical.

Like Birtwistle's whole oeuvre, *The Mask* is full of contradictions. It is the most interior of Orpheus operas, and the grandest in scope. It is the most technologically advanced, and also the most ancient-sounding. Some listeners might resist the idea that a piece this abstract can be thought of as an opera at all, but from another perspective, it's the only genuinely Orphic opera ever written.

⟨ᗒᴥ⟩

The Mask of Orpheus is also more nearly impossible in the *literal* sense—that is, impossible to perform—than any other opera considered in this book. The piece calls for a large, unconventional orchestra: nineteen wind players; sixteen brass players; three harpists; electric guitar, bass, and mandolin; seven percussionists; and sophisticated pre-recorded electronics. This orchestral palette includes a number of ancient or otherworldly instruments: the antique oboe d'amore; a Japanese Noh harp; and three conch shells, which speak with a hair-raising, shofar-like squall. Unusually for a large-scale opera, there are no string instruments other than the plucked ones (harps, guitars), but the piece's texture is so rich that the first time I listened through it I didn't even notice the strings' absence. (They are "not in the nature of the piece," Birtwistle has said. "What would the strings bring to this? They're too lyrical." Their omission enacts a rejection of the Romantic orchestra along with the Romantic idea of Orpheus.) In addition to a large cast of singers, the piece also calls for actors, puppets, and a troupe of mimes. The music is so complex that it requires two conductors.

These extreme logistical complexities make *The Mask of Orpheus* staggeringly difficult to produce. Nearly two decades passed between the opera's conception and its first performance, and along the way the project became something of a poisoned chalice: practically every major British opera company committed at some point to presenting the piece, but the endeavor repeatedly foundered. In the end, the English National Opera undertook the huge effort to bring *The Mask* to life in 1986, thirteen years after the opera was supposed to have premiered at London's other leading company, the Royal Opera at Covent Garden.

This near-impossibility of performance has also translated into a confounding difficulty of access for would-be listeners. *The Mask of Orpheus*'s music and its libretto do not work hand in hand, as they do in most operas, but instead move on parallel, semi-independent tracks: some key dramatic events are silently acted out without any corresponding evidence in the music of their having taken place. For this reason, *The Mask*, more than most operas, needs to be *seen* if it is to be perceived in its entirety, but as of 2021, the opera has never been performed outside London, there is no publicly available video, and none of the opera's London productions has presented it uncut. An excellent recording does exist, but even this makes a few substantial cuts, especially to the third act. Given that this act's ambitious structure is based on the ebb and flow of the tides, the cuts surely lessen its potentially mesmerizing effect.

Just as Birtwistle's entire output seems to consist of fragments of a mysterious, inaccessible whole, *The Mask of Orpheus* can, for now, be experienced only as a series of enticing but palpably incomplete parts. Nonetheless, it is well worth your time to immerse yourself in its world. I would urge the curious listener to abandon all hopes of comprehension at the door, and to give yourself over to *The Mask*'s overwhelming sonic power. This piece is closer to an ayahuasca ceremony than a night at the opera. It is an experience to be undergone, not understood.

IMPOSSIBLE PERSPECTIVES:
THE MASK'S DRAMATIC STRUCTURE

The Mask of Orpheus resists every attempt to boil down its action into a conventional plot summary, but it nonetheless communicates a clear sense of progression, and eventually regression, across its epic span. As Robert Adlington explains in his lucid study of Birtwistle's music, the opera's three acts "focus on, respectively, Orpheus as man, hero, and god."

The first act presents the birth of Orpheus and the primordial emergence of his music: our hero's father, Apollo, a frightening, electronically generated voice that speaks in an invented language, rumbles cryptic messages that seem to infuse Orpheus with a godlike life force. Once Orpheus has gained the power of song, he speaks of his youthful adventures: his voyages with Jason and the Argonauts, his love affair with Eurydice. We witness multiple contradictory versions of certain events: Orpheus and Eurydice's wedding; the pursuit, and in one version the seduction, of Eurydice by the beekeeper Aristaeus; Eurydice's death and funeral. Finally, Orpheus visits the Oracle of the Dead, and eventually tricks her into telling him the rules that will grant him access to the underworld.

Of the three acts, the second, which depicts the protagonist's journey to and from the underworld, has the clearest sense of forward motion. Orpheus's progress is marked by his passage through seventeen portal-like arches, each of which possesses different properties, dangers, and associations ("the arch of Secrecy," "the arch of Wings," etc.). Near the end of the act, Orpheus realizes, or at least comes to believe, that he has dreamed everything that has happened thus far. He commits suicide.

The opera's first two acts are complex enough, but Act Three takes things to an entirely new plane. This act depicts not so much events within the Orpheus myth as the long-term fate of the myth itself. Its structure is based on the motions of tides on a beach: we seem to be standing on some shore at the edge of the ocean of time as the waves disgorge long-buried events from past millennia. Substantial segments of music from the previous acts are treated as mysterious objets trouvés, hunks of waterlogged wood or seaworn glass that wash ashore seemingly at random. The myth has been transformed into an inscrutable relic, a stone carved with messages in some lost tongue. We witness its degeneration, the loss of its original meaning. Eons of rot, corrosion, and decay accumulate into something new, something rich and strange.

I hope some enterprising company will someday tackle the challenge of presenting this act uncut—perhaps in a space other than a conventional theater. With the composer's permission, an endlessly looping recording of its music might make for an engrossing sound installation, a kind of shoreline of eternity, like the site-specific John Cage and John Luther Adams pieces that were built to unfold for centuries to come.

TEEMING ECOSYSTEMS: THE MUSIC OF *THE MASK*

Since *The Mask of Orpheus* is anything but linear in its construction, I would recommend that listeners approach the piece in a nonlinear way. For now, the BBC Symphony's stellar audio recording is the fullest document we have, apart from the score itself, and I find that Act Two makes for a more coherent aural experience than either of the outer acts. The first act is full of confounding involutions and interruptions, and the cuts to Act Three make it hard to get a full sense of its impact. But Act Two, with its exhilarating sense of momentum and its relatively clear structure, has the satisfying wholeness of a fifty-minute symphony. A good place to begin your listening odyssey is Orpheus's initial vision of the seventeen arches at the end of Act One ("I remember the arches. I can see a deep valley"), which is accompanied by a deliciously weighty sequence of chords in the winds and brass. From here, I would listen straight through to Act Two's devastating conclusion.

Birtwistle has spoken of *The Mask of Orpheus* as "one of the most complex works of art ever devised," a description that would sound immodest if it weren't, surely, objectively true. The opera's musical fabric consists of numerous textural layers, many of which display a stubborn aloofness, an unwillingness to play nicely with the others. These layers are sometimes required to line up precisely, like the whirring and ticking of some diabolically intricate clock, but more often the relationship between them is left somewhat fluid. The resulting impression is of a teeming ecosystem, an ocean or fertile rainforest full of fantastical creatures. I don't know another composer who achieves quite Birtwistle's blend of precision and openness: he lavishes extreme care on each individual layer, but he smears them together with a certain abandon. The image of the earth's strata—discrete layers interfusing and exerting pressure on one another—is again relevant. (I'm also reminded of the advice that Jean Sibelius supposedly gave a conductor who was wrestling with the question of how to tease out the nuances of his scores: rather than obsessing over every individual detail, Sibelius said, performers of his music should simply "swim in the gravy.")

The music for Orpheus's passage through the first arch is a

striking example of Birtwistle's unlikely instrumental superim-positions. Orpheus is just setting out on his journey into the underworld. As he describes what he sees ("Water flows over the edge of the arch. Green shoots cover the rock walls"), his music is fluid, notated almost without barlines; it is only occasionally that Birtwistle draws an arrow to alert the singer to line up with the orchestra. In contrast to Orpheus's lyrical line, the winds play a hesitant staccato figure; they seem to be tentatively knocking on a stone wall to test for a sign of hollowness, a point of entry. Beneath them, four stopped horns and a bass clarinet wheeze like a macro-accordion. A trio of soprano saxes, the instrumental analogue to the three Furies who will appear later in the act, wails deliriously. (Birtwistle's blisteringly intense soprano sax writing will purge your memory of all traces of Kenny G.) When Orpheus sings of water flowing over the arch, a liquid effluence of percussion bubbles up subliminally: congas, temple blocks, bongos, log drums, and suspended cymbals burble and whisper.

As Orpheus moves through the arches, the music grows more intense. Often a change in texture is announced by an abrupt gesture in the percussion that feels like the flipping of a switch, or a signal-sound in a video game, a sign that you've made it to the next level.* Sometimes this "signal" is a cascade of violent slaps from a cadre of whip-wielding percussionists. Elsewhere, it is a rapid upward sweep on xylophones, marimbas, and vibraphones.

The passage through the arches mostly blends together into a sequence of overwhelming, hallucinatory power, but the sixth

---

* The use of percussion gestures as starting-gun-like "signals" that trigger abrupt shifts in musical texture might remind some listeners of the American composer Andrew Norman (b. 1979), who has used such techniques still more explicitly, and to memorable effect, in orchestral works like *Play* (2013).

arch stands out for the vast evolution that the music undergoes in a span of barely more than two minutes. At first, Orpheus sings with palpable effort over an ominous texture of shifting choral lines, sputtering trombones, and quiet pinpricks in the guitars and harps; he could be a TV journalist yelling over the whir of helicopter blades. Eventually, two musical "signals" interrupt him: the alarming cry of a sort of orchestral fire engine composed of three soprano saxes and four horns; and a lightning-fast scattering gesture in percussion and plucked instruments. This percussion gesture begins to mutate, to grow longer and more elaborate. As it does, loud sustained notes begin accumulating in the winds and brass, creating a claustrophobic effect. When this texture reaches its breaking point, it splits open into a classic Birtwistle orchestral dance: it is one of his many rites of spring, feral and percussive, built out of multiple overlapping rhythmic cycles. Orpheus finally interrupts with a shout ("I remember falling through the jewelled water"), and the orchestra snaps into place. The rhythms remain violent, but now they are much blunter and simpler. Orpheus briefly seems to be calling the shots, leading the dance. Then he is interrupted by an electronic snarl from the depths: Apollo takes the reins once again.

Though Birtwistle's musical voice is what makes *The Mask of Orpheus* hang together, the piece could not have been realized without major contributions from two other artists, the electroacoustic composer Barry Anderson and the opera's polymathic librettist, Peter Zinovieff. Both Anderson and Zinovieff pushed Birtwistle to explore new musical spaces: Anderson helped Birtwistle devise new sound worlds through cutting-edge techniques of electronic sound production, and Zinovieff concocted radical formal structures whose labyrinthine complexities invited and enabled an analogous density in Birtwistle's music.

The Mask of Orpheus is unique in Birtwistle's output for its prominent use of electronics, and Anderson, the architect of its electronic sounds, deserves more credit than he has received. Avant-garde electronic music, like cinematic special effects, does not tend to age well, but Anderson's work is as breathtaking today as it must have been in 1986. He mercifully avoids the kind of space-age, science-fiction-esque effects that make some twentieth-century electronic music sound, to borrow the composer Nico Muhly's phrase, "like straight up R2D2."

The piece's electronic sounds take several distinct forms. There are "auras," gentle soundscapes that hum, sometimes all but inaudibly, throughout the whole opera. There is Apollo's oracular growl. And there are six self-contained interludes, each about three minutes long: three of these are called "Passing Clouds of Abandon," while the other three are "Allegorical Flowers of Reason."

These interludes reveal alluring traces of a deep collaborative process between Birtwistle and Anderson, the nature of which remains mostly obscure. (Anderson died the year after the opera premiered, and Birtwistle has never offered a detailed account of their working methods.) According to the scholar Jonathan Cross, the interludes' sound material consists of "four simple groups of sampled harp sounds," refracted images of "Orpheus' lyre," but without reading Cross's study, there's no way I would have guessed I was listening to a harp. We seem, rather, to be in the presence of some alien percussion ensemble. The sounds sometimes burst into a scalding, fizzing foam, like a sparkler; sometimes they crumble into a pile of burbling molecules; sometimes they lurch forward with an aggressive stutter.

The rhythmic gestures are recognizably Birtwistle's in their fierceness and their frequent self-interruptions, but the sound material could hardly be more different from his usual earthy palette. Birtwistle evidently notated the interludes' rhythms in detail: "I don't know where the scores are now," he told Cross. "They're impossible rhythms for a human, but for a machine they're easy." The result is a rare hybrid of two highly inventive composers' worlds. It's as if one of Alberto Giacometti's pencil sketches had been colored in by Francis Bacon.

By all accounts, Anderson was a notably self-effacing collaborator, but Zinovieff stands among the most brilliantly bossy librettists in operatic history. The ambitious formal scheme and nested plays-within-a-play—the "Passing Clouds" and "Allegorical Flowers," which depict fragments of other myths—are all Zinovieff's inventions, as is the third act's "tidal" structure. The text for Act Two, in particular, is unlike any other libretto I've encountered: it contains precise instructions, *down to the second*, for how long each musical event should be.

Given Birtwistle's inveterate stubbornness—he's a hedgehog, remember—it is perhaps surprising that he was willing to work from so minutely prescriptive a text. But he seems, in fact, to have relished the process: "Harry loves being told what to do," Zinovieff told Cross, "even if he doesn't do it!" Birtwistle evidently valued Zinovieff's schemata not because he found some mystical order inherent in them but rather because they proved capable of generating unexpected musical forms. There can be a special liberation in temporarily ceding creative control.

Zinovieff also palpably enjoys subverting all possibility of straightforward comprehension; he has a fondness for Russian-doll complexities, riddles wrapped in enigmas. My favorite of these is Orpheus's "Third Song of Magic," in Act Three. The song opens with Orpheus responding to a recurring musical fragment called the "Fossil Shell." Orpheus speaks cryptically: "Earth-pressed into time mould / This tree-dance. / Fruit-flower from day found. / Death-grey into nightfall." Cross notes that, according to commentary in the libretto, Orpheus is referring to events from Act One: his wedding ceremony and the subsequent dance. Well, that's a bit hard to grasp, but maybe a discerning listener could make the connection. Ah, I forgot to mention that the above text is sung in Orphic, a language invented by Zinovieff. You all had two years of Orphic in high school, right?

All this might seem unbearably pretentious if it were comprehensible, but thankfully, it's all sublimated into music. And this entombment of meaning, this burial of signification in a wash of pure wonderment, is one of *The Mask*'s deepest achievements. The "meaning" of the Orpheus myth is the inaccessible and possibly nonexistent pearl within the oyster on the ocean floor. But who cares about the pearl, when Birtwistle, Zinovieff, and Anderson managed to build an entire ocean around it? The impossibility of understanding, of ever looking behind the mask of *The Mask*, is the most fruitful impossibility of all.

THREE

The Firewood and the Fire

Words, Music, and Stravinsky's
The Rake's Progress

W hat is the nature of the relationship between music and words, whether in opera, song, or any other medium that brings music together with language? Are they lovers, business partners, rival siblings, mortal enemies? Does one matter more than the other, and if one medium assumes a dominant role, is the other automatically weakened or undermined? Opera's oldest adage on this subject asserts the primacy of music: *prima la musica, poi le parole*. But many a singer, coach, and composer has insisted that if opera is to be experienced not just as music but also as theater, clear communication of the text ought to be the performers' priority.

Though this tension is inherent in the relationship between these two media, this relationship is often framed in terms of mutual reverence: look how sensitively Fauré illuminates this poetic image with a single fragrant chord; look how modestly the text of this Schubert song effaces itself before the music; and so on. But from the composer's perspective, the relationship between music and words is not just one of respectful deference: it is also a battle of wills. The music and the poetry should each, ideally, manifest a certain stubbornness; their desires should even be somewhat at odds with each other. The relationship must be dynamic for the music to be worth listening to. After all, if the music had exactly the same desires as the poetry, there would be no need for music in the first place.

The more fraught the relationship between words and music, the richer the result can be. This paradoxical dynamic is exemplified by the collaboration between Igor Stravinsky and W. H. Auden on *The Rake's Progress* (1951), one of the most rewarding operas in the repertoire. Throughout *The Rake*, Stravinsky's music and Auden's poetry seem to perpetually subvert each other, but the relationship is in fact mutually reinforcing. The vocal lines that result from the tension between their respective textures is a singularly vivid musico-poetic compound, a strong yet ductile substance that brims with energy and life. Stravinsky exerts such steady friction on the sharply hewn firewood of Auden's text that the whole thing bursts brilliantly into flame.

Some composers prefer to work with librettists whom they can push around, and Stravinsky himself had displayed this tendency in his earlier theater pieces. He had no compunctions about ordering Jean Cocteau to repeatedly overhaul the text for the opera-oratorio *Oedipus Rex* (1927), early drafts of which Stravinsky found too "Wagnerian" and which he insisted must be simpler (he ordered Cocteau to make it "very banal!"). But he never made such a demand of Auden, whom he came to view as a peer. According to Stravinsky's amanuensis, Robert Craft, some of *The Rake*'s fustian philosophical digressions puzzled Stravinsky when he first read the libretto, but when he set it to music, he "treasured every word . . . and cut or changed very few of them."

The Rake is thus a rare example of a major composer and a major poet engaging as equals in a deep collaborative effort. What's more, Stravinsky's voice as a composer and Auden's as a poet have certain essential qualities in common, especially a chiseled, lapidary clarity. It would be hard to find two artists with a stronger allergy to vagueness or obfuscation; they each prefer pure, unfiltered sunlight to impressionistic cloudiness. One of the miracles of *The Rake* is the coexistence of their respective lucidities. Both the composer's and the poet's voices remain audible, even as Stravinsky refracts the light of Auden's poetry at an impossible angle, setting it deliciously askew.

The Rake's Progress is loosely based on the eighteenth-century British painter William Hogarth's pictorial series *A Rake's Progress*, engravings of which Stravinsky saw at the Art Institute of Chicago in 1947. Stravinsky was attracted to Hogarth's rococo aesthetic as well as his lavishly satirical depiction of a debauched, Sodom-like London, and he told Auden that he wanted to write a piece with all the trappings of Classical-era opera. Auden, working in collaboration with his life partner, the writer Chester Kallman, was glad to oblige him: their libretto is an elaborate morality tale, written in brilliantly wrought Augustan verse.

At the story's beginning, the idle young Tom Rakewell is engaged to the virtuous Anne Trulove. One day, Tom speaks aloud his desire to be rich. As soon as he does, the mysterious Nick Shadow appears and informs Tom that a previously unknown uncle has died and bequeathed his vast wealth to Tom. Shadow offers to work as Tom's servant for "a year and a day," at which time he will claim whatever wages they agree are fair. Tom unquestioningly follows Shadow to London, where he soon forgets his commitment to Anne and, having claimed his fortune, gives in to every temptation he encounters—drinking, gambling, prostitutes. Hounded by his ever-increasing guilt, and by a misguided impulse to prove his freedom from both passion and rational thought, Tom marries Baba the Turk, the bearded lady at a local circus. When he grows tired of his life with Baba, Tom ruins himself by investing his fortune in a bogus machine that he is convinced is capable of miraculously turning stones into bread. At the end of the agreed-upon term, Shadow attempts to claim his wages: Tom's soul, of course. Tom is rescued at the last moment by the grace of Anne's enduring love for him. But he doesn't escape unscathed: though he will not be damned, from this moment forward he will be insane. In the final scene, Anne visits Tom in Bedlam, where it is implied he will spend the rest of his days.

On the surface, *The Rake's Progress* seems to be, well, all surface. It can feel, on a first encounter, like a stiflingly stylized fable, one that risks preciosity at every turn: its protagonists are literally named "Rakewell" and "Trulove," and the music seems to be little more than a parade of self-conscious allusions to Handel and Mozart. The whole thing must be a joke, right?

Not quite. Hard as it is to see past the piece's powdered wigs and three-cornered hats, its heroic couplets and twangling harpsichord, *The Rake's Progress* is much more than a period piece. Through their loving attention to intertwined details of characterization, harmony, and prosody, Stravinsky and Auden set themselves the daunting task of proving that pastiche does not necessarily equal parody.

The Rake's Progress was the first opera I participated in as a performer: a student production of the piece during my freshman year of college initiated me into the joys and struggles of bringing an opera to the stage. I remember my bemusement, when I first studied the piece, at its curlicued ornateness, as well as my trepidation at having to negotiate the score's sadistic, finger-twisting difficulties at the piano. My task was to coach the cast and direct the chorus—in this production an ensemble of no more than eight singers—but when a tenor dropped out, I was also conscripted to *sing* in the chorus. As a result, I got to know the opera from many angles: playing it at the piano, conducting chorus rehearsals, and finally performing it onstage.

Before long, my perplexity gave way to amazement and love. Like the best Mozart operas, *The Rake's Progress* grows richer with every day you spend in its company. The opera's characters, who seem at first glance to be cardboard figures in a mock morality play, turn out to be flesh-and-blood human beings; and the plot, which can seem frivolous right up to the final scene, has a way of breaking your heart at the last second.

I'm hardly alone in having been nonplussed by *The Rake* when I first encountered it: critics and commentators have condescended to the piece ever since its premiere, though there's little consensus among them on the question of whether its cardinal sin is its modernistic chilliness, as well as the perceived ungainliness of Stravinsky's rhythmic and harmonic dislocations, or its unforgivable backwardness. Olin Downes, writing in *The New York Times* about the opera's American premiere, articulated the former view: "Stravinsky has long since shown that he has a paucity of melodic inspiration," he declared. "Much of the vocal line . . . is essentially unvocal," and "the moments of real feeling and inspiration are very few." Howard Taubman found a certain chilliness in both music and libretto: the music manifested "the Stravinsky point of view—cool, objective, intellectual," and the libretto seemed to be no more than "a carefully calculated intellectual conception." The young Pierre Boulez, in whose eyes any hint of neo-Classicism constituted a damning regression into musical infancy, sneered "What ugliness!" in a letter to John Cage. Even the writer Paul Griffiths, in his book-length study of the opera, claims that the musical approach Stravinsky took, with its references to past idioms, "could only be taken by a composer for whom both tonality and opera were dead."

Now that I know the piece better, I find these judgments mystifying. I dare anyone to listen to, say, Bryn Terfel singing "I burn! I freeze!"; or Dawn Upshaw as Anne; or any performance of the Act Two trio ("Could it then have been known"), and still dismiss this piece as a heartless intellectual exercise. My hunch is that many critics who mistrust *The Rake* are listening in one of two ways: either they can hear only the piece's top layer, and are suffering an allergic reaction to the use of eighteenth-century tropes; or else they made up their minds five minutes into the first scene, and stopped listening at that point. (The opera's first scene, which depicts a false and unsustainable utopia, is intentionally its most heavily stylized.)

But *The Rake* is beloved by a community that knows the piece far better than most critics do: that is, artists who have performed it. The singers, conductors, and directors I know who have essayed *The Rake* invariably speak of it as an opera that has a special place in their hearts. This bodes well for the piece's future health. I remember the pianist Robert Levin saying once that many of Mozart's works entered the bloodstream of the international repertoire not due to the approbation of either critics or audiences but rather because musicians felt in their bones that they *had* to play this music. *The Rake*, which feels to me like a long-lost sibling to the Mozart operas, has a similar effect on many musicians. In the life cycle of an opera, this one is still quite young. It's just barely coming into focus.

☌

We are lucky to have a rich bounty of documents from throughout *The Rake*'s development. There is Stravinsky and Auden's initial exchange of letters from October 1947, in which Auden, after a no-nonsense list of practical questions about Stravinsky's preferences ("it is the librettist's job to satisfy the composer not the other way round"), permits himself a curt expression of excitement about the project: "I need hardly say that the chance of working with you is the greatest honor of my life." We also have a detailed initial outline of the opera's structure, created by Stravinsky and Auden after a week spent working together in Los Angeles in November of the same year. Soon after that, Auden (unbeknownst to Stravinsky) invited Kallman to collaborate with him on the libretto. From this point on, most of the work between librettists and composer was done long-distance, in writing: two draft typescripts of the libretto have survived, each of them marked up with the creators' edits and marginalia.

My impression from studying Stravinsky and Auden's early correspondence is that both artists initially intended to write a piece that would actually have had the faults that many critics have ascribed to the final product: heartlessness, chilliness, artificiality. The writer Alan Ansen reports (evidently quoting Auden from memory) that the poet initially intended for the opera to have seven characters, who would correspond to the seven deadly sins:

"The hero, of course, will represent Pride, the young girl Lust . . . The rich old woman will be Avarice, the false friend Anger, the servant Envy and so on." At that time, Auden identified the prideful title character with Lucifer, and he imagined the opera's final scene in Bedlam as a Satanic coronation service: "He ought to be anointed with a chamber pot . . . Piss is the only proper chrism."

For his part, Stravinsky initially seemed inspired by a combative impulse to redefine the medium of opera, to fight Wagnerian bloat with Apollonian leanness: he intended to compose "*not* a Musical Drama, but just an Opera with definitely separated numbers." The storyboard-like quality of Hogarth's pictures, the way that each of the sequence's eight scenes occupies its own frame, strongly appealed to him. As Griffiths relates in his study of *The Rake*, Stravinsky originally wanted each musical number to be framed by spoken dialogue, and he planned on writing "a Choreographic Divertissement in the first Act's finale." Auden, having grasped that Stravinsky was on the hunt for antiquated theatrical devices, suggested that "between the two acts, there should be a choric parabasis"—that is, an interlude in which the chorus directly addresses the audience about a topic entirely irrelevant to the main narrative.

None of these ideas made it into the opera. Once they got started, it seems that all three creators—but especially Stravinsky—found that they couldn't stick to their principles without compromising something vital, something unexpected: the humanity of the characters and the story's essential tenderness. Tom Rakewell is not a mere allegory of Pride, nor is Baba the Turk the embodiment of Avarice. And there's certainly no room for a "choric parabasis" or a "Choreographic Divertissement." Once the opera revealed its true nature, it made its own demands.

I want to track two of *The Rake*'s metamorphoses, two of its transformations from firewood into fire. First, there is Stravinsky's loving subversion of Auden and Kallman's text, the way he ignites the raw material of the poetry into music, seemingly by breaking the poetry's every rule. The other is the transformation of Hogarth's stop-motion morality play into a drama filled with living, breathing characters.

This latter transformation is itself a two-part process. First, Auden and Kallman turned Hogarth's anemic Rake into a person with agency: Hogarth shows a debauched society swallowing up a seemingly passive victim, whereas the opera's libretto is full of individual human beings making the decisions that will determine their fates. The second stage of this transformation is the way Stravinsky imbues Auden and Kallman's characters, some of whom look a little stilted on the page, with life and warmth. The final result, with its suppleness and buoyancy, bears little resemblance to Hogarth—but then, a fire doesn't look much like the wood it was kindled from, either.

AUDEN AND MUSIC

When Stravinsky, acting on the recommendation of Aldous Huxley, invited Auden to write *The Rake*'s libretto, he may not have known that he was inviting one of the most devoted of opera aficionados to finally make a substantial contribution to an artistic medium he had long adored as a spectator. Auden's one previous foray into music-theater had been his libretto for Benjamin Britten's operetta *Paul Bunyan* (1941), an endeavor that everyone involved seemed to feel, after its premiere in New York, was best swept hastily under the rug. The notion of two hyperliterary, fresh-off-the-boat gay British expats writing a ready-for-Broadway light opera about the manliest man in American folklore might sound like something out of *The Producers*, and alas, the Britten-Auden *Paul Bunyan* is as preposterous as the phrase "Britten-Auden *Paul Bunyan*" would suggest. With this experience behind him, the prospect of writing an opera set in Hogarth's London, in sumptuously Popian verse, must have struck Auden as a welcome return to familiar turf.

Auden loved opera, as he loved myths and fairy tales, for its ability to cut to the bedrock of the human psyche; certain operatic roles, like Don Giovanni, recur throughout his work as psychological touchstones, ur-emblems of essential human types. The noisy, no-holds-barred spectacle of operatic performance also provided him with a welcome contrast to the solitary work of writing. Indeed, Auden's love of opera was founded on what he perceived to be music's fundamental difference from his own art form, poetry—a difference that he articulated, with his trademark bossiness, as a strict circumscription of the two art forms' respective functions. Music, for Auden, was a playground of pure catharsis, while poetry was the proper arena for investigations and litigations of humankind's duties to itself and to God. He loved music precisely because he believed it to be immune to the tortuous self-consciousness that was his daily bread.

Though I inevitably disagree with Auden's delimitations—his insistence that music is incapable of psychological ambiguity, for instance, strikes me as absurd—I find it energizing to wrestle with his ideas about music's essential nature. The clarity of his positions can help us clarify our own. It is, counterintuitively, *because* of Auden's fanboyish passion for music, and his attendant need to strip it of its complexities and treat it as an idealized Other, that he is an especially thought-provoking philosopher of the art form.

His theory of the prehistoric origin of music, for instance, is quietly revelatory. Auden proposes that music probably did not originate with the ear—that is, with the desire to imitate external sounds—but rather with humankind's "direct experience of his own body," the body's inner "tensions and rhythms." He draws a contrast between music and the visual arts, which he believes *are* dependent on the eye, and on a desire to represent external things. I think many musicians would agree that Auden's diagnosis rings true: music is the result of an inner physical need, as dance is, and its external realization in sound is an aftereffect rather than a cause.

Elsewhere, however, Auden's precepts about music are unhelpfully reductive. "Music cannot exist in an atmosphere of uncertainty," goes a typical dictum. "Song cannot walk, it can only jump." He also asserts that the essence of music-making is the expression of human willpower, the creation of a "self-determined history": "A succession of two musical notes is an act of choice." (He doesn't address the question of what makes a succession of two notes more distinctly an "act of choice" than a succession of two words in a poem.) If music is an expression of choice, then opera is "an imitation of human wilfulness," and opera characters are inevitably "monomaniac[s]."

With this established, Auden makes a rule: opera "cannot present character in the novelist's sense of the word, namely, people who are potentially good *and* bad, active *and* passive." When certain composers and librettists dare to do so—as, for example, Mozart and Da Ponte do in *Le nozze di Figaro*—Auden finds the effort unconvincing: the Mozart–Da Ponte Figaro is "too interesting a character to be completely translatable into music." Rossini's depiction of the same character as a "maniacal busybody" is, for Auden, more credible, since he thinks music is better suited to manic perpetual motion than to psychological nuance.

Clearly Auden took a wrong turn along the way, because he's ended up somewhere absurd: he's literally faulting Mozart for the subtlety of his portraiture! But there's something to be learned from Auden even at his most exasperatingly dogmatic. To appreciate Auden's achievement in *The Rake's Progress*, we must first understand his concept of opera as proof of the irreducible reality of human willpower: "Every high C accurately struck utterly demolishes the theory that we are the irresponsible puppets of fate or chance." Auden believed, and needed to believe, that human beings possess some modicum of freedom, with all freedom's attendant risks and responsibilities: the possibility of real guilt, and of real salvation. In *The Rake's Progress*, he would put his philosophy of freedom to the test, in the medium that he believed best manifested the reality of that freedom.

In the decade after *The Rake*'s premiere, Auden wrote extensively about the craft of opera-making, and his essays about the role of the librettist are among the most perceptive ever published on the subject. He lovably sounds at once like a sober professional, generously sharing his tricks of the trade, and like a petulant, picky opera queen. Here is Auden on the nature of operatic plots: "No good opera plot can be sensible for people do not sing when they are feeling sensible." Operatic libretti should ideally feature "not one sensible moment or one sensible remark," a standard that is "very difficult to manage though Wagner managed it."

Auden also argues, in a more serious vein, that myths make the best subject matter for tragic operas because only mythic, archetypal characters genuinely invite the audience to imagine themselves as *participants* in the tragedy. Myths belong to all of us, whereas in contemporary stories, the audience perceives "a situation some people are in and others, including the audience, are not in." When we cannot imagine that the suffering depicted onstage could be our own, "the pleasure we . . . are obviously enjoying strikes the conscience as frivolous." This is the difference between empathy and voyeurism, a difference that makes all the difference. Auden's viewpoint provides a welcome and bracing corrective to the attitude that tends to prevail in the twenty-first century: we are too ready to assume that audiences are capable of empathizing *only* with characters in contemporary situations, characters who look, talk, and dress as they do.

As for his own role, that of the librettist, Auden is sternly matter-of-fact in his insistence on its modesty and contingency. The librettist's task is to serve the composer, period: "The verses which the librettist writes are not addressed to the public but are really a private letter to the composer," since only the composer will read the words *as words*; by the time they reach the public, they will have been transformed beyond recognition. Their "moment of glory" is "the moment in which they suggest to [the composer] a certain melody." Once the words have been set to music, "they must efface themselves and cease to care what happens to them." To hear Auden tell it, the librettist's presentation of a text to the composer is a kind of virgin sacrifice. When we listen to operatic singing, Auden doubts that we hear words at all: he believes we hear only "sung syllables," and as a result, "in song, poetry is expendable, syllables are not."

Because of this, Auden prefers the humble but expertly sculpted verses of the bel canto librettist Felice Romani, who collaborated with Donizetti and Bellini, to the libretti of a more ambitious writer like Hugo von Hofmannsthal. Romani knows his place: he is a reliable supplier of clean, dry firewood, ready to be set alight. By contrast, the wordy, winkingly allusive free verse that Hofmannsthal writes for Richard Strauss's *Der Rosenkavalier* (1911) has a waterlogged quality; it seems unwilling to give itself over entirely to the demands of the music. (Auden is also dismissive of Mozart's librettists, and clearly feels it's a shame Mozart didn't have the chance to collaborate with *him*.)

It probably won't come as a surprise that Auden the librettist rarely follows the prescriptions of Auden the theorist. He's too ambitious a poet and too sophisticated a thinker for that. The text of *The Rake's Progress* is much more than a self-effacing collection of singable syllables—and thank goodness! The piece is richer for the outrageous theatrical risks that Auden takes. These risks range from borderline-kitsch pageantry that wouldn't be out of place on *RuPaul's Drag Race* (one New York company refused to premiere *The Rake* because the bearded Baba the Turk no doubt represented some "perverse sexuality") to an ambitiously Kierkegaardian ethical program. And surely the most outrageous risk of all was to bring RuPaul and Kierkegaard together under one roof.

I have a feeling, however, that if Auden had been working alone, his inner censor might have nixed some of the opera's freakier ideas, Baba included. (In the original scenario, Baba was an "Ugly Duchess," often referred to by the irresistible abbreviation "Ugly D.") The difference between *The Rake's Progress* and one of Auden's sober poem-plays, like *The Age of Anxiety*, is that for *The Rake*, Auden found a partner in crime, a collaborator who would egg him on and dare him to scale opera's campiest heights. The partner Auden chose for this folie à deux was Chester Kallman, a fellow poet and opera fan, and one of the loves of his life.

FROM IMAGE TO WORD: AUDEN, KALLMAN,
AND THE LIBRETTO OF *THE RAKE*

Auden met Kallman in New York in the spring of 1939, and fell so deeply in love that he later wrote of having experienced a "Vision of Eros." The episode marked a turning point in the poet's life: at thirty-two, Auden believed for the first time that he was both capable of romantic love and deserving of it. Kallman, just eighteen at the time, was quick-witted and sophisticated beyond his years, and as a native New Yorker, he was already an experienced operagoer; he helped whet Auden's appetite for the art form by taking him on dates to the Met. Their love affair splintered when their respective ideas about fidelity proved irreconcilable (Kallman had no interest in monogamy), but their commitment to each other far outlasted their erotic relationship. In the fall of 1947, when Auden returned to New York after his exhilarating initial brainstorming sessions with Stravinsky, he eagerly showed Kallman the outline that he and the composer had devised.

Kallman had a keen instinct for what would and wouldn't work onstage, and he ventured a few criticisms. He suggested, for instance, that it probably wasn't a great idea for Tom Rakewell to summon Nick Shadow by yawning. Auden's original notion was that Tom's yawn, the gesture that betrayed his idleness, could serve as his unconscious invitation to his demon. But as Kallman pointed out, a yawn is unlikely to be visible from the cheap seats in a big opera house. Worse, it might even look grotesque, like a failed attempt to sing. Auden grudgingly admitted that Kallman was right; according to the latter's account, Auden grumbled that he shouldn't "point out little flaws if you have no idea what to put in their place." As it happened, though, Kallman *did* have an idea: he suggested that Tom could summon Shadow three times over the course of the opera by speaking three wishes, fairy-tale style. This was an indisputable improvement. Auden surely sensed that if he had Kallman by his side, he was much less likely to repeat the mistakes that had made *Paul Bunyan* unfunny and theatrically inert. And so, without telling Stravinsky, Auden hired Kallman as co-librettist.

Auden and Kallman's two biggest challenges, in adapting a series of paintings into a full-length theater piece, were to transform eight tableaux, eight frozen moments, into a drama with a coherent arc, and to turn the essentially passive figure of Tom Rakewell—who, in the paintings, is always being groped or manhandled by someone or other—into a dynamic character. They did not merely overcome these hurdles but went so far as to treat these challenges as the central subjects of the work: *The Rake*'s two deepest themes are the issue of free will—whether it exists at all, and if it does, how it manifests—and the question of what a mortal human being's relationship to time, and eternity, ought to be.

Tom Rakewell suffers from what Emerson would have called a "disease of the will." When we first meet Tom, we hear him convince himself that free will is an illusion, and that he is therefore justified in his laziness:

> Since it is not by merit
> We rise or we fall,
> But the favor of Fortune
> That governs us all,

Why should I labor
For what in the end
She will give me for nothing
If she be my friend?

This travestied Calvinism makes Tom easy prey for his demonic alter ego, Nick Shadow, who suddenly materializes to inform him of his mysterious inheritance. The role of Shadow, who does not appear in Hogarth, is a canny invention on Auden's part: he is the embodiment of Tom's diseased will, the fiendish force of unreason that Tom allows to lead him by the nose.

Accompanied by Shadow, Tom goes to London to claim his inheritance, and gluts himself on the many pleasures available to a wealthy, unworldly young man. When Tom admits that he is still not happy, Shadow tells him that he will be happy only if he is free, and he will be free only if he can overcome the "twin tyrants" of desire and reason. Tom must prove his freedom by performing a kind of stunt, an acte gratuit: he must do something that he neither wants to do nor is impelled to by a rational sense of duty. Shadow's suggestion is that Tom should marry Baba the Turk, the bearded lady at a local circus.

The acte gratuit is the mirror image of the forces that actually guided Auden in his artistic work (and Stravinsky too, for that matter). Tom rejects reason and passion in favor of freedom; Auden was skeptical of the idea that freedom is an unalloyed good, but his poetry depends on both passion and reason, held in equilibrium. Auden insisted on the reality of *free will*, of course, but he defined free will as the freedom to choose what is right, according to his idiosyncratic interpretation of Christian morality; nothing could be further from Tom's delusional framing of "freedom" as a militantly antirational, self-policing nihilism. To write his poetry, Auden needed a degree of *unfreedom*: he liked rules, both metrical and moral. Tom, on the other hand, "progresses" from a denial of the reality of free will to a desperate belief that freedom can be expressed only through a refusal of all rules, all cultural norms, all responsibilities. This way madness lies.

Tom's grotesque denial of his own agency is matched by his tragically unfulfilling relationship to time: he is incapable of living in the present moment, though the mirage-like prospect of future success is a constant source of anxious glee for him. Auden once suggested that Tom suffers from manic depression (that is, bipolar disorder), as Kallman did in reality: he is "a man to whom the anticipation of experience is always exciting and its realization in actual fact always disappointing," a person who is "elated by the prospect of the future and then disgusted by the remembrance of the recent past." In other words, Tom is the anti-Orpheus: plagued by a shame that he does not dare face, he cannot look back. As his regrets accumulate, he has to sprint ever faster into his illusory future in order to escape them. In the end, his punishment is not hellfire, but rather confinement to an eternal present tense in which he is left with nothing.

Anne Trulove, Tom's fiancée, is his antithesis: she is selflessly devoted to Tom, and her unwavering sense of duty and responsibility for her actions verge on self-flagellation. A character as impregnably virtuous as Anne does risk being a bore, and I'm afraid there's a whiff of misogyny in Auden and Kallman's treatment of her: I can't help but hear, in her ever-righteous lines, the muffled sound of two male librettists trying to stifle their giggles at the *idea* of such an improbably saintly woman. (In a reflection on *The Rake* published a decade after the opera's premiere, Kallman snickeringly points out that the only thing Anne ever says to her father is "Yes, Father"—"but then, of course, she is a *very* good girl.") When Anne decides to go to London to find the wayward Tom, her aria displays an unambiguous resolve that serves as a counterweight to Tom's elaborate sophisms:

> I go to him.
> Love cannot falter,
> Cannot desert;
> Though it be shunned
> Or be forgotten,
> Though it be hurt
> If love be love
> It will not alter.

This blunt fixity of purpose might look one-dimensional on the page, but don't judge poor Anne just yet—she is the character who is most thoroughly transformed by Stravinsky's music. And the hint of mockery in the librettists' depiction of Anne was, to some degree, inwardly directed: the Auden scholar Edward Mendelson has pointed out that Auden, throughout his relationship with Kallman, himself played the long-suffering Anne to Kallman's recalcitrant Rake.

Auden has long received both the praise and the blame for *The Rake's* perceived strengths and weaknesses; the luster of his name has blinded many commentators to the reality that this libretto was a joint effort. To his credit, Auden did his best to share the glory: "Two librettists are not two people but a composite personality," he wrote. Though a given line may have been written by one or the other of them, "the censor-critic who decides what will or will not do is this corporate personality."

This rings true at the structural level: the piece's boldest departures from Hogarth are clearly the product of a giddy shared fervor ("the day that Baba the Turk was born and named," Kallman recalled, "we both laughed until we could no longer stand up straight"). But line by line and scene by scene, Auden's and Kallman's contributions are strikingly different. Many of the lines that have struck listeners as problematically vague were actually written by Kallman, whose knack for finding strong, direct theatrical gestures—Tom's three wishes, for instance—does not always translate to verbal clarity or conciseness. I wonder if any listener has ever understood what Shadow is saying when he warns Tom that his fortune brings with it complications like "Attorneys crouched like gardeners to pay, / Bowers of paper only seals repair," or when Tom, ranting about the young London ladies who court him for his money, says, "Cover their charms a little, you well-bred bawds, or your goods will catch their death of the rheum long before they learn of the green sickness."

Opera lovers owe Kallman a debt of gratitude for turning Auden on to opera in the first place, and for serving brilliantly as his familiar spirit. But I wish Auden had written a bit more of *The Rake* himself, because his half of the libretto magnificently displays something close to the full range of his Houdini-esque dexterity in a wide array of idioms and metrical forms: eclogue, folk ballad, lullaby, Edward Lear–style nonsense verse, austere Classical elegy.

In the hands of many poets, *The Rake* would have ended up as either a dull morality play or a mean-spirited satire; Auden avoids both extremes by injecting the piece with a heavy dose of camp.

After Tom and Baba consummate their ill-fated marriage, Tom sits at the breakfast table in glum silence as Baba babbles lines of a fabulously McGonagallesque irregularity:

I get so confused about all my travels.
The snuff boxes came from Paris, and the fluminous
  gravels
From a cardinal who admired me vastly in Rome.
You're not eating, my love. Count Moldau gave me the
  gnome,
And Prince Obolovsky the little statues of the Twelve
  Apostles,
Which I like best of all my treasures except my fossils.

On the rare occasions that Auden writes a clunker, the culprit is usually his fondness for treating verbal abstractions as if they were as tangible as a stone or a potato. This is no problem on the page, but it can create difficulties in the theater. Nick Shadow's references to "the unpredictable Must" of desire and "the inflexible Ought" of duty are mighty hard to understand when they're sung; I always hear "must" as "mast," especially when (as directors often choose to stage this moment) the baritone pantomimes his helpless enthrallment to a raging erection.

The opera's penultimate scene, in which Shadow leads Tom to a graveyard to claim his soul, functions as a kind of dramaturgical trapdoor: it gives a strong impression of being the opera's finale before opening unexpectedly into the surreal new space of Bedlam. The Bedlam scene is, I think, Auden's finest moment in the libretto, and one of the most powerful things he ever wrote, in any medium.

In the graveyard, Shadow tells Tom that his time is up: he

will be damned upon the stroke of midnight. First, however, Shadow unwisely decides to give Tom a final chance to save himself through a game of chance. (Evidently Shadow suffers from the overconfidence that has led many a supervillain to needlessly toy with their nemeses once they have them cornered.) Shadow will draw three cards at random; if Tom can guess all three, he will be saved. With the help of Anne, whose voice he hears in the distance, Tom correctly guesses that Shadow has cheated, and played the same card (the Queen of Hearts) twice. Shadow is furious—his prey has eluded him. Tom's many sins, however, do give Shadow some "power to pain": from this moment on, Tom will be insane. The grace of Anne's love can save Tom from damnation, but it can't give him the brains that he has lacked from the beginning.

The scene changes to Bedlam. Tom, who believes himself to be Adonis, irritates his fellow patients with his exhortations to prepare themselves for Venus's arrival. The Bedlamites first answer with singsong playground taunts ("Madmen's words are all untrue. / She will never come to you") before singing a chorus that I think deserves a place in Auden's *Collected Poems*:

> Leave all love and hope behind;
> Out of sight is out of mind
> In these caverns of the dead.
> In the city overhead
> Former lover, former foe
> To their works and pleasures go
> Nor consider who beneath
> Weep and howl and gnash their teeth.
> Down in Hell as up in Heaven
> No hands are in marriage given,

Nor is honor or degree
Known in our society.
Banker, beggar, whore and wit
In a common darkness sit.
Seasons, fashions never change;
All is stale yet all is strange;
All are foes, and none are friends
In a night that never ends.

This chorus is a dark mirror of Auden's 1937 poem "Lullaby" ("Lay your sleeping head, my love"). Both poems are in trochaic tetrameter, the four-beat meter whose crisp symmetries and fairy-tale connotations made it a favorite of Auden's (it is also favored by Shakespeare's Puck). In "Lullaby," Auden has a vision of the transience of earthly happiness, embodied by the fragile content-ment of his lover resting his head on Auden's arm:

Lay your sleeping head, my love,
Human on my faithless arm;
Time and fevers burn away
Individual beauty from
Thoughtful children, and the grave
Proves the child ephemeral:
But in my arms till break of day
Let the living creature lie,
Mortal, guilty, but to me
The entirely beautiful.
. . . .
Every farthing of the cost,
All the dreaded cards foretell,
Shall be paid, but from this night

Not a whisper, not a thought,
Not a kiss nor look be lost.

Auden is aware both of presence and of the transience of presence: I'm alive right now / it's all slipping away. This relationship to time finds its exact inversion in *The Rake*'s purgatorial chorus. In "Lullaby," the moment is fleeting but precious, and it may be preserved in memory, whereas the Bedlam-dwellers inhabit a boring, eternal present tense. In their lifeless limbo, both memory and love are impossible: nothing is precious because nothing can change. The world outside, they claim, has forgotten them.

But this turns out not to be true: Anne appears after all. She has come to visit Tom, and gamely plays along with his delusion, pretending to be Venus to his Adonis. For a moment, Tom is entirely happy. Anne sings Tom a lullaby, and bids him a tearful farewell. When Tom wakes up and asks where Venus has gone, his fellow asylum-dwellers tell him that no one has been to see him. He believes them. He is alone, and desolate.

The much-misused phrase "poetic justice" could have been invented for Auden: Tom, who refused to live in the present tense, is finally left with nothing *but* the present. We witness his newly childlike relationship to time in two iterations: total happiness, then total despair. He is both saved and not saved. Love and grace are real, but not omnipotent.

Part of the genius of *The Rake*'s libretto lies in the way Auden and Kallman hold a space open for music: their tale poses a kind of riddle that only music can solve, the challenge of proving, or manifesting, the reality of human agency. Tom might claim that free will is an illusion, but according to Auden's definition of opera as the purest, most concentrated form of human willful-ness, he proves himself wrong every time he opens his mouth to sing. Stravinsky's music is itself the best refutation of Tom's self-deceptions. I want to turn now to that music, which utterly transforms Auden and Kallman's text—and not, I would wager, in quite the way the librettists expected it would.

FROM WORD TO MUSIC: STRAVINSKY'S IGNITION OF THE TEXT

In the first few decades of his career, Stravinsky probably wouldn't have agreed with Auden that operatic characters are willful by their very nature: indeed, he had long since revealed an attraction to stories in which the possibility of personal autonomy is thrown sharply into question, and many of his earlier pieces seem to fe-tishize either the absence or the enacted destruction of individual free will. His earliest successes were ballets, and it's surely easier for a dancer, rather than a singer, to create the illusion of being an automaton pulled by invisible strings. Rightly or wrongly, *voice* remains a near-universal metonym for acts of self-determination, whether we're talking about giving underrepresented groups a voice in the political process or celebrating a young author's breakthrough, the story in which they "found their voice." A singer whose voice fills a four-thousand-seat auditorium is thus an embodiment of willed self-magnification, while the silent bal-let dancer has long been a symbol of self-effacement. (This trope persists even in its negation: the dancers I know who most thor-oughly reject these connotations are often those who, like Bobbi Jene Smith, allow themselves to vocalize while dancing, to let a grunt or a sigh announce their subjective existence, the reality of their pleasure and effort.)

Stravinsky's depictions of limited or liminal autonomy take two distinct forms: the individual whose autonomy is obliterated by a potent social collective; and the mechanistic sublime of the automaton. Examples of the former include *The Rite of Spring* (1913), with its ritual sacrifice of the Chosen One before the assembled elders; and *Les noces* (1923), which depicts a Russian peasant wedding. The singular power of *Les noces* derives from the sense that the celebrants who make up its cast are in the grip of some mysterious collective force that pulls them forward in a vertiginous, headlong rush: the sacred ritual of marriage has a will of its own, an impetus so powerful that it swallows up its participants, who submit to it with a giddy blend of joy and terror.

In the latter category—the self-effacing virtuosity of the automaton—there are *Petrushka* (1911), whose protagonist is a puppet brought to life by a magician; and *The Nightingale* (1914), whose title character is a magical bird that suffers the indignity of being temporarily replaced by a mechanical imitation. There is singing in both *Les noces* and *The Nightingale*, but at the premieres of both pieces, the characters were portrayed onstage by dancers. To put singers onstage would have been to suggest, misleadingly, that these characters are autonomous beings. Stravinsky preferred, instead, to create the sense that they were being manipulated by unseen higher powers. The oracular mouth of the singer had to be invisible.

None of this applies to *The Rake's Progress*, but when Stravinsky started writing the piece, he might have thought otherwise. The passivity of Hogarth's Rake, the sense that, in Kallman's words, he "is exclusively acted *upon*," might have been what attracted Stravinsky to the subject in the first place; Hogarth's paintings might have struck him as a grim secular counterpoint to the suffocating social rituals he had depicted in *Les noces* and *The Rite of Spring*. But Stravinsky ultimately embraced his librettists' focus on individuals and individual agency. This shift, subtle though it might seem, would transfigure the way he depicted human beings in music.

The finished score does, however, contain one tantalizing "ghost" of a possible earlier conception of the piece. Writing operas is a messy business, and composers often build them in anything but chronological order. Because of this, it can be revealing to look at the music that was *composed* first in a given opera: these passages can reveal traces of what the composer thought the piece was going to be before they found its true language.

The first music that Stravinsky wrote for *The Rake* was the eighteen-bar prelude to the graveyard scene in the opera's final act. He composed this music soon after his initial discussions with Auden, before he had received a word of the libretto. This little prelude is scored for string quartet alone, and as Griffiths notes, its dissonant twinges call to mind the music that Stravinsky would write in the years after *The Rake* more than they resemble anything else in the opera. What this suggests to me is that, absent the specific demands that *The Rake* would make on him, Stravinsky was already in the headspace of his post-*Rake* music (the austerely beautiful *Cantata* [1952], for example, or *Agon* [1957]). But when he received Auden and Kallman's libretto, he seems to have realized that he would have to write a very different kind of piece.

Anne Trulove, the most unflappably "willful" character of all, is the best example of this difference—even though, as we've seen, the piece's librettists found Anne to be a bit of a bore. Her lines tend to be blunt or didactic: "I go to him," "Every wearied body must / Late or soon return to dust." It would have been easy, had Stravinsky been so inclined, to make Anne into a caricature of piety.

But Stravinsky evidently found Anne sympathetic, and he takes her seriously: he manages to both embrace her goodness and complicate it. One of his most effective tools of characterization, curiously enough, is Anne's coloratura—that is, the virtuosic way that she embellishes her melodic lines. In some contexts, coloratura can have a merely ornamental function, but it can also be a kind of musical blowtorch, a means for the voice to blaze a trail through the orchestral texture. (See: Callas, Maria.) Anne's coloratura lines have this latter function: they communicate that she has her own demons to wrestle with, her own doubts and fears to overcome. A pious line like "A love that is sworn before Thee can plunder Hell of its prey" might sound cloyingly self-satisfied if it were set to music in a straightforward way, with one note per syllable. But look at what Stravinsky does with it:

This fierce, melisma-ridden phrase creates the sense that Anne is wrestling with some unseen foe. The music is full of textual repetitions that aren't present in the written libretto; as sung, the line is as follows: "A love—a love that is sworn—sworn before Thee—can plunder Hell—can plunder Hell of its prey . . . can plunder Hell of its prey!" It's evidently not *easy* for Anne to say this. She does so not merely because she believes it, but because she needs to *make* herself believe it. (Kallman ultimately acknowledged that Stravinsky deserved the credit for making Anne a credible, flesh-and-blood character: because of the music, "[Anne] has become quite real to me . . . I even rather like her.")

The pianist Craig Rutenberg, who was my boss at the Met when I worked on the company's music staff, met Stravinsky late in the composer's life, and Craig passed along a bit of advice that Stravinsky had given him. Stravinsky said that to perform *The Rake* properly, you have to get two things right:

1. Throughout the opera, every tempo should be a dance tempo. It should always be possible to dance to the music.
2. The singers should pronounce the words with the inflections of a native English speaker, even when the music seems to demand otherwise.

This second guideline is deeper and wiser than it sounds. Generations of critics have faulted Stravinsky's text-setting in *The Rake's Progress*, claiming that, as a nonnative English speaker, he must not have known what he was doing. *The prosody is awful!* (So they claim.) *The stresses are in all the wrong places!* But this criticism is founded on a basic misunderstanding of Stravinsky's rhythmic language. The fact that a particular syllable lands on an "on"-beat does *not* mean that it needs to be accented; by the same token, a syllable on an offbeat *can* be accented. What Stravinsky achieves in *The Rake* is a complete reversal, in the music, of the expected placement of the poetry's emphases, and this reversal is much too consistent to be merely the fumbling of a befuddled old Russian squinting through the Hollywood sunshine at an incomprehensible assemblage of foreign syllables. Indeed, his treatment of English poetry in *The Rake* is as canny, and as lovingly irreverent, as his treatment of innumerable musical forms throughout his career—the Baroque concerto in his Violin Concerto, or symphonic form in his Symphony in C and Symphony in Three Movements.

The challenge for any singer who essays *The Rake* is to articulate both rhythmic syntaxes at once: the rhythm of the poetry *and* the rhythm of the music. The singer should pronounce the words naturally even when the music thrashes like a bucking bronco beneath them. If they succeed in doing so, something magical happens: you can hear the ghost of Audenesque English within Stravinsky's transfiguration of it. For this musical cubism to have its full effect, the original object must remain visible through its refractions. This paradoxical effect is not unlike a textural sleight of hand that Stravinsky was fond of in his orchestrations: he will frequently have a pair of instruments—two clarinets, for instance—play a phrase together, but one of the players is instructed to play staccato, while the other plays legato. This creates a beguiling, impossible texture, somehow pointillistic and seamless at once.

In *The Rake*, Stravinsky's refractions/reversals of the text take two basic forms. First, he inverts the poetry's rhythmic patterns: on-beats become offbeats; "duple" time in the poetry becomes "triple" time in the music and vice versa; and the libretto is often re-lineated (or, in musical terms, re-barred). Stravinsky will take, for instance, three lines of poetry and add a "break" in the middle of the second line, so that three poetic phrases become two musical ones. Musicians might think of these transformations as

micro- and macro-hemiolas: they create an interior rhythmic dou-
bleness, either at the level of individual syllables or whole phrases.

The second kind of reversal, and the more surprising one, is
the way Stravinsky frequently upends the libretto's formal prescriptions. The composer had told Auden in no uncertain terms
that he wanted to write an opera with "definitely separated numbers," and his librettists delivered just what he'd asked for. But
Stravinsky ended up resisting his own strictures and blurring
the distinction between "numbers": he decided, for instance, to
transform several sections that the librettists had marked "recitative" into lyrical, through-composed music with orchestra. His
upending of our expectations runs in both directions.

Tom Rakewell's aria "Love, too frequently betrayed," sung to an
audience of Whores and Roaring Boys soon after his arrival in
a London brothel, is an especially clear example of Stravinsky's
subtle subversion of Auden's poetry. Shadow is showing Tom
off to the crowd, and demonstrates that his pupil is sufficiently
debauched by asking him to recite scornful definitions of Duty,
Pleasure, the Beautiful, etc. Tom obliges, but when he is asked
to define Love, he blanches. ("Presumably what he is supposed
to do," Auden said in a BBC interview, "is what Alberich does
in *Rheingold*, which is to renounce Love.") Far from renouncing
Love, though, Tom soon sings a desperately sad little ode to it.
Here is his aria's first verse, with text by Auden:

> Love, too frequently betrayed
> For some plausible desire
> Or the world's enchanted fire,

Still thy traitor in his sleep
Renews the vow he did not keep,
    Weeping, weeping,
He kneels before thy wounded shade.

This aria is in Auden's beloved trochaic tetrameter, a meter that translates in musical terms to 4/4, with most lines beginning on the beat:

Stravinsky unostentatiously reverses the poetry's every stress. The text's first word, "Love," is sung not on the downbeat but on the second eighth note of the bar; the second line begins on a pickup; and the third and fourth lines begin as the first one did:

The first time Auden begins a line with an unstressed syllable (what musicians would think of as a pickup) is the word "renews," and Stravinsky reverses this too: he places the "pickup" syllable *on* the beat. It's also clear from the poetry's formatting that the single indented line, "Weeping, weeping," has a special function.

Stravinsky highlights this: "Weeping, weeping" (and the corresponding line in the second verse, "Dying, dying") is the only line in the aria where the music's accents line up with the poetry's.

Throughout the opera, Stravinsky also consistently reverses duple- and triple-meter poetry in his setting of it. Tom's first aria, "Since it is not by merit," follows a rollicking triplet rhythm that might remind the reader of "'Twas the Night Before Christmas": "Why should I labor / For what in the end / She will give me for nothing / If she be my friend?" Stravinsky sets this text to a burbling duple rhythm. Later in the same scene, he does the opposite: Tom expresses his naïve joy about his unexpected inheritance in duple-rhythm poetry: "I wished but once, I knew / That surely my wish would come true." Stravinsky converts this section to a sleek 6/8.

The exceptions to this rule of inversion/subversion are exceedingly rare, and each has an obvious dramatic purpose. Anne's father, a dully virtuous Eeyore of a man, sings his first lines ("O may a father's prudent fears / Unfounded prove") in a plodding rhythm that unimaginatively obeys the stresses of the poetry. This clearly differentiates him from the young lovers on the other side of the stage. The other notable exception is the auctioneer Sellem, who sings in an unusually naturalistic way in the allegro section of his solo ("Who hears me, knows me"). Auden mentioned this latter example in a defense of Stravinsky's text-setting: only in the auction scene, Auden said, is it "dramatically essential that the sung rhythms conform pretty closely to the spoken," and in Stravinsky's music, "they do." Sellem's idiosyncratic rhythmic syntax is full of nervously jaunty little swinging gestures that land heavily on every stressed syllable. He sounds, fabulously, like a fast-talking American televangelist who has been beamed down into eighteenth-century London (where he is a huge hit with the ravenous and highly impressionable city folk).

ॐ

Auden's collaboration with Stravinsky was perhaps the only creative partnership of Auden's life in which he was not the bossy one; his reverence for Stravinsky's music, and the fact that he was twenty-five years the composer's junior, largely kept him in check. Even so, he and Kallman are unusually prescriptive librettists: they specify not only form ("Pantomime with Orchestra") but also tempo ("Prestissimo. Voices in canon."), and sometimes even minutely detailed musical instructions ("Baba's interjected interruptions become more and more frequent and gradually both faster and louder"). When Auden and Kallman mark a section "recitative," they often specify whether it should be orchestral recitative or secco (that is, with harpsichord alone). These sections are usually intended to be parodic or prosaic, as in the case of Tom's unconvincing promises that he will invite Anne to join him in London as soon as he's made himself the toast of the town.

As often as not, Stravinsky ignores the "recitative" marking altogether, transmuting a businesslike chunk of prose into a stretch of beguiling melody. Here, for example, is Baba the Turk's first entrance, in which she imperiously orders Tom to help her out of her carriage:

ORCHESTRAL RECITATIVE

BABA (*interrupting with vexation*): My love, am I to remain in here forever? You know that I am *not* in the habit of stepping from my sedan unaided. Nor shall I wait, unmoved, much longer. Finish, if you please, whatever business is detaining you with this person.

As admirers of Mozart's operas, Auden and Kallman probably had something specific in mind: a series of parlando outbursts, interrupted by slashing gestures from the orchestra ("My love [SLASH], am I to remain in here forever [SLASH]?" etc.). But Stravinsky takes the opposite tack: his setting isn't really recitative at all, but rather a sweetly lyrical line in which two bassoons, warbling voluptuously in the instrument's pungent upper register, wind around Baba's voice like a pair of pet weasels.

One of Auden and Kallman's most specific prescriptions, and also one of Stravinsky's clearest refusals, comes in the graveyard scene. According to the printed libretto, many of Tom's and Shadow's lines are "to be sung to one or more ballad tunes in the traditional manner without expression." Much of the scene is indeed written in ballad meter, with the standard end rhymes:

TOM RAKEWELL
How dark and dreadful is this place.
Why have you led me here?
There's something, Shadow, in your face
That fills my soul with fear!

NICK SHADOW
A year and a day have passed away
Since first to you I came.
All things you bid, I duly did
And now my wages claim.

At the end of the scene, the librettists also specify that Shadow's cry of despair when he loses the card game ("I burn! I freeze!") should be sung to the same tune, "resuming the ballad."

These directions are extraordinarily specific—Auden and Kallman seem to want to compose the scene themselves. Their idea isn't a bad one: in the hands of a different composer (Kurt Weill, for instance), the repeated use of a single ballad tune might have been eerie and effective. But Stravinsky had other ideas. Tom's lines are not at all ballad-like: over an inexorable trudging motion in the low strings, he sings nervous little bursts of coloratura, lines whose elaborate ornamentation seems to be a futile attempt to delay the approaching confrontation. Shadow's first lines *are* somewhat ballad-like in their jaunty tunefulness, but his aria at the end of the scene is altered beyond recognition; I doubt any listener would guess that "I burn! I freeze!" was intended to be a "ballad tune." Stravinsky explodes these lines into a formidable Handelian rage aria, one of the twentieth century's most gratifyingly melodramatic pieces of vocal writing. The trudging dotted rhythm that had quietly undergirded Tom's earlier lines now erupts into a desperate flailing, a helpless straining against some hellish leash.

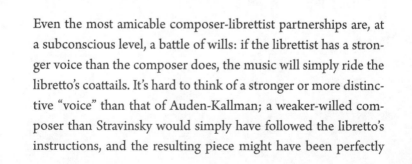

Even the most amicable composer-librettist partnerships are, at a subconscious level, a battle of wills: if the librettist has a stronger voice than the composer does, the music will simply ride the libretto's coattails. It's hard to think of a stronger or more distinctive "voice" than that of Auden-Kallman; a weaker-willed composer than Stravinsky would simply have followed the libretto's instructions, and the resulting piece might have been perfectly effective. But the special magic of *The Rake* derives from the mutual pressure that Stravinsky's and Auden-Kallman's voices exert on one another. Somehow, impossibly, this two-way subversion does not cancel itself out, but rather catches fire and comes to life.

I've talked about many things that I love about *The Rake*, but I haven't mentioned the best of all: the astonishing rightness of Stravinsky's harmonies, the physical satisfaction that every chord in this piece offers when you play it at the piano. His voice-leading has the inevitability of Mozart's or Bach's; you can drop a pin at any moment in the score, follow any instrument you like, and that instrument's part will manifest signs of an independent inner life. But when I try to talk about this, words fail me. Some of music's miracles remain impossible to describe.

FOUR

Verdi's Shakespeare Operas

Macbeth, Otello, Falstaff

In a memorable passage in Tom Stoppard's play *Arcadia*, a young mathematician reflects on the gulf between the aspects of our universe that humans have begun to understand and the things about which we're still in the dark. He muses that the twentieth century's landmark scientific advancements "only explained the very big and the very small":

> The ordinary-sized stuff which is our lives, the things peo-ple write poetry about—clouds—daffodils—waterfalls—and what happens in a cup of coffee when the cream goes in—these things are full of mystery, as mysterious to us as the heavens were to the Greeks.

In music, too, the twentieth century brought quantum leaps in our understanding of sound on micro- and macroscopic scales. We can put an individual sound under a kind of electron microscope, hear it for the teeming miniature world that it is, and separate its constituent elements. We can detect, and translate into sound, bursts of energy that might have originated millions or billions of light-years away. And when it comes to sheer force, a high-school garage band with a few cheap amps could easily overpower even the hugest orchestras of past centuries.

But in music as in science, the middle scale—the human scale—remains mysterious. We still can't explain why some melodies, and not others, lodge themselves unshakably in the mind's ear. We can't explain what musical effects are likely to raise goose bumps or cause our hair to stand on end. There is still no formula, no reliable way to predict, what will make a convincing musical embodiment of love, jealousy, or rage.

It is at this still-mysterious middle scale that Giuseppe Verdi operates with singular authority.

Among great composers, Verdi has the unusual quality of seeming great *only* from that middle distance, the scale of the theater. Put his music under a microscope, and you're unlikely to find intricate hidden patterns, as you might in Mozart or Bach. Zoom the camera way out, and you won't typically see a meticulously crafted total architecture, as you would with, say, Alban Berg's operas. Verdi's characters are not genetically engineered superheroes, as Wagner's are; he does not offer transcendent visions of universal brotherhood or pastoral utopia, like Beethoven or Gustav Mahler. But meet Verdi's gaze, listen to his music moment by moment, and you'll find that he is an artist of matchless honesty and directness. In the history of opera, the mature Verdi is the composer least likely to make a misstep in dramatic pacing or psychological portraiture.

His mastery as a musical portraitist owes a lot to his lifelong study of Shakespeare. Despite the differences in language and artistic medium, Shakespeare, more than any fellow composer, was his North Star, the awesome standard against which he judged his own progress as a dramatist. There are, of course, Italian composers out of whose musical language Verdi's palpably emerged (Donizetti and Bellini in particular), but at a technical level these composers provided models that he would eventually outgrow, rather than an ideal toward which he continued to aspire.

Verdi came of age during what has become known as the bel canto period of Italian opera, during which the glorification of the human voice was the composer's fundamental priority. Bel canto operas are distinguished by long, sensuously unspooling melodies and passages of fast, florid vocal gymnastics; their tonal palette is simple and their harmonic progressions few and familiar. An aesthetic whose central focus is the wonder of the beautifully produced voice inevitably lets some other aspects of the operatic art form fall by the wayside: one generally doesn't turn to bel canto for an evening of taut, seamless drama.

Verdi's early operas adhere, to varying degrees, to the idiom's structural conventions, and he had all the skills required to develop into a great bel canto composer—above all, the unteachable gift of inventing a melody that sounds inevitable, as though it had existed since the beginning of time. It is apparent even in his earliest works, however, that he is not entirely at home within bel canto's stylistic strictures. From the beginning, his music speaks with a blunt dynamism that demands different forms, different rules, a more flexible musical and dramatic language. Within the walls of the bel canto forms he inherited, the music of the young Verdi snarls and paces like a caged lion.

Shakespeare, on the other hand, provided an inexhaustible wellspring of inspiration: in none of his operatic predecessors could Verdi find such virtuosically free-flowing poetry in a stage work, or such an unpredictable and idiosyncratic sense of dramatic structure. The challenge for Verdi was to develop a musical language capable of matching Shakespeare's dramatic momentum. This was a slow process: Verdi loved Shakespeare throughout his life, but it took decades for his music to become Shakespearean.

At the risk of oversimplification, we might think of the composer's long engagement with Shakespeare as having three phases, which roughly map onto his three Shakespearean operas: *Macbeth* (1847), *Otello* (1887), and *Falstaff* (1893). When he wrote *Macbeth*, the young Verdi hadn't yet found a way to translate either the wildness or the fluidity of Shakespearean dramaturgy into his musical language. Over the decades that followed *Macbeth*, he absorbed many of Shakespeare's techniques and became a dramatist of supreme sophistication in his own right, creating a kind of Shakespearean pathos in middle-period operas like *Rigoletto* (1851). He brought this experience to bear in his second Shakespeare adaptation, *Otello*, which matches the original play in nuance and power. By the end of his life, his relationship with Shakespeare had become an improbably symbiotic one: with *Falstaff*, Verdi arguably goes beyond what Shakespeare achieved with the same material.

Verdi could not have done this alone. In fact, to translate the messy richness of Shakespeare's plays into the language of Italian opera, he needed a partner whose temperament was more or less the opposite of his own. One of Verdi's great strengths was his canny pragmatism: he had a catlike instinct for leaping only when he knew he'd land on his feet, for innovating only at a rate his audiences could handle. Part of what makes Verdi a consummate theater composer is his rage for clarity and compression: he had no patience for poetic grandiloquence, and he had a knack for boiling a given drama down to a hard, irreducible kernel. This is a virtue in most circumstances, but when it came to Shakespeare, it was also a liability. Leave a Shakespeare play too long in the extreme heat of the Verdian oven, and its poetry might just evaporate.

By contrast, Arrigo Boito, the librettist of *Otello* and *Falstaff*, was by nature an overreaching idealist, a polyglot intellectual who tried his hand at every imaginable art form: music, poetry, drama, fiction, criticism. In his own music, Boito ran a risk diametrically opposed to the risks inherent in Verdi's approach: Boito's operas tend toward the unwieldy and the hyperinflated. He had a weakness for building upon the shaky foundations of a grandiose poetic or philosophical ideal, rather than the firmer ground of clear musical ideas.

Given their very different aesthetic outlooks, it's probably no surprise that the Verdi-Boito relationship was not love at first sight: when the self-important young Boito burst onto the Italian scene, Verdi scrutinized him with a wary mistrust, the way a lean, street-hardened dog might eye a peacock that had obliviously strutted onto its turf. It was only after decades of coolness that Verdi came around to the notion that Boito's artistic personality might serve as the perfect counterweight to his own.

I want to explore both Verdi's ever-evolving relationship with Shakespeare and also the curious alchemy by which Verdi's temperament, fused with Boito's, yields music of a genuinely

Shakespearean richness. Neither Verdi nor Boito could have achieved the wonders of *Otello* and *Falstaff* on his own. We're lucky they finally joined forces, because these two operas provide the best possible case studies in what happens when a play is made to stand up and sing.

Verdi's Warmth

I'm sure we all have a few artists whose work we love unconditionally and irrationally. Verdi is one of those artists for me. I feel such a visceral sympathy with his music that I can ignore aspects of it that I might find inexcusable in other composers. In his earlier operas, his craftsmanship is sometimes crude; his instrumental music, in particular, tends to be painted with quite a broad brush (I've never met a string player who enjoys playing the tiring repetitive gestures that are endemic to the orchestral writing in those early operas). Plenty of lesser composers would have little difficulty coming up with richer harmonic voicings, smoother transitions, or more colorful orchestrations than you will find in operas from the first quarter or so of Verdi's career. Though in his maturity he achieved impressive technical fluency, Verdi remained disarmingly modest about the question of his musical prowess; once, when asked to become president of a newly formed chamber-music society, he asked the founders to "please leave me out. You know that when it comes to music I am a jackass."

Verdi's habit of brusque self-deprecation belies an absolute, unshakable trust in his own instincts regarding what works and does not work onstage. His specialty is the bold embodiment of primal states of human psychology—jealousy, rage, loyalty, love—and the potent floods of animal emotion that seethe beneath the masks we wear in the social world. He speaks both *from* and *to* a mysterious glowing coal in the human soul, a fierce core that is both human and animal: human in its limitless capacity for compassion, animal in its latent ferocity and its imperviousness to reason. It's not the "lizard brain," the part of our minds that is susceptible to mob mentality, that Verdi addresses; but neither is it the reasoning, language-making mind. Rather, Verdi addresses something ancient and warmly mammalian in our psyches. His music is made of the warmth that floods the body in extreme emotional states, moments of overwhelming rage, shame, or love. It is helplessly passionate, monomaniacally direct, utterly alive.

Of all the qualities I admire in Verdi, three stand out. First, I'm in awe of his instincts: he knows just what to trust, and what not to trust, in a work of music-theater. Verdi trusts opera's vivid impossibilities—the things that no one would say or do in life, but which are perfectly reasonable onstage—and has no patience for the blandly plausible, or for anything that has to explain itself. Curses, blood oaths, spontaneous outbursts of love or rage—these are his raw materials, as natural in opera as a handshake is in life. But anything that takes a few extra sentences to explain itself, anything that reeks of abstract or idealized conceptions of Beauty or Goodness—Verdi has no time for such things.

Second, I love the paradox that Verdi was an intensely practical person working in the least practical of art forms; he was an unsentimental master of human sentiment. His temperament enabled him to treat opera with a refreshing pragmatism, as if it were a concrete, humbly workable substance, like timber or stone. In letters to collaborators, he comes across as a clear-sighted, no-nonsense master craftsman, nothing at all like the Romantic archetype of the flighty tortured genius. With his librettists, he could be a ruthless, needling taskmaster: "POCHE PAROLE" ("FEW WORDS"), he wrote repeatedly, with a blaring insistence, to one hapless wordsmith. Singers who worked with him describe an unwaveringly exigent coach who demanded a speechlike precision of diction. I find, in Verdi's pragmatism, an invigorating confirmation of the *reality* of music and language, a sense that they're not made of some imaginary ether but rather are physical substances that must be approached with workman-like diligence and respect.

The third thing that amazes me about Verdi is the enviable trajectory of his artistic life. His career was one of slow, steady growth across more than half a century, a career in which practically every new opera quietly refines and improves on the previous one. Composers' biographies are rife with dysfunction, madness, and premature death; among them, Verdi is a rare example of good sense and dogged determination. There is a tortoise-and-the-hare dynamic between Verdi and his more overtly revolutionary contemporaries, most of whom he outlived: his innovations were so subtle and so gradual that they often went unnoticed. He never announced what he was doing, never published a manifesto or formulated an aesthetic system; he just carried on slowly, surely cracking open, then abandoning, the bel canto models that he had grown up with, his music growing richer and more daring with each new piece. In the history of classical music, perhaps only Haydn followed a similar path, from workmanlike competence in his first pieces to sparkling, quick-silver brilliance—and, like Verdi, a hard-won sense of *joy*—in old age.

Let's walk a bit of that path with him. We don't have space here to start at the *very* beginning, so let's start with Verdi's first attempt to make Shakespeare sing.

Raw Material: Macbeth

There was a time when Verdi's *Macbeth* was underrated to the point of being almost forgotten. The opera's final, revised version was first performed in the United States only in 1941, and the Metropolitan Opera did not produce the work until 1959. In recent decades, the pendulum has swung sharply in the opposite direction: even if, by Verdi's formidable standard, *Macbeth* has hardly achieved the permanent ubiquity of *La traviata* (1853) or *Aida* (1871), it has become at least as frequent a presence at major opera houses as middle-period masterpieces like *Un ballo in maschera* (1859) and *La forza del destino* (1862).

What accounts for this shift? It surely has something to do with the seismic impact of Maria Callas's blazing mid-twentieth-century Lady Macbeth, and with the contemporaneous increase in interest (which is also partly attributable to Callas) in the bel canto composers whose influence is so palpable in Verdi's earlier works. And of course the work's popularity can be justified by its many musical highlights. But I am mistrustful of *Macbeth*'s resurgence: I suspect it has a lot to do with the reliably salutary box-office impact, especially in the English-speaking world, of the word "MACBETH" lighting up a marquee, and with opera companies' desire to lure theatergoing audiences with the promise of an evening of Shakespeare. A number of prominent Verdians have added fuel to the fire by overstating *Macbeth*'s revolutionary qualities: the conductor Gianandrea Noseda's rhapsodic assertion that "with [*Macbeth*], Verdi jumped musically 50 years ahead" is typical.

Much as I love *Macbeth*, I don't think this approach does the opera any favors. Verdi's first Shakespeare adaptation is a bloody prime cut of Italian opera, full of visceral satisfactions that are unique to his early period, but it's not especially Shakespearean in its construction: my appreciation of *Macbeth* tends to correlate inversely with my awareness of its source material. When he wrote *Macbeth*, Verdi was still beholden to certain inflexible bel canto conventions—long, static arias; grand choruses—that are fundamentally at odds with the play's nimbleness and its ferocious, spiraling momentum. He had not yet found a librettist who had a deep knowledge of Shakespeare's plays, or who was capable of emulating the molten flow of the Bard's dramaturgy. And it would be decades before he would fruitfully wrestle with the music of his German rival Richard Wagner, from whom he would borrow certain chromatic techniques that would allow him, in his last operas, to weave seamlessly Shakespearean transitions from scene to scene and emotion to emotion.

I don't want to underestimate *Macbeth*'s many strengths, or its importance in Verdi's musical trajectory: the act of engaging with the sheer *weirdness* of Shakespeare's drama helped Verdi to break certain long-ingrained bel canto habits, and the plot's fantastical elements allowed him to make use of eerie musical colors that he'd never had an excuse to experiment with before. But in the long perspective of Verdi's career-long Shakespearean project, *Macbeth* is only the first step.

Verdi's partner in the creation of *Macbeth* was the librettist Francesco Maria Piave, a selflessly devoted collaborator whose stoicism in the face of Verdi's frequent, withering bursts of vitriol proved essential to their working relationship. A more sensitive or self-involved writer would have stormed away at the first sign of the hectoring tone the composer was liable to take with librettists, but the saintly Piave patiently weathered every Verdian storm. For all his day-to-day grumpiness, Verdi did recognize the rarity of Piave's gift for unobtrusively helping composers do their best work: the pair ultimately collaborated on ten operas, including *Rigoletto* and *La traviata*.

Piave's self-effacing craftsmanship made him the ideal partner for most projects, but *Macbeth* was hardly a typical subject. At the time, Shakespeare's plays had barely been performed in Italy,* and *Macbeth* was an especially odd fit for the country's mid-nineteenth-century operatic idiom. For one thing, it has no love story, unless you count the ungodly pact that binds the Macbeths, and an Italian opera without a love story is almost a contradiction in terms. (In Italy, *Macbeth* became known colloquially as *l'opera senza amore*, "the opera without love.") The play is also dramaturgically thorny—the murderous momentum of its first two acts can lead to a sense of anticlimax in the following three—and full of bizarre coups de théâtre: witches, apparitions, an army disguised as a moving forest. Translating such a play into the stand-there-and-sing conventions of post–bel canto opera would be no easy task.

As a result, Verdi's letters to Piave from throughout the process of writing *Macbeth* are—even by his standards—startlingly

---

* A couple of leading Italian composers had written Shakespeare-adjacent operas, but in each case the connection to the Bard's work is shaky at best. Bellini's setting of the Romeo and Juliet story, *I Capuleti e i Montecchi* (1830), is based on an Italian source rather than on Shakespeare, and Rossini's *Otello* (1816) is based so tenuously on Shakespeare's play that the story is barely recognizable.

harsh. We might detect a warning sign in the composer's declaration, early on, that he had the color and "general character" of the opera in his head "just as if the libretto were already written." With that Shakespearean "color" in his head, surely any concrete realization according to the rules of Italian-opera versification was bound to disappoint him. The scholar Julian Budden summarizes Verdi's complaints:

> The whole of Lady Macbeth's recitative, including the letter, was too long and not sufficiently "lofty" in style; the first line of her adagio was too commonplace and took away all the energy of her character. There were too many lines in the duet between Macbeth and Banquo; as for the chorus of witches—something was wrong though Verdi could not exactly say what.

If we ignore for a moment that the source material is Shakespeare, it's hard to see just what Verdi found so infuriating about his librettist's work. Piave was, it seems, delivering modest, effective verses of the kind that had worked so well in his earlier libretti for Verdi, and that conformed to the expectations both of Italy's composers and its public. Verdi, however, was asking for something new, without knowing quite *how* to ask for it; his frustration is palpable in his slightly incoherent demand that the witches' texts "must be trivial but in an extravagant original way." The gap between what he heard in his head and what he was capable of articulating seems to have enraged him.

Piave's work looks rock-solid if we're judging it as an Italian-opera libretto, but if we unwisely remember the fleetness and ferocity of the Shakespearean original, we might understand why it made Verdi apoplectic: in some places, Piave seems to have been perversely seeking to drain the play of its best qualities. Take, for example, the title character's first meeting with Lady Macbeth, after he has informed her by letter of the witches' prophecies. In Shakespeare, Macbeth says little, while Lady Macbeth weaves a tantalizing web around him:

MACBETH

> My dearest love,
Duncan comes here to-night.

LADY MACBETH

> And when goes hence?

MACBETH

To-morrow, as he purposes.

LADY MACBETH

> O, never
Shall sun that morrow see!
Your face, my thane, is as a book, where men
May read strange matters. To beguile the time,
Look like the time; bear welcome in your eye,
Your hand, your tongue; look like th' innocent flower,
But be the serpent under't. He that's coming
Must be provided for; and you shall put
This night's great business into my dispatch,
Which shall to all our nights and days to come
Give solely sovereign sway and masterdom.

MACBETH

We will speak further.

LADY MACBETH

> Only look up clear:
> To alter favor ever is to fear.
> Leave all the rest to me.

An exchange like this certainly requires some trimming for it to be libretto-ready, but Piave boils the original down ad absurdum:

MACBETH
Oh my Lady!

LADY MACBETH
Cawdor!

MACBETH
Soon you shall see the king.

LADY MACBETH
And he'll depart . . . ?

MACBETH
Tomorrow.

LADY MACBETH
Never shall the sun that morrow see!

MACBETH
What are you saying?

LADY MACBETH
Don't you understand?

MACBETH

I understand . . . I understand!

LADY MACBETH

Alright then?

In a couple of places, Piave and Verdi clearly wanted to include a beloved line from Shakespeare, but they evidently felt it would be tedious to keep the entire speech from which that line is drawn. The result is that certain lines are awkwardly torn (or rather, "untimely ripped") from their context. When Macbeth learns of his wife's death, he skips nine-tenths of the "Tomorrow and tomorrow and tomorrow" speech and jarringly jumps straight to its climax: "What does life matter?" he snarls. "It is a tale told by a poor idiot—wind and sound, signifying nothing!"

In spite of the un-Shakespearean behavior of large swaths of the libretto, *Macbeth* clearly fired Verdi's creative imagination. The opera's dark-hued orchestral writing broods and seethes with an intensity that had only been hinted at in his earlier operas. And his depiction of the leading couple is largely triumphant: the role of Lady Macbeth in particular, which requires a singer to command a vast range of vocal and dramatic effects, has no real precedent in Italian opera.

This is apparent from the first sound Lady Macbeth makes. She enters amid a boiling orchestral introduction that foams with string tremolos and violent offbeat accents. Once this agitation subsides, the orchestra rolls out a velvety carpet of sound for her, but instead of singing, she *speaks*. It's hard to overstate how unusual this would have sounded to Verdi's audience. The leading lady in a bel canto opera typically announced herself with a languidly beautiful recitative, followed by a *cantabile* aria. Here, by contrast, Lady Macbeth seems oblivious to music itself as she recites, with grim focus, the letter from her husband that tells her he has been named Thane of Cawdor. She then erupts into a blazing, incantatory a cappella line, a musical summons from the depths of Hell.

Over the course of the opera, Lady Macbeth shows that she is capable of delicate, devastating sarcasm—she mockingly reproaches Macbeth for his lack of resolve with a playful little dance in 3/8 time—as well as fearsome displays of strength. At times, she sings with an eerie, childlike purity; elsewhere, she displays an unnerving sexual magnetism. In the aria "La luce langue", which Verdi added for his 1865 revision of the opera, the orchestra purrs seductively as Lady Macbeth insists to herself that the dead no longer care about holding power: the phrase "a loro un *requiem*, l'eternità" ("for them a requiem, and eternity") contains an alluring hint of a specifically late-Verdian harmonic warmth that typically connotes religious or erotic yearning.

It can't be easy to be married to such a Lady, and the role of Macbeth does pale somewhat in comparison. Lady Macbeth's role is full of bold musical analogues to the huge range of tones with which she speaks in the play, whereas with Macbeth, one is more keenly aware of what has been lost. Shakespeare's Macbeth tends to brood and simmer; Verdi's tends to explode. Verdi and Piave do not quite find an equivalent for the gnawing inwardness that characterizes Macbeth's blackest moods, his tendency to wallow masochistically in his self-inflicted misery. For long stretches of the play, Shakespeare's Macbeth is a kind of introvert, and the terms "introvert" and "dramatic baritone" are almost mutually exclusive.

On its own terms, however, Verdi's Macbeth is a magnificent role, full of burnished, vocally gratifying melodies. If the highlights of Lady Macbeth's role are the sections that stray furthest from bel canto conventions, the glory of Macbeth's part lies in his self-pitying outbursts, which demand an entirely conventional beauty and strength of tone: his terror and fury when confronted with Banquo's ghost, or his emotional whiplash as he hears the paradoxical prophecies of the apparitions in Act Three. In such moments, Verdi invests Macbeth with the kind of sympathetic grandeur to be found in his depiction of the Biblical king Nebuchadnezzar in *Nabucco* (1842), another opera about a flawed ruler brought to the brink of madness. The sheer beauty of Macbeth's music makes him arguably a more sympathetic figure in Verdi than in Shakespeare; his roughest edges, his bleakest self-confrontations, tend to be excised or smoothed over. This is both his limitation and his strength: there is little that's specifically Shakespearean in either his ranting or his crooning, but there is in this role a solid, warmly Verdian core.

One feature of *Macbeth* that might sound odd to twenty-first-century ears is a particular use of major-key music that Verdi inherited from his bel canto predecessors. There's a popular notion that major and minor keys can be partitioned into a simple binary, according to which major keys are "happy" and minor keys are "sad." There's really no musical idiom for which this dichotomy is accurate; from Schubert to Radiohead, many of the saddest songs ever written are in major keys. But the major-key mood I'm referring to in bel canto opera has nothing to do with that Schubertian lump in the throat. Counterintuitive though it might seem, early-Romantic Italian composers often used major keys for music of rage and anxiety. When it works, music in this mode embodies the irrational pleasure that can accompany feelings of extreme anger—the giddy sensation of blood rushing to the head. When it doesn't work, the listener might wonder why the character is swearing bloody vengeance with the can-do perkiness of a Sousa march.

This bel canto–inflected use of major-key music is present at many points in *Macbeth*, and its highly variable effectiveness makes it a useful lens through which to examine Verdi's growth as a dramatist. Whenever he uses this flippantly breezy kind of musical motion, we might ask: Does Verdi transcend the fundamental mismatch of harmonic palette and dramatic situation? Does he successfully create a sense of the uncanny, an intimation of dangerous, rapturous abandon? Or are we merely in the clutches of bel canto prettiness?

The moments when Verdi succeeds by this metric are among *Macbeth*'s highlights. Lady Macbeth's sleepwalking scene, for instance, is in D-flat major starting at her vocal entrance. I usually think of that key as a lushly comforting one, but in this case, it's obvious from the first notes that something is deeply wrong. The strings enter with a jagged, teeth-chattering stutter, and Lady Macbeth's long vocal phrases are warped at every turn by sudden shifts in dynamics, from forte outbursts to caressing pianissimo murmurs. In this scene, Verdi gives his leading lady an unusual number of disparate instructions: *sotto voce* (quiet, as if to herself); *spiegata* (full-voice); *con forza* (forcefully); *con dolore* (sorrowfully, in pain); *cupo* (dark); and at the end of the scene, *un fil di voce* (very delicately, with a single "filament" of voice).

Throughout the sleepwalking scene, Verdi thrillingly has it both ways: he both breaks and does not break the rules of bel canto composition. He writes long, classically beautiful melodic lines, but ruptures them with unstable dynamics and articulations. Without these violent affective shifts, a melody like the one at the words "Arabia intera / rimondar sì piccol mano" ("All Arabia's perfumes / could not clean this little hand") would be unambiguously lovely. But with Verdi's exquisitely specific markings, and accompanied by the strings' clipped, machine-gun giggling, this line becomes something more: it is somehow both itself and a grotesque parody of itself. Verdi wields the sickly sweet beauty that is native to the bel canto idiom as an improbably keen-edged weapon.

Not every major-key moment of high drama is as effective as this one, however, and it's telling that the weaker ones tend to belong to Macbeth rather than his wife. At the end of the banquet scene in Act Two, once Macbeth has recovered from the terror of seeing Banquo's ghost, he initiates the act's concertato finale with a meandering E-major melody, accompanied by limping triplets in the orchestra. And in the final act, as his world falls apart around him, Macbeth pauses the action to sing "Pietà, rispetto, amore," a slow and mournful cantabile aria whose emotional content is so generic, it might as well be the aria of a proud father, or an old man nostalgically recalling a lost love, or really anyone at all other than the play's anguished antihero. In moments like these, the listener might feel that the air has been sucked out of the room, that the dramatic thread has gone slack.

When Verdi returned to Shakespeare decades later, he had

figured out how to avoid such lapses. But to write his first fully Shakespearean music, he would need the help of a poet-composer who was only five years old at the time of *Macbeth*'s premiere. This uncommonly gifted Renaissance man was named Arrigo Boito.

The Overreacher: The Singular Career of Arrigo Boito

> As long as we roam in the world of ideas, everything
> smiles upon us, but when we come down to earth, to
> practical matters, doubts and distresses arise.
>
> *—From a letter from Verdi to Boito*

L et us take a moment to acknowledge a basic fact: writing
operas is fiendishly hard. If a composer focuses exclusively
on their own medium, music, and ignores the demands of
opera's other constituent art forms, their opera is unlikely to get
off the ground. But it is equally risky for a composer to treat all
the art forms out of which operas are made as one big goulash,
which the composer, through sheer force of will, single-handedly
disgorges. We might call this "the Wagner method." Wagner was
better at it than almost anyone, and it was dicey even for him.

In his youth, Boito was surpassingly confident about the virtues of this latter method. He was the ultimate multihyphenate,
a composer-poet-librettist-playwright-novelist-critic-conductor-
translator—and even, late in life, a senator—who refused throughout his career to focus his energies in one medium or another. An
artist who spreads himself as thin as Boito did is probably doomed
to work in opera, the only art form messy and generous enough to
encompass so many disparate interests. And indeed Boito made
a range of contributions to opera that no other single artist could
have made. His libretti for other composers manifest a wisdom
that comes from experience writing music himself; his virtuosity
with poetic forms and fluency in multiple languages enabled him

to translate Wagner into Italian and adapt Shakespeare for the operatic stage. His poetry is campily theatrical; his theater pieces are campily poetic.

But Boito is also a poignant figure, a cautionary tale for the overambitious. If the trajectory of Verdi's artistic life is one of patient, incremental growth, the graph of Boito's career is full of jagged leaps and crashes. His skill as a composer did not quite match his gifts as a wordsmith, yet he announced himself, early in his career, as Italy's answer to Wagner—that is, as a composer-poet whose loftily literary music dramas would elevate Italian music, which he viewed as hopelessly retrograde, into the Wagnerian ether. He riskily announced his ideas about the music of the future before he had shared much music with the public: by the time he unveiled his first large-scale creation, the opera *Mefistofele* (1868), he had already become a figure of some notoriety, and expectations were feverishly high. Perhaps because of this excessive hype, *Mefistofele* was a dud at its premiere, and the traumatic experience of bringing it to the stage seems to have stymied Boito's musical creativity. Though he worked on another epic opera, *Nerone*, for nearly sixty years, he could never quite bring himself to finish it.

Boito and his friend Franco Faccio, a fellow aspiring composer-conductor, began to make waves in Italy's music scene while they were still students at Milan's conservatory. Upon their graduation, the two young *avveniristi* ("futurists") won prestigious traveling fellowships, and were given letters of introduction to an enviable list of the day's leading composers: Berlioz, Verdi, Rossini, Gounod. Perhaps puffed up by this surfeit of institutional support, Boito was soon making pronouncements about the state of music and the other arts in Italy. His prose from this period tends toward the deep purple:

> Indeed, the Sublime is simpler than the Beautiful ... Only the great form is suited to the Sublime, the eternal, universal, divine form: the spherical form. The horizon is sublime, the sea is sublime, the sun is sublime. Shakespeare is spherical, Dante is spherical, Beethoven is spherical ...

And so on.

It didn't take long for the hype surrounding Boito and Faccio to reach Verdi's ears, and he responded at first with cautious skepticism. When a friend showed him the Boito essay quoted above, Verdi's reaction was curt and irrefutable: "Fine things!! Too bad I don't understand them ... To write music one very simple thing is needed: *Music*." The more the rhetorical provocations of the *avveniristi* outshone their musical accomplishments, however, the more annoyed Verdi became: "I think at present and will continue to think next year that to make *a shoe* you need some *leather* and some *skins*! ... To make an opera you must first have music in your body." Verdi took pains to emphasize that he was not antiprogressive; he would gladly support the young *avveniristi*, he said, "provided they make some music for me ... in whatever form, with whatever system, etc., but it must be music!"

Boito's rashest move, the blunder that caused a nearly irreparable rift with Verdi, came at a dinner following the premiere of one of Faccio's operas. Boito had written a provocative poem for the occasion, an ode to Italian art, which he delivered as a toast. The poem expressed Boito's hope that Italian art would escape "from the chains of the old and the idiotic ... Perhaps that person is already born who will raise Art up, chaste and pure, upon that altar which is soiled like the wall of a whorehouse." Verdi was not Boito's explicit target, but as Italy's most prominent composer, he took personal offense. "If I . . . have befouled the altar," Verdi wrote to his publisher Tito Ricordi, with his inimitable blend of self-deprecation and Olympian disdain, "then let [Boito] clean it and I will be the first to light a candle there."

Boito's *Mefistofele* has always had its fans. The piece is especially beloved by basses, who relish, in the title role, the rare opportunity to be the star rather than singing the supporting parts to which opera's deepest voices are often consigned (aging kings and fathers, faceless high priests, etc.). With a great bass snarling and sneering to his heart's content, *Mefistofele* can make for irresistibly over-the-top grand opera, and because of this—as well as the familiarity and relative bankability of the Faust story—the piece is still revived with some regularity.

By naming his opera *Mefistofele* rather than *Faust*, Boito displayed a preference for antiheroes, a Miltonic sympathy for the devil, that would recur throughout his career: his next protagonist was the mythically depraved Roman emperor Nero, and when he came to collaborate with Verdi, Boito wanted to name their opera *Iago* rather than *Otello*. But *Mefistofele* is not the radical dramaturgical reimagining that its title seems to imply: at heart, it is a conventional setting of the Faust story that mostly follows the contours of its source in Goethe. There's a kind of punk-rock flippancy in Boito's decision to name his first opera after the devil, but in neither his music nor his dramaturgy does Boito make good on this provocation.

Mefistofele's music sounds like it was written by someone who has certainly *had* ecstatic musical experiences, and who wants very badly to create them, but who doesn't quite have the patience to develop his material such that these experiences might occur organically. Boito has a habit of attempting to create extreme climaxes very suddenly out of very little; this happens right from the outset, in the opera's orchestral prelude and first chorus, which are full of unprompted would-be orgasms, angels shouting their allegiance to the Holy Father with an incongruous insistence. And for all Boito's public proclamations about the music of the future, his harmonic palette is pretty bland. Wagner-inflected chromatic harmonies make occasional cameos, but Boito's music stops and starts too frequently to sustain the kind of slow-burning foreplay that these harmonies are capable of.

The rare moments that feel full of genuine *musical* energy, rather than abstract poetic ambition, largely belong to Mefistofele himself. His first aria, "Son lo Spirito che nega sempre tutto" ("I am the spirit who negates everything, always"), is a deliciously campy manifesto of nihilism, full of whirling strings, cackling winds, and vocal lines that brilliantly show off a broad swath of the bass's range. There are also flashes of musical vividness in Mefistofele's declaration of allegiance to Faust, which has a creepy chromatic warmth, and his swaggering proclamations at the witches' sabbath.

But elsewhere, the music rides the libretto's coattails, and even in this early piece, Boito is a confident and sure-handed librettist. He is a master of the bustling, busily polyphonic crowd scene, a feature that he would develop further in his libretti for *Otello* and Amilcare Ponchielli's *La Gioconda* (1876). Line by line, Boito's libretti also display a poetic ambition that is uncommon in opera. He wields classical verse forms with unerring dexterity, and he takes a virtuoso's delight in wordplay. Among his many linguistic tricks, aficionados of English poetry will recognize an echo effect favored by George Herbert: Boito sometimes treats the final syllable or two of a word as an echo, which reveals a different word and a different meaning. In *Mefistofele*'s Prologue, for instance, "soave" ("gentle") is echoed to become "ave" ("hail").

These effects sometimes sound clever; sometimes they're merely precious. Boito also lapses at times into an arid, abstracted idealism: *Mefistofele*'s fourth act, in which Faust is transported to ancient Greece for a quick tryst with Helen of Troy, is stuffed with dull extended harp solos, faux-Attic ceremonial music, and Faust's bloodless professions of love for Helen ("Purest ideal form / Of eternal beauty!"). It's the kind of theatrical miscalculation that Verdi would never have made: if he'd been presented with *Mefistofele*'s libretto, he probably would have cut the whole fourth act with an impatient "POCHE PAROLE."

Boito, so confident in his youth, was almost paralyzed by doubt about his musical abilities later in life. This is a shame: I find his unfinished second opera,* *Nerone*, much richer than *Mefistofele*, even if *Nerone* is also the more unwieldy of the two. In the later piece (which was completed and premiered posthumously thanks to the efforts of the conductor Arturo Toscanini), Boito successfully crafts a decadent, overripe musical language to depict a correspondingly decadent moment in Roman history. The

---

* Boito also wrote the text for a mythological opera, *Ero e Leandro*, and evidently came quite close to completing his own musical setting of it in the early 1870s. He abruptly destroyed the music before it could be performed, however, and ultimately gave the libretto to the composer Giovanni Bottesini.

work's music is an eccentric mélange of mid-nineteenth-century French influences, Italian verismo, and the soft-textured, rotting-on-the-inside chromaticism of Wagner's *Parsifal* (1882). It's a combination of qualities that would be suited to precious few subjects, but it's a perfect match for the story of Nero's fall, which Boito sets against the rise of a radical, cultlike early Christianity.

As usual, however, Boito went about things in a curiously self-sabotaging way: he published the opera's ambitious libretto long before the music was written, needlessly ratcheting up the pressure on himself. And he continued to spread himself thin. Verdi seemed aware of Boito's difficulty staying focused on composition, and touchingly insisted in the early stages of their collaboration on *Falstaff* that Boito commit to undertaking this new project only if he was sure that he could finish his own work: "If you, while writing *Falstaff* had . . . to distract your mind from *Nerone* . . . I would be blamed for this delay, and the thunderbolts of the public's ill will would fall upon my shoulders." Boito assured him that it would be no problem, but Verdi was right to worry: Boito never saw his extravagantly nightmarish opera come to life.

By committing himself to Verdi, however, Boito was hardly wasting his time—and still less was he inviting "the public's ill will."

FULL CIRCLE: VERDI AND BOITO
RETURN TO SHAKESPEARE

Before Verdi and Boito could work together, Boito had to outgrow his messianic tendencies, and Verdi had to get over the grudge he bore Boito over his insulting "ode to Italian art." This took many years. By the time Verdi was ready to take a fresh look at Boito, both artists had changed profoundly.

In the operas that followed *Macbeth*, Verdi tested and ultimately broke apart many of the vestigial structures that he had inherited from the bel canto generation. One essential difference between the bel canto aria and its nearest equivalent in Shakespeare, the soliloquy, is that in bel canto opera, an aria is rarely a vehicle for dramatic action; more often, it is the musical embodiment of a single, fixed state of mind. The Shakespearean soliloquy, by contrast, is not a static articulation of something the character already knows; it's a locus of self-interrogation and epiphany. In his middle-period operas, Verdi found new ways to treat the aria more and more like the Shakespearean soliloquy.

In *Rigoletto*, the title character's searing aria "Cortigiani, vil razza dannata," is a prime example of this newfound formal dynamism. It begins with Rigoletto's outburst of blind rage against the men who have abducted his daughter; the strings, repeating a ferocious sextuplet figure, seem to be straining to break free of invisible shackles. When this effort fails, Rigoletto changes tack and abjectly begs his tormentors, the music limping woundedly along; when this fails too, he collapses and sings a heartrending lament. This aria is an X-ray of Rigoletto's soul, and it's more Shakespearean than anything in *Macbeth*; in his volatility, vulnerability, and pathos, Rigoletto resembles no one so much as King Lear.

Boito, too, was honing his skill as a Shakespearean, notably in his early libretto for Franco Faccio's *Hamlet* adaptation, *Amleto* (1865). After an 1871 production at Milan's Teatro alla Scala, Faccio's *Amleto* went unperformed throughout the twentieth century and was next revived, through the excavatory efforts of the conductor Anthony Barrese, only in 2014. I'm grateful that *Amleto* is available to us today: though Faccio's blocky, sharp-hewn music is little more than competent, Boito's libretto is a revelation. The college-age Boito somehow managed the tightrope act of deftly condensing Shakespeare's huge text (Rosencrantz and Guildenstern are nowhere to be found) without seeming to lose anything essential. The libretto's poetry is a brilliant blend of tight Italian verse forms and convincingly idiomatic approximations of Shakespearean pentameter. It's so good, in fact, that I wish Verdi had thought to take a chance on the young Boito for the 1865 revision of *Macbeth*, since Boito, even as an undergraduate, evidently knew Shakespeare better than Verdi's other collaborators did.

As things turned out, the Verdi-Boito partnership would take quite a bit longer to crystallize. Verdi first hired Boito for the relatively modest task of revising the libretto of his 1857 opera *Simon Boccanegra* in 1880–81; this was surely a test to see if Verdi could imagine building an opera with Boito from scratch. Verdi seems to have been pleased by the dynamic of their working relationship: Boito had grown up, and the qualities that had irritated Verdi a couple of decades earlier were no longer in evidence. Their first complete collaboration, *Otello*, would turn out to be well worth the wait.

Expansion and Contraction: Otello

The process of adapting a play into an opera is a little like forcing the original text to drink a concoction out of *Alice in Wonderland*: some features of the original shrink or evaporate, while others are magnified to unrecognizable dimensions. *Otello*, which has the rare distinction of being a masterpiece based on a masterpiece, is my favorite example of this dynamic. The drama's three principal characters—Othello, Desdemona, and Iago—are each affected differently by this fickle alchemy: in the opera, Otello is an even richer and more sympathetic figure than he is in the play, while Desdemona is mostly unchanged. Iago, on the other hand, is diminished: his nuances somehow drain away when he's forced to sing. I want to examine why and how the rocky passage into music has such disparate effects on each of the principal characters, since I think these differences illuminate certain unwritten but fundamental principles of operatic characterization.

I mentioned earlier that Boito originally wanted to call the opera *Iago*: his *Faust* adaptation was called *Mefistofele*, after all, and Iago is every bit as essential to *Othello* as Mephistopheles is to the Faust story. Iago is a psychological black hole, a scene-stealer who ends up stealing the whole play: he speaks more lines than Othello; he orchestrates the drama's whole tragic trajectory. Why not acknowledge, in the title, that he's the star?

Verdi's unyielding resistance to this idea encapsulates the difference between his temperament and Boito's. Yes, Verdi acknowledged, Iago is an unstoppable engine of destruction, but Othello is the drama's beating heart: "It is Otello who acts," and the blood is ultimately on his hands. Though Verdi did not articulate this, he might also have felt that naming the opera *Iago* would have been misleading, an unjustified provocation: it would imply a thorough dramaturgical reworking of the play, a reweighting of the drama such that we see the world through Iago's eyes. (Boito's failure to make good on just such a provocation is one of the disappointments of *Mefistofele*.)

In reality, far from weighting the drama in Iago's favor, Verdi's opera does the opposite: Verdi amplifies Otello's voice and presence at the expense of Iago's. I think the reasons for this go deeper than some pedantic belief that a tragedy must be named after its hero: Verdi seems to have felt a profound sympathy with his protagonist. The composer's personality, in music if not in life, is palpably similar to Otello's; their salient shared qualities include a disarming emotional directness and vulnerability, an earnestness and single-mindedness that preclude all irony, and a capacity for overwhelming passion and power. If there was ever a role Verdi was born to set to music, it's this one. As a result, even if *Othello* sometimes feels like Iago's play, *Otello* is unquestionably Otello's opera.

OTELLO'S STRUCTURAL INNOVATIONS

In *Otello*, Verdi's and Boito's very different sensibilities—the former's insistence on tautness and economy, the latter's tendency toward density and discursiveness—balance each other to create a unique hybrid structure. There are plenty of set pieces (arias, duets, etc.), but the architecture of the drama absorbs them with ease; for the first time in a Verdi opera, the dramaturgy as well as the music is capable of real legato. In his earlier operas, Verdi had no problem letting the seams show; even a masterpiece like *Un ballo in maschera* contains some music that's bluntly functional, music that trots on like a stagehand and cheerfully announces, *Excuse me, I just have to fill these fifteen seconds while so-and-so makes his entrance.* Such music is not inherently problematic, but there's just no room for it in *Otello*, which moves with a molten swiftness from its first notes.

When familiar operatic devices do appear in *Otello*, their purpose is often subversive. Iago leads a drinking song in Act One, for example, but it's not exactly *La traviata*'s exuberant "Libiamo": Iago's drinking song spirals further out of control with each verse, eventually bursting open into mass panic. Verdi subtly builds the potential for violence into the song's musical materials, which are off-kilter and harmonically unstable from the start; the superficially cheerful ditty's descent into chaos feels natural and inevitable.

In Verdi's hands, radical stasis is every bit as effective as violence. In Act Two, just when Iago has planted a seed of doubt in Otello's mind, a band of locals inconveniently arrives to present flowers to Desdemona. They praise her beauty with a blithely lovely (and rather long) chorus, accompanied by a mandolin. Iago croons mock-soothing advice in Otello's ear over the beginning of this chorus, and then Otello is forced to stand back and watch: for as long as this maddeningly leisurely ceremony lasts, there's nothing he can do. It's like being stopped at an intersection while a parade processes unhurriedly in front of you, the participants smiling and waving as your car grumblingly idles. All the while, beneath the music's sunny, gently swaying surface, Iago's words are taking root.

The most grotesque use of a set piece comes at the end of Act Two, when Otello and Iago swear allegiance to each other in "Sì, pel ciel," a very conventional duet of friendship. This duet is structured in quite an old-fashioned way: Otello sings a verse, Iago sings a verse, and the two of them sing a verse together. By this point in Verdi's career, the tenor-baritone bromance was a familiar trope, and Verdi often had his two male stars declare their loyalty to each other in just such a duet (there are good examples in *La forza del destino* and *Don Carlo* [1867]). After the lavalike flow of the previous twenty minutes, the blatant conventionality of "Sì, pel ciel" feels grotesque, as it should: the whole thing is a lie. After Otello's final would-be-triumphant high A, the brass-heavy orchestra snarls the curtain down behind his back.

Even the huge concertato finale of Act Three—the kind of pageant-like ensemble scene that was a tried-and-true Verdian specialty—has tricks up its sleeve. In this scene, Otello slaps Desdemona in front of a large group of visiting dignitaries, and Desdemona initiates the music of the finale while lying prostrate on the ground. In *Macbeth*, too, the protagonist loses his cool in public just before a big ensemble finale; and the image of a mistreated woman surrounded by a confused, sympathetic crowd would have been familiar from the Act Two finale of *La traviata*. But in both of those operas, once the music of the ensemble begins, the act's dramatic action is clearly over. In *Otello*, by contrast, Iago continues to stir the pot throughout the finale, muttering instructions to Otello and Roderigo; and Verdi creates the sense that the chorus's music, which builds and builds, is driving Otello over the edge. Eventually, Otello snaps, and orders everyone to leave. The stage empties: Verdi deconstructs the concertato finale before our eyes. Otello collapses. In a disorienting reversal of perspective, the chorus is momentarily heard singing offstage. By the end of the act, Iago is the only man standing.

OTELLO

In the play, we're always hearing about Othello's heroism, but in the opera, we don't have to take anyone's word for it: one well-struck high note is worth a thousand words, and Verdi makes sure we know who we're dealing with right from Otello's first entrance.

Since Verdi and Boito cut the entirety of Shakespeare's first act, *Otello* begins with the storm scene that opens the second act of the play: the first sound we hear is a fierce crash of orchestral thunder, which I like to think of as Verdi's announcement to his public that the old man had plenty of piss and vinegar left in him. Having defeated the Turkish fleet, Otello's ship is caught in a storm off Cyprus, and a crowd watches anxiously from the shore. The music of the opera's first four minutes lurches queasily from key to key as dozens of voices narrate the ship's unsteady progress with fragmentary, overlapping exclamations. For Verdi, this was a wholly new way to begin an opera: even relatively late works like *Aida* typically begin with a scene-setting orchestral prelude. In *Otello*, by contrast, the very first chord hurls us into the deep end.

In Shakespeare, once Othello has safely landed, he first greets Desdemona and then, in passing, offhandedly addresses the assembled crowd: "News, friends: our wars are done; the Turks are drown'd." A single line of pentameter is all this rather important news bulletin gets; it might as well be a chyron at the bottom of a CNN broadcast. Verdi and Boito thrust this little aside center stage and explode it into arguably the most thrilling first entrance of any operatic character, the "Esultate!" ("Rejoice!"). Otello cuts through the storm's blustery, chilly chromatic instability with an ascending major sixth—a gesture that, in Verdi, is always redolent of romantic or heroic aspiration—that lands in a burnished D-flat major. His voice shines like a beacon. After four minutes of seasick swirling, it's thanks only to Otello that we know we're on solid ground.

Verdi's Otello is not just more palpably heroic than Shakespeare's; he is also more sympathetic. Of all Shakespeare's protagonists, Othello's language, with its rolling rhythm and rich, archaic vocabulary, comes closest to pure music, and once Othello's jealousy takes hold, Shakespeare seems to chafe at language's limits (all those cries of "O!"). In depicting Otello, the explosive properties of Verdi's musical language give him an unfair advantage. *All* his characters have an inbred tendency to heat up and boil over— it's just what Italian-opera characters do! As a result, Otello's loss of self-control seems more credible in Verdi's music than it does in language alone.

The excision of the play's first act has the collateral effect of deemphasizing, to a degree, the fraught racial dynamic that is so inescapable in Shakespeare. It is in this deleted first act that Iago goads Desdemona's father, Brabantio, with grotesquely racist descriptions of the sex acts Othello is surely performing with Desdemona, and it's also in this act that Brabantio publicly denounces Othello and Desdemona's relationship in front of Venice's highest-ranking officials. In the opera, Brabantio doesn't appear at all, and as a result we have little sense of the obstacles Otello and Desdemona had to overcome to marry each other. Another effect of Verdi and Boito's condensation of the play is that, in the opera, there are far fewer of the offhandedly racist statements that are so omnipresent in Shakespeare that they form a kind of maddening background hum. When overtly racist language does appear in the opera, it's usually voiced by Iago, and because of this, there's a persistent association of such slurs with Iago's general despicableness.

To be clear, this is still an *Othello* adaptation: some aspects of the title character will inevitably feel problematic to modern audiences, especially the combination of Otello's credulousness with the antique ideal of "nobility" that he embodies. But compare Otello with any of Verdi's other tenor leads (Manrico in *Il trovatore* [1853], the Duke in *Rigoletto*, etc.) and the others look like empty shells, 2D posterboard cutouts. Otello is by far the richest, most dynamic, most lovingly detailed of Verdian tenor roles, and out of *all* Verdi characters, I think he lavished a similar care only on Rigoletto and *La traviata*'s Violetta.

Verdi also notably avoids, in his depiction of Otello, the prefabricated musical exoticisms that were readily available to him. Otello is described as a "Moor," and nineteenth-century audiences might have expected him to be depicted through familiar "Moorish" musical tropes: piccolos, chiming triangles, sinuous dance rhythms. Verdi had in fact made use of such tropes in *Don Carlo*, whose "Veil Song," a ballad about a randy Middle Eastern king, is full of exactly these sounds. But Otello is, for the most part, not made to sound like an Other. To my ears, he sounds as close to Verdi's own voice as any character Verdi ever created.

Otello's Act Three aria "Dio! mi potevi scagliar tutti i mali" ("Lord, Thou couldst have tried me with every affliction") concentrates the role's every emotional extreme into a four-minute span. In the previous scene, Otello had exploded with rage and accused Desdemona of infidelity, calling her a whore to her face. She has just run away from him. Left alone, Otello realizes that whether or not Desdemona is guilty, he has disgraced and degraded himself. The strings slide wearily downward. Unusually for the aria of a tenor protagonist, Otello begins with sixteen repetitions of the A-flat below middle C, a dully unshowy middle-range note, before descending to the even less glamorous low E-flat. ("Voce soffocata," Verdi writes on the first note—"with a suffocated voice.") The aria remains within this narrow range for nearly two minutes. By denying his tenor the gift of melody, Verdi creates the sense that Otello is desperately clinging to a single note for stability as his world nauseatingly shifts around him. At the line "Ma, o pianto, o duol!" Otello finally ascends into a more gratifying register. Describing the "mirage" of his happiness, Otello sings a tremulously beautiful, slowly unfurling melodic line that, mirage-like, evaporates midphrase before restarting and expanding. At this line's conclusion, the strings start to stir uneasily; the harmonies mutate from a lush E-flat major into unstable, endlessly refractable diminished chords. The music's blood has started to boil. Otello sings a series of loud, jagged phrases, which Iago interrupts to announce that Cassio is nearby. Otello answers with a jarring outburst of joy (we are again in E-flat major). Hearing his own frenzied glee, Otello is disgusted all over again. He collapses back into his lower register, and Iago takes advantage of his exhaustion to seize control, accompanied by a jittery, urgent line in the strings.

A piece like "Dio! mi potevi" shows the mature Verdi at his all-assimilating best. Though it is clearly an aria, it has the Wagnerian quality of having no obvious beginning or ending; it organically emerges from and returns to the liquid flow of the drama. In just a few minutes, it traces a dynamic psychological arc, from revulsion and despair to nostalgia to fury to joy to renewed self-disgust. And it contains the entirety of the title role's wide musical range: austerely elegant for its first two minutes, meltingly beautiful at its core, and, by the end, unstoppably volatile.

IAGO

Shakespeare's Iago is one of his scariest creations, a chameleonic psychopath who operates by implication and insinuation. He is among Shakespeare's most virtuosic talkers, one who accomplishes diabolical feats of persuasion with an exquisitely subtle affective palette that ranges from poisoned-honey sweetness to chummy good humor to wounded self-pity. He is capable of a dizzying range of tones, and above all he's an unstoppable fountain of *words*, thousands and thousands of words. This slippery prolixity makes him an awkward fit for Verdi, the man who implacably demanded "FEW WORDS" of his librettists, and whose greatest strength is his emotional honesty. Iago's every word drips with toxic irony, and is there any other composer whose musical language is as free of irony as Verdi's? "I am not what I am," says Iago; but Verdi's music can never be anything other than what it is.

Boito is partially responsible for the operatic Iago's relative lack of subtlety. In his adaptations of Othello's and Desdemona's parts, Boito largely remains true to Shakespeare's characterizations, but I think Boito's Iago shares some DNA with his own earlier villains, Mefistofele and the grotesquely evil Barnaba, in *La*

Gioconda. Iago's big solo scene in the opera is his "Credo," an aria whose heavy-metal bravado is irresistible but whose text Shakespeare's Iago would never speak:

> I believe in a cruel God, who created me like unto Him,
> And who, in wrath, I name.
> From the vileness of a germ, or of an atom,
> I was born vile.

When Shakespeare's Iago is left alone, he reveals that he has no core: like the villain in a morality play, all he knows how to do is brood over his machinations and marvel at their success. The "Credo," with its showy braggadocio, sounds less like Shakespeare's Iago than Boito's Mefistofele. In its articulation of a nihilistic theology, this aria is a direct descendant of Mefistofele's "Son lo Spirito che nega sempre tutto," to the extent that some of its lines could easily have been spoken by that devil. The aria's final, climactic line—"Death is nothingness, and heaven an old wives' tale"—is also borrowed: it was originally intended for an aria of Barnaba's in *La Gioconda*.

This recycling of tropes from earlier Boito antiheroes spills over into Verdi's music: with its blaring orchestral introduction and jerky, stop-and-start motion, parts of the "Credo" sound nothing like the rest of *Otello*, and indeed they sound curiously like the young Boito—surely the only instance of Boito the *composer* influencing Verdi. The "Credo" is undeniably effective, but it creates the sense that Iago is a familiarly unctuous kind of Italian-opera villain rather than the transcendent nihilist who stalks the stage in Shakespeare. The operatic Iago might have retained more of his mystery if he were deprived, as Mozart's Don Giovanni is, of ever singing an aria of vehement self-definition.

Much of Iago's other music, however, is spellbindingly potent. After his drinking song rouses the chorus into a frenzy, Iago comments on the action with a manic staccato line that sounds plausibly like both terror and glee. And the extended sequence in Act Two during which he convinces Otello of Desdemona's supposed infidelity is a tour de force, one of the best things Verdi ever wrote. Listen to the drawling, unfinished musical phrases Iago sings to irritate Otello; listen to the toxic lullaby he croons into Otello's ear just when he knows Otello has passed a psychological point of no return ("Non parlo ancor di prova"). One of Iago's finest moments is a cruel musical joke: when Otello, having decided to murder Desdemona, asks Iago for poison, Iago says Otello should not poison his wife but rather should strangle her in bed, "dove ha peccato" ("where she sinned"). Verdi sets these words to a descending line that is nearly identical to, and nearly rhymes with, Otello's line "ancora un bacio" ("one more kiss"), from his love duet with Desdemona.

DESDEMONA

Of the three principal roles, Desdemona is least altered by the precarious journey from speech to song. In Shakespeare and Verdi alike, she possesses a quiet strength, a stronger backbone than she is sometimes credited with. Some of her edges are softened in the opera because of the absence of Shakespeare's first act; we do not witness her crucial gesture of rebellion, her public profession of love for Othello. Elsewhere, however, the shortening of her role in the opera may actually improve the drama. I'm surely not alone in feeling that, in the play, Desdemona's insistence to Othello that he pardon Cassio feels exaggerated for effect; her implausible fixation on this point seems engineered to make the audience wince. In the opera, the dynamic is reversed: Desdemona's request on Cassio's behalf is brief and perfectly reasonable, and Otello's annoyance at it seems out of proportion.

The surer Otello becomes of Desdemona's infidelity, the more blindingly beautiful her music is. In Act Three, when Otello commands Desdemona to swear that she has been faithful to him ("swear, and damn yourself!"), the music stops in its tracks. As the orchestra gasps and shudders like a death march, Desdemona tells Otello that she does not understand where his anger is coming from. For three phrases, her line remains fixed on the soprano's low E; her music seems pinned to the ground. This note requires her to use chest voice, an earthy and primal kind of vocal production that is not so different from Broadway "belting." To linger so long in this mode is unusual for a lyrical role like Desdemona, and when she finally leaves that low E, she jumps more than an octave up to a blazing F-sharp on the word "furia" ("fury"). Desdemona then changes tack and sings a long, painfully beautiful melodic line that climaxes on a high B-flat before making a steep descent back into chest-voice terrain. This is not the behavior of a shrinking-violet soprano heroine. Once Desdemona finishes singing, the strings continue to play her music with a voluptuous intensity; as the melody swirls around him, Otello says, "If your demon saw you now, he'd think you were an angel, and would not take you." Verdi creates the sense that we are inside Otello's head, and from this perspective the sheer beauty of Desdemona's music is sickening, full of the bright heat of a pounding headache.

The highlight of Desdemona's role, and one of my two or three favorite moments in *any* opera, comes in the final act. Desdemona is in her bedroom with her maid Emilia, waiting uneasily for Otello. Numb from the traumas she has endured, she must remain numb so as not to confront her fear. She vacillates between distractedly going through the motions of her nighttime toilette and unintentionally expressing her mounting anxiety. At one point, she erupts with seemingly excessive irritation about a song that's stuck in her head: the "Willow Song," a tune she remembers her mother's maid singing when she was a child.

Verdi subtly teases out this song's unsettling implications: the woman Desdemona heard sing it was named Barbara, which identifies her with what Europeans called the Barbary Coast of North Africa: at one point in the play, Iago calls Othello a "Barbary horse," and in some editions of Shakespeare, the maid is named Barbary rather than Barbara. Verdi hints at the song's North African origins, and at the racial anxiety to which Desdemona is unconsciously giving voice, by employing a harmonic language that is familiar from *Aida*. Desdemona's first line ("Piangea cantando") bears a strong family resemblance to the oboe melody that accompanies Aida's plea to Radamès to flee Egypt with her ("Fuggiam gli ardori inospiti").

As it progresses, the song reveals an extraordinary form. With each verse, the orchestral motion grows more uneasy and the instrumental textures more transparent; by the third verse, the music has a gossamer, wind-like insubstantiality. It is clear that Desdemona has forgotten her surroundings and entirely entered the world of the song: at the line "E gl'occhi suoi piangean tanto, tanto, / da impietosir le rupi" (the equivalent in Shakespeare is "Her salt tears fell from her, and softened the stones"), the music takes on a sudden, frightening intensity. The airy string texture morphs into a fiery, concentrated tremolo, like mist cohering into a ghostlike outline: Desdemona seems to be confronting a specter, the weeping Barbara as an image of herself. Then, unexpectedly, the orchestra falls silent. In the quiet, Desdemona takes a ring off her finger and abstractedly asks Emilia to put it away. The orchestra hovers with a "Now where was I?" uncertainty; then Desdemona impulsively cries "Poor Barbara!" It's clear from these irregular pauses and whiplash-inducing swerves that Desdemona is in a state of shock and dissociation: she's not quite conscious of her actions or the profound psychic unease that they manifest.

After the "Willow Song" ends, Desdemona shakes herself out of her reverie and wearily wishes Emilia good night, accompanied by a reprise of the song's opening melody. As Emilia turns to leave, the orchestra softly repeats the same warm F-sharp major chord, which throbs strangely, like something unsayable rising to the throat and falling back again and again. Finally the dam bursts: Desdemona unleashes a tidal wave of sound, this time singing not "buona notte" but "addio"—"farewell." It is an overwhelming release of energy—terror, love, and grief pouring out with devastating force. When Desdemona sings this line, we realize that the entire "Willow Song" had been an act of repression, an ultimately hopeless attempt to distract herself; and we feel with painful clarity that she knows exactly what is in store for her.

With *Otello*, Verdi triumphantly emerged from retirement to realize a seemingly impossible goal: he created a Shakespeare adaptation that matches and in some ways magnifies the expressive power of the original drama. What could possibly remain for him to do after that, especially given that he was nearing his eightieth birthday?

It turned out that Verdi had the appetite to attempt a still-more-improbable goal: in their next collaboration, he and Boito sought to *expand* on Shakespeare by achieving something Shakespeare never managed to do. They wanted to finally give one of the Bard's most beloved characters, Sir John Falstaff, a piece that would be big and bold enough for his irrepressible spirit.

A Last Step, A First Step: Falstaff

Falstaff is a long-pent-up belly laugh of a piece, an unexpected late-inning about-face for a composer who had written nothing but tragedies for more than half a century. In the story of Verdi's musical life, *Falstaff* is the last and most satisfying plot twist—the big reveal, the unmasking. This opera brings Verdi's lifelong engagement with Shakespeare to a heartily satisfying conclusion: having been nourished for decades by the Bard's work, in this piece Verdi manages (impossibly) to *give back* to Shakespeare.

After *Otello*, Verdi was once again presumed to have retired, so he was able to write *Falstaff* in secret, at a leisurely pace. Even to his publisher, Giulio Ricordi, Verdi revealed the piece's existence only once composition was well underway. This difference in creative process is palpable in the opera itself, which has no sure-fire hits—no conventional showpiece arias, no big love duets or heart-stirring choruses. Some of *Falstaff's* early listeners found the piece unmelodic; to my ears, it consists of practically nothing *but* melodies, but they are often micro-melodies, lasting no more than a second or two before bursting like a soap bubble. Whereas in earlier operas Verdi tended to isolate his musical ideas so that each one would be firmly emblazoned on the listener's mind, in *Falstaff* the ideas interrupt and pile on top of one another with a Mozart-ean profusion. This has something to do with the faster pacing that is inherent in comedy, but it has more to do with the fact that Verdi was, for the first time in his professional life, composing primarily for his own pleasure. Far from being a grand summation of his long career, *Falstaff* is something much more special: it is the octogenarian Verdi's experimental first step in a new direction.

Verdi had not written a comedy since his unsuccessful second opera, *Un giorno di regno* (1840), which had its premiere fifty-three years before *Falstaff*'s. The experience of writing *Un giorno* was a traumatic one for the twenty-six-year-old Verdi: both of his young children had died shortly before he began work on the piece, and his wife, Margherita, died during its composition. He was hardly in a frame of mind to write a lighthearted comedy of mistaken identities, and *Un giorno* flopped at its premiere. Exhausted and depressed, Verdi swore he'd never compose again. That resolution didn't last long, but when he returned to the profession the following year, with *Nabucco*, he devoted himself exclusively to tragedy. He nevertheless resented any assumption, over the following decades, that he *couldn't* write comedy. In the 1870s, the sculptor Giovanni Dupré published a memoir that quoted Rossini, the most influential Italian composer of comic operas, as having once said that Verdi, with his "melancholy, serious character" and his "dark and sad" color palette, would surely never write an opera buffa. Verdi reacted with indignation, claiming that he'd been looking for a good comic libretto for decades. In the end, it was only in the twilight of his career that he'd find one.

Falstaff, unlike *Otello*, is not based on a single, unimpeachably sturdy source. The opera's plot is that of *The Merry Wives of Windsor*, one of Shakespeare's weaker plays, but Verdi and Boito, in their depiction of the title character, also draw on the Falstaff of the much stronger *Henry IV* diptych. Theatrical legend has it that Shakespeare wrote *The Merry Wives* at the direct request of Queen Elizabeth, who so enjoyed Falstaff's presence in *Henry IV* that she wanted to see him in a comedy. Shakespeare supposedly had only two weeks to write it. This story may well be apocryphal, but its persistence is telling in itself: generations of Shakespeareans have eagerly sought an excuse to explain away *The Merry Wives'* shortcomings. In *Falstaff*, Verdi and Boito carefully cherry-pick Falstaff's most memorable moments from all three plays in which he appears. The result is a kind of best-of compilation, a big Falstaffian banquet.

Falstaff's many musical pleasures have little to do with sophisticated character studies or a coherent dramatic architecture. In spite of Boito's canny condensation of the play—there are ten fewer singing roles in the opera than there are speaking parts in Shakespeare—*Falstaff*'s plot is still that of *The Merry Wives*, in all its banality. The first two acts build toward Falstaff's first public humiliation at the hands of the "merry wives"; the third act starts over and organizes itself around Falstaff's *next* public humiliation. In a letter to Boito shortly after they had begun work on the opera, Verdi lamented these structural weaknesses: "A pity that the interest (it's not your fault) does not increase until the end," Verdi wrote.* "The culmination is the finale of the second act; and the appearance of Falstaff's face amid the laundry, etc., is a true comic idea." Compared to this comic climax, Verdi feared "that the last act . . . will end up weak." Boito agreed: "No doubt, the third act is the weakest. And in the theatre this is a serious mistake." (Inveterate mansplainer that he was, Boito's letter continues with a lecture

---

* By "the end," Verdi seems to have meant the end of the middle act (Act Two).

about the basic nature of drama: "Unfortunately, this is a general law of comedy. Tragedy has the opposite law ... Thus the last acts of tragedies are always the most beautiful ones." He seems to have forgotten he was writing to *Giuseppe Verdi*.)

In addition to the piece's built-in structural awkwardness, Boito's genteel literary style is an odd fit for bedroom comedy. No Boito libretto is entirely free of pretentiousness or overwrought poetry, but this tendency is more glaring in a farce like *Falstaff* than in a tragedy like *Otello*. To listeners with only a passing grasp of Italian, *Falstaff*'s libretto probably sounds like a beguiling deluge of bubbling comic patter. Fluent Italian speakers, however, might find its constant wordplay, its many mythological allusions, its Boccaccio quotes, etc., a little wearying. Boito evidently sought to create an Italian equivalent for Elizabethan English, with its rich potential for punning, but he can't quite match Shakespeare's tonal dexterousness, his gift for toggling between poetic refinement and virtuosic bawdiness. At one point in *Falstaff*, Bardolfo, a hard-drinking lackey of Falstaff's, warns Ford that his wife might be cheating on him in the following terms: "La corona che adorna / D'Atteïn l'irte chiome / Su voi già spunta" ("The crown that adorns / Actaeon's bristling hair / Now appears upon you"). Ford understandably has no idea what Bardolfo is talking about, and asks him to clarify. Shakespeare can make even a moment like this work by deploying one of his raunchier registers, but in Boito, Bardolfo inexplicably sounds like he's quoting Dante.

These flaws are barely palpable in practice however, because Verdi's music—especially the music for Falstaff himself—*does* have a Shakespearean breadth of tone. Verdi's Falstaff is the anti-Iago, as indefatigably life-affirming as Iago is nihilistic, and paradoxically, because of this diametric opposition, the two characters resemble each other profoundly. The roles make similar vocal demands, and were written with the same singer, Victor Maurel, in mind; many subsequent singers (Tito Gobbi, Giuseppe Taddei, Renato Bruson, Cornell MacNeil—the list goes on) have had success portraying both characters.

No other Verdi character sounds like these two. Falstaff and Iago are capable of a different kind of *agency*, which manifests as a different form of musical motion and a different relationship between singer and orchestra. In their arias, Iago and Falstaff do not simply ride the surges of orchestral sound, as other characters do; rather, they lead the orchestra around by the nose. Their arias wander searchingly from idea to idea in accordance with the character's reflections; they are full of musing a cappella sections and sudden, agitated recitatives. This unpredictable, irregular motion creates the sense that the character is guiding the orchestra, rather than the other way around. The through-line of these arias is not any given melodic thread but rather the train of Iago's or Falstaff's *thought*. Other characters might sometimes seem to be mere vessels for the melodies that surge through them, but Iago and Falstaff both conduct and stage-direct every scene they appear in.

The two roles also share the same harmonic DNA, a sweet and sticky chromaticism that contemporary listeners might recognize through its influence on early Disney soundtracks. Especially when Iago and Falstaff go to extremes of violence or delicacy, they are almost indistinguishable from each other. Listen to Iago at his most purringly seductive, in a mini-aria like "Era la notte," in which he claims to have overheard Cassio murmuring in his sleep about his supposed affair with Desdemona; then listen to Falstaff in his would-be ladies'-man mode, in a brief passage like the moment in the opera's first scene in which he claims that he's still in his prime ("Io sono ancora una piacente estate di San Martino"). Such passages share a fundamentally comic, almost cartoonish quality—a quality that I find just slightly wrong for Iago, but that is perfect for the infinitely extroverted Falstaff.

The rest of the cast is a stock comedy ensemble, no member of which has anything close to Falstaff's capacity for vivid, brooding introspection. The "merry wives" are the Real Housewives of Windsor, bored and vindictive; their conversations mostly consist of plots to ensnare Falstaff or get back at Alice Ford's jealous, hot-tempered husband. (The merry wives' scenes decisively fail the Bechdel test.) The music of the young lovers, Fenton and Nannetta, is curiously wistful for a pair of horny teenagers: both of their arias in the opera's final act glow with an aching, autumnal melancholy that surely expresses Verdi's own state of mind more than theirs. Only the fabulously throaty contralto role of Mistress Quickly is, at her best, a real match for Falstaff. This pervasive two-dimensionality is, for Verdi's purposes, not an obstacle but an opportunity. *Falstaff*'s characters may not be especially interesting as individuals (Falstaff aside), but when they speak as an ensemble, their collective voice is irresistibly vivid. The opera's ensemble music has a giddy, quicksilver brilliance that forges a one-of-a-kind marriage between the tongue-twisting virtuosity of Rossinian patter and the increased horsepower of the late-nineteenth-century orchestra.

Falstaff also has a rare quality in common with Mozart's *Così fan tutte* (1790): it is full of passages that are much more beautiful than they have any right to be, moments when a seemingly trivial dramatic situation opens, for an instant, onto a radiant alternate world. Some of the opera's most beautiful music may actually be found in its most mean-spirited scenes, its moments of mockery or deception. When the "merry wives" read Falstaff's love letter aloud in order to make fun of it, the music is genuinely wonderful in spite of their sarcastic intentions. Near the end of the letter, Alice spins one particularly pompous phrase into a long, gorgeous cantabile line. At the melody's final cadence, she sings a scornful, faux-Classical trill, and the other women join her in a burst of staccato laughter, popping the bubble, breaking the spell.

In the opera's final scene, Verdi pulls one more rabbit out of his hat: he ends the opera with a jubilant fugue, led by Falstaff and sung by the whole cast, on the words "Tutto nel mondo è burla" ("All in the world's a joke"). Early in their collaboration on *Falstaff*, when Verdi fretted in a letter to Boito about whether he had the energy to write yet another opera, Boito tempted him with the prospect of a surprise happy ending to his career: "Having made all the cries and lamentations of the human heart resound, to end with an immense outburst of cheer! That will astonish!" This final fugue is that "immense outburst of cheer." Verdi, through Falstaff, addresses the listeners who had followed him across those decades of tragedy after tragedy: remember, he seems to say, don't take any of it *too* seriously.

This final number also contains the subtlest, most telling parallel between Falstaff and Iago. Near the end of his "Credo," Iago, like Falstaff, summons the trope that life is one big joke: "Vien dopo tanta irrision la Morte" ("After all this mockery comes death"). And then what? "La Morte è il Nulla" ("Death is nothingness"), he sneers, a cappella. This phrase contains three pitches that span a minor third, between the baritone's low B-flat and the D-flat above it. Near the end of *Falstaff*'s final fugue, something very similar happens. The orchestra and chorus suddenly fall silent, and Falstaff, with exaggerated, menacing glee—is he parodying someone?—sings the words "Tutti gabbati" ("We're all fools"). This phrase, like Iago's, is sung a cappella, and like Iago's it lies low in the baritone's range and contains three pitches that span a minor third.

Falstaff, by expressing the same sentiment as Iago, also mocks him, and offers a kind of cheerful cosmic refutation. In the "Credo," Iago's statement is answered only by the hysterical laughter of the orchestra, but Falstaff is warmly echoed by a chorus of his fellow human beings. Then the whole cast, which had stood silently spellbound throughout Falstaff's faux-solemn declaration, starts to giggle. The music builds giddily and achieves liftoff, the sopranos sharing one last high C. The orchestral outro is wonderfully brief and no-nonsense: *Okay, okay, basta*, the brass seem to say, with a very Verdian impatience. *Show's over, everybody go home*. What more can any composer hope for than this: having spent a lifetime writing unforgettable expressions of rage and pathos and grief, to have the grace and good humor at the end of the day to turn around and laugh it all off?

FIVE

Walt Whitman's Impossible Optimism

Walt Whitman is more operatic than opera itself. He attempts, in his poems, to channel the surging, boundary-bursting force of the burgeoning American nation, in all its chaotic self-contradiction. He yearns to speak on behalf of the whole continent, to unite opposites and smooth over differences, as if the country could be gathered into a gigantic choral collective. He introduces himself as a "kosmos"; he would like both to speak for everyone and to be no one in particular. He is a chameleon, a shapeshifter, a self-appointed national cheerleader. Everything about him is impossible.

Because of this—because he's an opera in himself, and also because I (maybe unwisely) dared to put him onstage as the protagonist of my first opera, *Crossing* (2015)—Walt gets a chapter of his own in a book that otherwise concerns itself exclusively with operas and their creators. (I think he'd be thrilled to find himself in the company of Orpheus, Falstaff, and the rest of the art form's outsize personalities.)

The idea of surrounding Whitman's geyser-like poems with the orchestral sound that they seem to demand is—I see now—an all-but-unattainable endeavor, but it seemed like an irresistible challenge to me around the time I graduated from college. When I set out to write the opera that would become *Crossing*, however, I didn't know that my excavations of Whitman's contradictions and paradoxes would hit so close to home: I'm a Whitmanian optimist at heart, and *Crossing* turned out to be an interrogation of the limits of that optimism. And I couldn't have guessed that Whitman would seem so relevant to the reckonings America would face throughout the years the opera was being developed.

Crossing was first produced by Boston's American Repertory Theater (A.R.T.) in 2015, and that production, directed by Diane Paulus, traveled to the Brooklyn Academy of Music in the fall of 2017. By the time *Crossing* reached New York, Whitman's inveterate optimism seemed both naïve and all too familiar. Back in 2016, a lot of us had assumed, or obstinately insisted, that the nation's better angels would surely win the day; the alternative seemed nightmarish and inconceivable. And then, of course, that nightmare became our everyday reality. Throughout the first half of 2017, during those awful months when the Trump administration was rolling out policy after grotesque policy, I remember feeling, as I revised *Crossing* in advance of its Brooklyn production, that Whitman was telling me things I'd never noticed before. He seemed to embody both America's best qualities and its most self-deceiving, self-aggrandizing ones. Engaging with Whitman suddenly felt like an uncomfortable self-examination, an X-ray that analyzed the stress fractures within my own misplaced optimism.

My goal in *Crossing* was both to look at America through Whitman's lens and to scrutinize that lens, to hold it up to the light. Whitman has diffused himself so pervasively into the language through which America understands itself (even our concept of selfhood owes much to his expansive definition of the self) that he is often all but invisible. His generosity, his messiness, his blind spots—and above all his unshakable, irrational optimism—are our own.

This chapter has a double impossibility: my impossible attempt to capture Whitman's spirit in operatic form, and the generative impossibility that is Whitman's optimistic worldview, which doggedly endured beyond all disillusionment.

When the team at the A.R.T. invited me, in 2012, to write an opera for the company's 2014–15 season, which was to have a year-long focus on the American Civil War, I wasn't sure I was the right person for the task. In many ways, the invitation was enticing. I had just graduated from Harvard, where the A.R.T. shares its rehearsal and performance spaces with student theater groups, and the theater's artistic leadership had seen some of my student work performed on their main stage. Commissioning a full opera from me was a huge leap of faith on their part. And given that I'd just moved to New York for a job on the Met's music staff, it was comforting that the A.R.T.'s theater already felt like home to me, a space of learning and experimentation.

But—the Civil War? Really? That moment in history felt somehow both distant and overfamiliar; to immerse oneself in Civil War studies was, I thought, to risk exposure to various kinds of musty, unhealthy nostalgia. The music I associated with that historical moment was hardly appealing, either. The aural image that the war conjured for me was a twangy unaccompanied fiddle whining away behind a Ken Burns voice-over, some grainy-voiced actor reading a soldier's sad letter home. Midway through our first Black president's eight years in office, what could be urgent or fresh or relevant about *that*?

Whitman was the key that unlocked that era for me. The poet's vividly personal account of the war, recorded in the diaries he kept during his years working as a volunteer nurse in Virginia and Washington, D.C., provided the window I needed to see the Civil War on a human scale. Whitman knew that the war's casualty count was so staggering that the enormity of the loss couldn't be *felt*, except as an impersonal statistic, by anyone reading about it from afar. Because of this, his diaries maintain a stubborn focus on individual lives and individual experience. He insists that the war's most important events were the countless quiet acts of love and heroism that typically go unrecorded: "The real war will never get in the books," he writes, even as he attempts to write a book that would tell the story of that "real war." If I was going to explore this moment in American history, I needed Walt Whitman as a spirit guide.

Whitman's decision to devote years of his life to volunteering in field hospitals was an act of unfathomable generosity, and one that would severely test the optimism that was his natural state of being. The first thing the poet describes upon his arrival at a makeshift hospital in Virginia is "a heap of amputated feet, legs, arms, hands, &c., a full load for a one-horse cart," with "several dead bodies" lying nearby, covered in blankets. But this gruesome sight, and the carnage that he would subsequently witness on an almost daily basis, did not deter him. Whitman had both a strong stomach and a limitless capacity for sympathy; he was born to be a nurse. As we'll see, some of his pre–Civil War poems show traces of a poignant inner struggle to understand what a queer poet's role in society could be, especially in wartime. He had no desire to be a soldier—can you picture Walt Whitman aiming a rifle at his fellow man? But he was also no ivory-tower writer; he wanted to *be there*, at the heart of the crisis, helping however he could.

In the hospitals, Whitman channeled his creative exuberance into the multiform work of healing. Depending on different soldiers' needs, he served at various times as a nurse, a companion, a bedside scribe, a garrulous raconteur, and a shamanic source of spiritual comfort. This varied and extroverted work arguably suited him better than the solitary labor of writing poetry. One can often sense a frustration, in Whitman, that his poems can't burst off the page and metamorphose into an embrace, a kiss, a communal sing-along. The war created a unique opportunity for Whitman to translate his artistic principles into action. Instead of writing poems for an imagined future reader, he could tell stories and write letters for individual after individual, face-to-face. The bedside encounter is the ideal locus for Whitman's art.

The more I studied Whitman's diaries, poetry, and biography, however, the more certain things bothered me. Wasn't there something odd about the way Whitman spent practically all his time with helpless soldiers—often mere boys, as the poet exclaims over and over in the diaries—and in his frequent physical expressions of affection? ("I loved him much, always kiss'd him, and he did me," Whitman writes of one young soldier, in a typical description.) Did Whitman perhaps need the radical intimacy of these wartime friendships as much as, or more than, the soldiers he tasked himself with comforting?

The war also had a curious impact on Whitman's artistic work: his experience in the hospitals seems, at some level, to have cured him of the need for poetry. He continued to write, of course, but his most ambitious poems—"Song of Myself," "Crossing Brooklyn Ferry," "The Sleepers"—date from before the war, and his poems *about* the war usually strike me as pale echoes of experiences that were, for him, too intense for words. The line between the transcendent and the terrible, the inspired and the merely bombastic, is always quite thin in Whitman, and even in his pre-war prime, there are arguably more weak poems than great ones. But after the war, his batting average is much lower; the wind seems to go out of his sails. Whitman called the war "the most profound lesson of my life"; did that "lesson" lessen his need for creative work? And where did the vast ambition of the pre-war years come from in the first place? What was that boundless hunger that needed to express itself in poetry?

WHITMAN AND OPERA

Whitman's poetry is not just "operatic" in the generic sense: he was a devoted opera fan, and his experiences attending live opera in New York substantively influenced his development as a writer. It might come as a surprise that the self-proclaimed bard of American democracy, the poet who wanted to burst free of the shackles of received verse forms and who had a declared allergy to any art that reeked of Continental decorum, unabashedly worshipped at opera's altar. Whitman thought of opera as an emancipatory volcanic force, one that was capable of precipitating transformative spiritual experiences in listeners who submitted to its power. In one of the extravagant catalogues of human experience in "Song of Myself," a series of earthy work-sounds ("the heave'e'yo of stevedores unlading ships by the wharves," "the steam-whistle," etc.) is followed by a euphoric vision of opera:

> I hear the trained soprano . . . she convulses me like the
> climax of my love-grip;
> The orchestra whirls me wider than Uranus flies,
> It wrenches unnamable ardors from my breast,
> It throbs me to gulps of the farthest down horror,
> It sails me . . .

Whitman experiences the art form with his whole body: opera invades and overloads his nervous system, prompting an ecstasy so extreme that it verges on trauma. The experience of operatic performance, for Whitman, seems barely distinguishable from sex, or an acid trip.

Like many of the art form's aficionados, Whitman grew to love opera only after overcoming an initial aversion to it. In his youth, he preferred unpretentious, homegrown music, like brass bands and touring family vocal groups. He initially found the European classical singing style "stale" and "second-hand . . . with its flourishes, its ridiculous sentimentality, its anti-republican spirit." What changed his mind was his experience of the spectacle of fully staged live opera. In the many opera houses that popped up in mid-nineteenth-century New York City, Whitman heard the bel canto operas of Bellini, Donizetti, and Rossini, as well as Verdi's earlier works, and evidently underwent a kind of conversion. Here at last was an art form as big and bold and *loud* as he imagined the American spirit itself to be! (As a Verdi lover, and as someone with a taste for high-decibel live performance, I'm tickled that Whitman's poetic bluster may owe something to the earthshaking intensity of the Verdian orchestra playing at full throttle, "which we privately confess . . . is one of the greatest treats we obtain from a visit to the opera.")

Once he had been "converted," Whitman proselytized enthusiastically on the art form's behalf. In a touching letter from 1863, Whitman describes opera to a group of young soldiers in a Washington war hospital. Whitman was volunteering in the hospitals at the time but had gone home to Brooklyn to visit his mother. "Two or three nights ago," he writes, "I went to the N Y Academy of Music, to the Italian opera. I suppose you know that is a performance, a play, all in music & singing, in the Italian language, very sweet & beautiful." He then writes a detailed, blow-by-blow plot synopsis—it's clear from his description, which makes the opera sound like an action movie, that he's writing for an audience of teenage boys—at the end of which Whitman reminds his young friends of the basic facts of the art form:

> Comrades, recollect all this is in singing & music, & lots of it too, on a big scale, in the band, every instrument you can think of, & the best players in the world, & sometimes the whole band & the whole men's chorus & women's chorus all putting on the steam together—& all in a vast house, light as day, & with a crowded audience of ladies & men. Such singing & strong rich music always give me the greatest pleasure.

Whitman's description of the opera house's atmosphere—the men and women singing together, the vast theater, the bright light, the crowded audience—resembles the sweeping American panoramas that fill his poems, those impossible snapshots that aim to describe the seething activity of a whole continent. A letter like this illuminates the way that opera, in its attempt to create an all-encompassing, communally shared sensory experience, provided Whitman with a model that no other art form could. Other poetry might aspire toward the condition of music, but Whitman's aspires toward the condition of opera.

THE CODED REVELATIONS OF "THE SLEEPERS"

As I prepared to write *Crossing*, I combed Whitman's early works for clues about the poet's state of mind in the years preceding the Civil War. No poem proved more revealing than "The Sleepers," which is both a phantasmagorical vision of sleep as the ultimate democratizing force, and also an atypically vulnerable portrait of the man behind the curtain of the "Walt Whitman" persona. "The Sleepers" throws into sharp relief the contradiction that is central to Whitman's poetry: the way that his sense of his own apartness and difference mingles uneasily with his desire to be Everyman, to live everyone's life. I think it is both his most personal (and most obliquely encrypted) examination of his queerness—it's a far cry from the joyous poems of flagrantly homoerotic camaraderie for which he is most famous—and also a kind of coded testament, an account of a question that quietly tormented Whitman in the 1850s: What role could he possibly play in the society he lived in?

The ethical quandaries of Whitman's whole poetic project

are on vivid display here. In his insistence that sleep, by return-ing us to a state of primal innocence and helplessness, is capable of dissolving human difference, Whitman himself attempts to annul certain distinctions that are likely to strike the reader as indissoluble: for example, the relationship between master and enslaved person. The poet reveals a poignant, troubling desire to see humanity through the leveling "dim light" of sleep: "I swear they are all beautiful," he says, protesting too much. "Ev-ery one that sleeps is beautiful . . . every thing in the dim light is beautiful . . ."

The poem is full of quintessentially Whitmanian catalogues of people from all over the globe, and from all walks of life: ba-bies, criminals, young lovers, people in insane asylums. These catalogues have something in common with a children's book like *Goodnight Moon*, both in the lulling quality of Whitman's ca-dences and in his attempt to list, to account for, the whole wide world of sleepers. But the poet's desire to name and to know ev-ery imaginable human type also has something in common with more sinister kinds of catalogues: Don Giovanni's list of his con-quests, for instance; or the notebooks that Cormac McCarthy's Judge Holden carries with him in *Blood Meridian*, recording every natural phenomenon of the American West as ever more of the territory is subdued.

Between these lists, which appear near the beginning and end of the poem, there is a series of enigmatic dream visions: the speaker first sees a swimmer drowning at sea; then he witnesses a shipwreck; he has a vision of George Washington bidding fare-well to his troops; and he tells a story from his mother's youth about an encounter with a Native American woman. (The origi-nal 1855 version of the poem also contains a bizarre fifth vision in which the speaker announces that he is Lucifer's "sorrowful terrible heir"; Whitman wisely cut this section for the "death-bed" edition of *Leaves of Grass*.)

I think all four of these dream visions evince a deep, perhaps unconscious struggle: the speaker fears that he is powerless, uselessly and unacceptably passive, compared to the men of action—swimmers, sailors, soldiers—who populate his dreams. Whitman seems to be confronting fundamental questions of what his social responsibilities are as an artist and a queer person. The picture that emerges, however fragmentarily, is of Whitman as a would-be healer, comforter, and mourner. Though this poem was written in the decade before the Civil War, "The Sleepers" is full of intimations of the path the poet would follow throughout the war years.

Whitman tellingly opens his paean to sleep by announcing that he "wander[s] all night." This establishes a basic opposition: others might sleep, but the poet is awake.

> I wander all night in my vision,
> Stepping with light feet, swiftly and noiselessly stepping
>   and stopping,
> Bending with open eyes over the shut eyes of sleepers

Since Whitman treats night and sleep as allied forces of restorative oblivion, there is something unnatural about this compulsion to "wander all night." Whitman seems to see himself as a kind of Flying Dutchman or Melmoth figure, a solitary spirit who possesses some special "vision" but who is condemned to wander, to bear witness to suffering, and who is denied the peace that seems to be granted to all other beings:

Wandering and confused, lost to myself, ill-assorted,
  contradictory,
Pausing, gazing, bending, and stopping.

How solemn they look there, stretch'd and still,
How quiet they breathe, the little children in their
  cradles.

The wretched features of ennuyés, the white features of
  corpses, the livid faces of drunkards, the sick-gray
  faces of onanists,
The gash'd bodies on battle-fields, the insane in their
  strong-door'd rooms, the sacred idiots, the new-born
  emerging from gates, and the dying emerging from
  gates,
The night pervades them and infolds them.

After a conventional image of serenity—young children peace-fully sleeping—we expect that this montage of disturbing pic-tures ("gash'd bodies," etc.) will be deployed in opposition to that first image. But Whitman's point, instead, is that night and sleep embrace and contain *even* these extremities of human suffering. The entire life cycle—that fantastic image of the newborn and the dying both "emerging from gates"—is enclosed within the wider womb of night and sleep. The poem continues with a catalogue of sleepers:

The married couple sleep calmly in their bed, he with his
  palm on the hip of the wife, and she with her palm on
  the hip of the husband,
The sisters sleep lovingly side by side in their bed,

The men sleep lovingly side by side in theirs,
And the mother sleeps with her little child carefully
    wrapt.

The blind sleep, and the deaf and dumb sleep,
The prisoner sleeps well in the prison, the runaway son
    sleeps,
The murderer that is to be hung next day, how does he
    sleep?
And the murder'd person, how does he sleep?

The female that loves unrequited sleeps,
And the male that loves unrequited sleeps,
The head of the money-maker that plotted all day sleeps,
And the enraged and treacherous dispositions, all, all
    sleep.

I stand . . .

"I stand." Everyone else sleeps—the prisoner, the blind,
the deaf, the dumb—but not the poet, who stands and keeps
watch:

I stand in the dark with drooping eyes by the worst-
    suffering and the most restless,
I pass my hands soothingly to and fro a few inches from
    them,
The restless sink in their beds, they fitfully sleep.

This is an uncannily clear image of Whitman's work during the
Civil War: it is a vision of the poet as comforter and witness, a

lonely figure who is denied sleep's comfort, yet who believes he can soothe the "restless," the ones who "fitfully sleep."

Whitman then launches into his familiar Everyman mode: I am X, I am Y, I am Z too. Somewhat uncharacteristically, however, his identity-hopping here takes on a fantastical guise; the poet imagines that he is assisted by a playful band of spirit guides. The poem transforms momentarily into a light-footed Mendelssohnian scherzo:

> I am a dance—play up there! the fit is whirling me fast!
>
> I am the ever-laughing—it is new moon and twilight,
> I see the hiding of douceurs, I see nimble ghosts
>   whichever way I look,
> . . . .
> Onward we move, a gay gang of blackguards! with mirth-
>   shouting music and wild-flapping pennants of joy!

In the company of these "journeymen divine," Whitman is Oberon and Puck at once ("I reckon I am their boss and they make me a pet besides"). With their help he can become anyone: "the actor, the actress, the voter, the politician, / The emigrant and the exile."

But this playfulness, and this barrage of possible identities, are just a prelude to the one transformation Whitman lingers over. He assumes the identity of a woman waiting in the darkness for her lover, and imagines a double erotic encounter, with a male lover and with darkness itself. This encounter is so intense, and breaks so many taboos, that I wonder if the main purpose of the scherzo that precedes it is to contextualize this passage as "unreal," and to distance the speaker from it. (For this section only,

I quote from the original 1855 edition of the poem, since Whitman later cut the passage's revealing final stanzas.)

> I am she who adorned herself and folded her hair
>   expectantly,
> My truant lover has come and it is dark.
>
> Double yourself and receive me darkness,
> Receive me and my lover too . . .

Three figures are present: the woman, her lover, and "darkness." Darkness ultimately "takes the place of my lover," and proves irresistibly attractive:

> Darkness you are gentler than my lover . . . his flesh was
>   sweaty and panting,
> I feel the hot moisture yet that he left me.
> . . . .
> Be careful, darkness . . . already, what was it touched me?
> I thought my lover had gone . . . else darkness and he are
>   one

Darkness is depicted here not as an all-embracing womb, as it is elsewhere in the poem, but as a male spirit, a kind of incubus. Whitman does not tell us exactly what has happened—obscurity is intrinsic to the scene being described—but it's clear that the encounter unexpectedly intensifies; Whitman's ellipses, like Emily Dickinson's dashes, are blanks whose meanings we may fill in ourselves. The rest of this section, which was eliminated in the "death-bed" edition, removes all doubt that the speaker has had a confusing, overwhelming sexual encounter:

O hotcheeked and blushing! O foolish hectic!
O for pity's sake, no one must see me now! . . . my clothes
    were stolen while I was abed,
Now I am thrust forth, where shall I run?

The poem's deep, incantatory rhythm ("Double yourself and receive me darkness") breaks down into panicky vernacular babbling ("O for pity's sake, no one must see me now") to give vivid voice to the speaker's sense of shame, which changes into wonderment:

I feel ashamed to go naked about the world,
And am curious to know where my feet stand . . . and
    what is this flooding me, childhood or manhood . . .
    and the hunger that crosses the bridge between.

"The hunger that crosses the bridge between" the states of childhood and manhood is erotic desire. And that question, "what is this flooding me, childhood or manhood," exactly captures the mingled feelings of innocence and shame, youthful freshness and newfound maturity, that follow a transformative sexual encounter.

But the way that Whitman poses the question complicates our understanding of who is speaking. Is this still a woman, "she who adorned herself"? Or has Whitman tipped his hand and revealed that this is a gay male persona? The mysteriousness of the encounter is matched by a beguiling, confounding ambivalence on the part of the speaker. These lines are notably free of the sense of achievement that (as we all learn in adolescence) is supposed to accompany heterosexual loss of virginity: now I'm a real man. Instead, the speaker's encounter takes the form of *being flooded* by some incomprehensible force. It is a frightening, disorienting experience, but it also enables a kind of negative capability: the images of flooding and crossing are not far from the liberated openness of "Crossing Brooklyn Ferry."

The poem's first section, in which only the poet remains awake as the world sleeps, and the boundary-blurring "darkness" fantasy establish in different ways Whitman's strong sense of his own difference, his radical distance from a life lived within a single masculine identity. The subsequent sequence of dream visions constitutes Whitman's attempt to wrestle with the implications of that difference; these visions strike me as tea leaves that hint at the poet's future course of action. How might a person with Whitman's sensibility fit into, and contribute to, the world outside his imagination—a world that all too often seems defined by suffering and violence?

These four dream visions evidently relate the speaker's own experiences, since they are not preceded by one of Whitman's usual announcements that he is assuming some other identity ("I am she who . . . ," etc.). The first vision is of a swimmer drowning at sea:

> I see a beautiful gigantic swimmer swimming naked
>   through the eddies of the sea,
> His brown hair lies close and even to his head, he strikes
>   out with courageous arms, he urges himself with his
>   legs,
> I see his white body, I see his undaunted eyes,
> I hate the swift-running eddies that would dash him
>   head-foremost on the rocks.

What are you doing you ruffianly red-trickled waves?
Will you kill the courageous giant? will you kill him in
    the prime of his middle age?

Steady and long he struggles,
He is baffled, bang'd, bruis'd, he holds out while his
    strength holds out,
The slapping eddies are spotted with his blood, they bear
    him away, they roll him, swing him, turn him,
His beautiful body is borne in the circling eddies, it is
    continually bruis'd on rocks,
Swiftly and out of sight is borne the brave corpse.

Some readers of Whitman have taken this swimmer to be an image of the poet himself, in part because Whitman was a shameless affirmer of his own virility (he was, in contemporary terms, exceedingly body-positive), and partly because the swimmer is "in the prime of his middle age," as Whitman was when he wrote the poem. But the vocabulary doesn't resemble that of the poet's overt self-descriptions; he was hardly prone to calling himself a "courageous giant." This swimmer has more in common with Whitman's descriptions of ideally masculine American men: "I behold the picturesque giant and love him," he says of one working man in "Song of Myself." The crux of this anxiety dream is the unbridgeable distance the speaker feels between himself and the "giant," the man of action who is out there braving the waves. The speaker is helpless to save him; he cannot take action; he watches passively from the shore.

Shaken by this vision, Whitman writes a potently inarticulate couplet:

I turn but do not extricate myself,
Confused, a past-reading, another, but with darkness yet.

This is language that staggers under the force of some psychic pressure; alter the punctuation a little, and the second line could have been written by Paul Celan. I take these lines to mean something like this: *I turn away from this vision, but do not extricate myself from these dream-confrontations. Confused as I am, I will look again into the darkness and attempt another "past-reading."*

When he looks again into the darkness, he has another anxiety-provoking vision of a disaster at sea:

The beach is cut by the razory ice-wind, the wreck-guns sound,
The tempest lulls, the moon comes floundering through the drifts.

I look where the ship helplessly heads end on, I hear the burst as she strikes, I hear the howls of dismay, they grow fainter and fainter.

I cannot aid with my wringing fingers,
I can but rush to the surf and let it drench me and freeze upon me.

I search with the crowd, not one of the company is wash'd to us alive,
In the morning I help pick up the dead and lay them in rows in a barn.

This is perhaps both a nightmare and a memory; the Whitman scholar Karen Karbiener suggests that this section was inspired by a shipwreck that the poet witnessed off Long Island in 1840. As in his previous vision, the speaker stands helplessly on the shore as the ship runs aground: "I cannot aid with my wringing fingers." This time, however, he imagines himself taking part in the recovery effort: he does the sad work of gathering and laying out the bodies of the dead. He is newly able to channel his energy into the work of mourning.

The third vision is a very Whitmanian snapshot of George Washington:

> Now of the older war-days, the defeat at Brooklyn,
> Washington stands inside the lines, he stands on the
>   intrench'd hills amid a crowd of officers,
> His face is cold and damp, he cannot repress the weeping
>   drops,
> He lifts the glass perpetually to his eyes, the color is
>   blanch'd from his cheeks,
> He sees the slaughter of the southern braves confided to
>   him by their parents.
>
> The same at last and at last when peace is declared,
> He stands in the room of the old tavern, the well-belov'd
>   soldiers all pass through,
> The officers speechless and slow draw near in their turns,
> The chief encircles their necks with his arm and kisses
>   them on the cheek,
> He kisses lightly the wet cheeks one after another, he
>   shakes hands and bids good-by to the army.

Surely no one but Whitman would depict George Washington exclusively through images of our first president weeping and kissing his troops! This vision clearly has little to do with Washington, and a lot to do with Whitman himself. It is an image of the role Whitman would want to assume during a war: a kind of comforter-in-chief.

The fourth vision, which tells of Whitman's mother's encounter with a Native American woman, is less illuminating; it's even a little embarrassing in its account of the poet's mother all but salivating over the woman's physical beauty. The scene is striking, however, as an image of sudden, unexpected same-sex attraction: "The more she look'd upon her she loved her."

This last dream vision is followed by one of Whitman's less inspired "catalogues": "The Swiss foots it toward his hills, the Prussian goes his way, the Hungarian his way, and the Pole his way" is a representative excerpt. But the poem's eighth and final section is rapturously beautiful, and troubling:

> The sleepers are very beautiful as they lie unclothed,
> They flow hand in hand over the whole earth from east to
>   west as they lie unclothed,
> The Asiatic and African are hand in hand, the European
>   and American are hand in hand,
> Learn'd and unlearn'd are hand in hand, and male and
>   female are hand in hand,
> The bare arm of the girl crosses the bare breast of her lover,
>   they press close without lust, his lips press her neck,
> The father holds his grown or ungrown son in his arms
>   with measureless love, and the son holds the father in
>   his arms with measureless love,

The white hair of the mother shines on the white wrist of
    the daughter,
The breath of the boy goes with the breath of the man,
    friend is inarm'd by friend,
The scholar kisses the teacher and the teacher kisses the
    scholar, the wrong'd is made right,
The call of the slave is one with the master's call, and the
    master salutes the slave . . .

That last line is likely to grind any sentient reader to a halt.
"The master salutes the slave"!? No, he doesn't! No, the "call" of
one is not "one with" the call of the other! In this moment, the
poem tilts from dream into lie. Whitman's conception of sleep as
a potent leveling force reveals its dark side when he specifies
exactly what differences he is ready to smooth over.

It's clear from the context that Whitman does think of slav-
ery as an evil, indeed as a kind of disease; he follows it with images of other wrongs being righted and illnesses cured ("the
insane becomes sane, the suffering of sick persons is reliev'd,"
etc.). But there's something disturbing in his decision to include
the unbridgeable gap between master and enslaved person in
his hypnotic litany of human relationships. He asks us, in this
poem, to *not* focus on the injustices that human beings visit upon
one another when they are awake; he invites us to dwell, instead,
in an imagined subterranean realm of innocence and nondiffer-
entiation. It is not so different from a preacher telling his flock
that all earthly sorrows will be righted in heaven; "the myth of
heaven," Whitman says elsewhere in the poem, "indicates peace
and night." He is telling us that all will be well. And we may not
be convinced.

FANATICAL OPTIMISM

A moment like this one, which sticks out of the poem like a blade, is a manifestation of what I've come to think of as Whitman's fanatical optimism. I use the term "optimism" more in its philosophical sense—it's not so far from the notion that we live in "the best of all possible worlds"—than its quotidian one. Whitman wants his readers to be aware of the blazing sacredness of all things, and he expresses his faith in this total beatitude through the celebration and reconciliation of opposites. He will say that one particular thing is good—and then he will hasten to add that *everything else in the universe* is also good. "Clear and sweet is my soul, and clear and sweet is all that is not my soul," he says in "Song of Myself." In "The Sleepers," the earth is beautiful, and "what is not the earth is beautiful." Elsewhere, "what is called good is perfect, and what is called bad is just as perfect." In short: *it's all good.*

This habit of Whitman's, this perennial attempt to obliterate all difference with a steamroller of positive energy, has long bothered his more discerning readers. William James, in *The Varieties of Religious Experience*, classified Whitman among the writers in whom he found "the presence of a temperament organically weighted on the side of cheer and fatally forbidden to linger . . . over the darker aspects of the universe. *In some individuals optimism may become quasi-pathological* [emphasis mine]. The capacity for even a transient sadness or a momentary humility seems cut off from them as by a kind of congenital anaesthesia." James quotes a friend of Whitman's who put it plainly: "Perhaps, indeed, no man who ever lived liked so many things and disliked so few as Walt Whitman." Skeptical of contemporary claims that Whitman was a "pagan," a "mere natural animal man," James highlights the poet's ode, in "Song of Myself," to the supposed serenity of the lives of animals: "Not one is dissatisfied, not one is demented with the mania of owning things . . . / Not one is respectable or unhappy over the whole earth." No true pagan, James says, would sentimentalize the animal kingdom like this. There is a discrepancy between the personae Whitman claims to inhabit and the lived experience that his poems imply.

In a way, Whitman goes beyond even Leibniz's "best of all possible worlds" formulation, which at least admits the undesirability of suffering, even if suffering is supposedly at its absolute cosmic minimum. Whitman, in his all-encompassing pronouncements, insists that even sickness, suffering, and death are sacred and vital. The blinding force of this optimism is at once his superpower and his biggest ethical liability. His capacity to find beauty in the direst circumstances sustained him throughout his years working in war hospitals; he continued his unpaid and often traumatic work long after many people in his position would have given up and returned home to Brooklyn. But his stance also raises thorny ethical questions. If everyone and everything in the cosmos—life and death, master and slave, Northerner and Southerner—bodies forth an innate and omnipresent holiness, what impetus do we have to change things for the better? Doesn't such a stance risk being an argument for the status quo? How can anyone claim, as Whitman does in one of his sketchbooks, to be "the poet of slaves and of the masters of slaves"?

If Whitman's poetry sometimes sweeps moral distinctions aside in a tsunami-like "flood-tide" of praise, his Civil War diaries, collected as *Memoranda During the War*, helpfully complicate the picture of Whitmanian optimism. In this prose chronicle of the war years (though the line between poetry and prose barely exists in Whitman), he proves himself capable of a more nuanced attitude, sometimes giving voice to anxieties that his poetry, with its scriptural cadences, could not admit: misgivings about the Union's future prospects and about the ways that America's military and medical bureaucracies had failed the country's soldiers. If "The Sleepers" is Whitman's richest and most suggestive account of his prewar state of mind, his Civil War diary is the truest document we have of his social life, and his sense of the times he lived in.

THE DIARIES

Whitman's *Memoranda* is not long—it's roughly seventy pages—but I find reading it through to be a draining experience, since many of the diary's entries are violently expressed responses to violent experiences. Near its end, Whitman frets that this little book "would prove, at best, but a batch of convulsively written reminiscences." That's not an inaccurate description of the end result, but this "convulsive" quality is appropriate to the book's subject, as are its wearing repetitions: wave after wave of patients arriving in the hospitals, battle after battle, death after death. Whitman records it all with unstinting vigor and a gruesome lavishness of detail.

Some sections might seem unusually sober-minded to readers who are familiar only with Whitman's ecstatic mode. Early in the war, once the extent of the conflict had become apparent, he takes himself to task for his own earlier optimism: "The dream of humanity, the vaunted Union we thought so strong, so impregnable—lo! it seems already smash'd like a china plate." By the war's end, he had grown witheringly critical of the military as an institution, having witnessed its day-to-day functioning firsthand: "In the present struggle . . . probably three-fourths of the losses, men, lives, &c., have been sheer superfluity, extravagance, waste," he writes in 1864. He is appalled by the army's dehumanizing hierarchies, its treatment of rank-and-file soldiers as expendable: "The current military theory, practice, rules and organization," having been "adopted from Europe from the feudal institutes," are "not at all consonant with the United States, nor our people, nor our days." On the medical front, too, he finds the country's infrastructure sorely lacking. He notes that though many individual doctors are "full of genius," America's primitive health-care system fails to support them: there are "serious deficiencies, wastes, sad want of system . . . Whatever puffing accounts there may be in the papers of the North, this is the actual fact. No thorough previous preparations, no system, no foresight, no genius." (As of 2021, "no genius" remains a fair assessment of America's health-care system.)

In his accounts of the battles he witnessed and the suffering he saw in their wake, his tone could hardly be further from his insistence, in some of his poetry, that everything that happens on earth is good. "Reader, did you ever try to realize what *starvation* actually is?" he writes after seeing a group of emaciated Union soldiers newly released from Confederate prisons. For Whitman, the consummate lover of abundance and vitality, the sight of those prisoners, who resembled "mummied, dwindled corpses," was "worse than any sight of battle-fields." Elsewhere, there are gory narrations of battles and skirmishes, including a grisly Confederate attack on a train of wounded Union soldiers. He does not glorify these experiences. "Future years will never know the seething hell and the black infernal background of countless minor scenes . . . and it is best they should not," he writes near the diary's end.

But it wouldn't be Whitman if there were no contradictions, and at times he veers uncomfortably close to ogling or merely aestheticizing the young men he seeks to comfort. "I often come and sit by him in perfect silence," he writes of one soldier:

> He will breathe for ten minutes as softly and evenly as a young babe asleep. Poor youth, so handsome, athletic, with profuse beautiful shining hair. One time as I sat looking at him while he lay asleep, he suddenly, without the least start, awaken'd, open'd his eyes, gave me a long, long steady look, turning his face very slightly to gaze easier—one long, clear silent look—a slight sigh—then turn'd back and went into his doze again. Little he knew, poor death-stricken boy, the heart of the stranger that hover'd near.

The diaries are also full of a very Whitmanian insistence that the Southerner is as brave as the Northerner, that he is as glad to tend to the wounded Confederate as the wounded Union man. Just as, in his poetry, Whitman stubbornly refuses to admit difference, during the war he refuses to fight; he wants only to heal, and to heal indiscriminately. "I hardly think you know who I am," one wounded soldier says to him guiltily, after growing friendly with Whitman. "I don't wish to impose upon you—I am a rebel soldier." Whitman reassures the dying boy that this couldn't possibly matter to him.

Amid so much suffering and exhaustion, this gray-bearded, exuberantly affectionate personage must have been the object of much curiosity in the hospitals. We don't get a clear sense of this from Whitman's own account, but there are a couple of stray hints of it:

> Met John Wormley, 9th Alabama, a West Tennessee rais'd boy, parents both dead—had the look of one for a long time

on short allowance—said very little—chew'd tobacco at a fearful rate, spitting in proportion—large clear dark-brown eyes, very fine—didn't know what to make of me.

"Didn't know what to make of me"! Plenty of other soldiers must have felt the same way. This John Wormley, though his presence in the *Memoranda* consists entirely of this brief cameo, lodged himself in my mind. In a book that is full of Whitman looking at others, Wormley is a rare example of someone else *looking at Whitman* with what seems to be bemusement or skepticism. Since *Crossing* is in part an interrogation of Whitman's legacy, it felt essential for the opera's cast to include an anti-Whitman—a pessimistic, almost nihilistic presence, someone who could look at Walt with an X-ray gaze, cast doubt on the purity of his motives, and ask the old man what he's doing in the hospitals in the first place.

I named this character John Wormley. In addition to the lean, tobacco-spitting Wormley of the diaries, the opera's Wormley has certain qualities in common with the aforementioned soldier who confessed his Confederate allegiance to Whitman before he died; and with Peter Doyle, the former Confederate soldier who became Whitman's companion after the war's end. A tortured, self-hating Confederate escapee, the fictional John Wormley ended up being almost as essential to the opera as Whitman himself.

I originally thought that *Crossing* would be an ensemble piece, a composite portrait of the inhabitants of the purgatory-like space of the hospital—a little like Janáček's *From the House of the Dead* (1930), with its depiction of life in a Siberian prison camp. In the end, however, the Whitman-Wormley connection, an adversarial relationship that becomes a love affair, consumed more and more of the piece and became its central thread. The more intensely—the more uncomfortably—I put Whitman in contact with his polar opposite, the more clearly I could see him.

MAKING WHITMAN SING

Whitman was a huge, operatic personality who would no doubt relish the chance to stand center stage in his very own opera. But did his poetry really want to be set to music? And what could that music possibly sound like?

It turns out that setting Whitman to music is often impossible, a fool's errand. The very features that make his poetry so explosively musical on the page, or recited aloud, all seem perversely engineered to thwart further musicalization. Some of Whitman's lines are almost too long to *speak* in one breath, never mind singing them, and they're often riddled with forceful accents, like an Anglo-Saxon boast. Any given line might also contain half a dozen sharp rhythmic twists and turns; I open *Leaves of Grass* at random and am confronted by unsingable mouthfuls like "I find I incorporate gneiss and coal and long-threaded moss and fruits and grains and esculent roots." There is a rugged irregularity to his lines, like rapids crashing down jagged rocks. His epic lists—"everything only connected by 'and' and 'and,'" as Elizabeth Bishop would say—also don't translate well to music: such lists, especially when sung with a Whitmanian urgency, tend to sound comical, like the list of diseases that the quack doctor Dulcamara promises to cure in Donizetti's *L'elisir d'amore*.

None of this stopped me from trying. Before starting work in earnest on *Crossing*, I wrote a few songs based on Whitman poems, both as preparatory character sketches and to be sure that I wouldn't find it creatively paralyzing to engage with his poetry.

In the case of "The Sleepers," I took a tiny slice of that huge poetic canvas to create an intimate miniature, and for "Crossing Brooklyn Ferry," I tried to craft a musical idiom to match the poem's thundering intensity.

I chose a section of "The Sleepers" that sounded as if it could have been written during the war, at a soldier's bedside, rather than a decade earlier. Three moments from early in the poem—just seven lines total—seemed to me to have their own little song-like arc. The song's text is a collage of those moments:

> ... the new-born emerging from gates, and the dying
>   emerging from gates,
> The night pervades them and infolds them.
>
> I stand in the dark with drooping eyes by the worst-
>   suffering and the most restless,
> I pass my hands soothingly to and fro a few inches from
>   them,
> The restless sink in their beds, they fitfully sleep.
>
> The earth recedes from me into the night,
> I saw that it was beautiful, and I see that what is not the
>   earth is beautiful.

The song begins with a wandering, searching piano line that weaves its way around the voice throughout that mysterious first image, the being-born and the dying each crossing into a new world. (In the opera, Whitman sings these lines as he wanders the hospital wards in the middle of the night, the patients all asleep.) The harmonies flicker around key after key without firmly establishing any of them:

In the troubled, uneasy middle stanza, Whitman alternates between singing very tenderly, as though standing over a bed, settling a blanket around someone's shoulders, and evincing signs of a quiet, private grief:

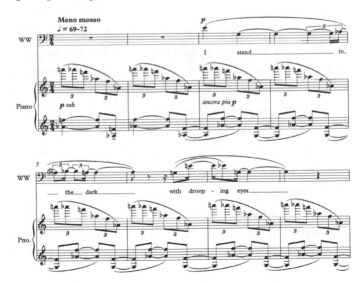

The first real musical turbulence comes near the end of this section. As "the restless" toss and turn in sleep, the music briefly surges forward, as though sitting up in pain. Then comes a kind of release: the fever breaks, the intensity slowly drains away. In the afterglow, Whitman sings words of serene acceptance:

This serenity is both hard-won and precarious: it is only with effort that Whitman is able to claim that death, absence, "what is not the earth," are all beautiful. He speaks these words not out of certainty, but to reassure himself. He speaks the words to make them true.

"The Sleepers" neatly organized itself into this brief interior drama, but "Crossing Brooklyn Ferry" turned out to be an untamable beast. I could hardly write a Whitman opera without, at least once, really letting Walt loose—at some point I had to unchain him, let him sing his wildest words, and "Crossing Brooklyn Ferry" seemed like the perfect opportunity. The poem recounts an epiphany Whitman experienced on the brief ferry ride between Brooklyn and Manhattan. Aboard the boat, myriad sensory experiences—the churning of the water, the ferry's rocking, the view of both shores at once and the awareness of being tenuously suspended between them, the presence of the other passengers packed close together—combine to create a rare moment of existential déjà vu. Whitman feels a visceral sympathy with everyone who had ever made, or would ever make, a similar passage from shore to shore, from birth to death. He is seized with a sudden desire to speak to everyone who would make this crossing in the future, to assure them that he's been there ("I am with you") and their experience is shared, no matter how distant he may be from them in time or space ("distance avails not, and place avails not").

The poem wavers poignantly between revelation and tautology. Whitman's impossible address to a still-unborn future reader achieves, in flashes, an uncanny directness; reading the poem, you might have the sense that Whitman really is talking about *you* when he says, "I consider'd long and seriously of you before you were born," or when he asks, with a conspiratorial wink, "We understand then do we not? / What I promis'd without mentioning it, have you not accepted?" Sometimes I glance at this poem and feel a shock of recognition, as if the page had turned momentarily into a mirror, or the mirrorlike surface of the waves.

But seen from another angle, "Crossing Brooklyn Ferry" is almost devoid of content. What exactly does Whitman's epiphany consist of? That fundamental human experiences—living, dying, walking a city's streets—are shared? Is that really such an epiphany? His lists of the activities that, he says, you and he have both experienced—"I too lived, Brooklyn of ample hills was mine, / I too walk'd the streets of Manhattan island, and bathed in the waters around it"—are, in spite of his authoritatively biblical cadence, pretty banal.* The poem's meaningfulness flickers; sometimes it's transcendent, sometimes merely insistent.

---

* Poor Walt couldn't have guessed how outlandish future generations of New Yorkers would find the notion of bathing in the waters around Manhattan.

"Crossing Brooklyn Ferry" proved ferociously difficult to set to music; the poem is a moving target, barely visible amid its foaming waves. I knew from the outset how the song would begin—with a churning motion in the lower strings, the piano, and the percussion, an open fifth evoking the frothing, seething water around the ferry. But after that first line ("Flood-tide below me! I see you face to face!"), the poem's instability, the way that it wanders from outburst to wild-eyed outburst, totally flummoxed me. I must have given Rod Gilfry, the valiant baritone who first sang the role of Whitman, seven or eight different versions of "Crossing Brooklyn Ferry" by the time the opera reached its final form.

Rather than recount my struggles to wrestle this poem into a coherent musical shape, I'll highlight one moment that I feel halfway okay about. I mentioned earlier that one challenge in setting Whitman is the sheer length of his lines, the way they spill over the side of the page and exceed the span of the human breath. For the central section of "Crossing Brooklyn Ferry," I decided to lean into this quality, to exaggerate it, to *lengthen* these already impossibly long lines. Starting at the line "Just as you feel when you look on the river . . . ," I slowed the pace of the vocal rhythm way, way down. Some syllables last an entire bar; each line of poetry is divided into multiple vocal phrases. Though the tempo remains propulsive and the orchestral music is virtuosic and busy, Whitman sings in slow motion. I wanted to create the sense that his voice is the calm, still center around which the orchestra revolves—that he is speaking to us from the eye of the storm:

GOOD HEALTH NEVERTHELESS

I must have changed my mind about Whitman five times a day while I was writing *Crossing*. Was there something predatory about his lingering presence in the hospitals? Was he a little too sure of his own saintliness, too convinced that his presence was desired, was necessary? And his belief in the unstoppable righteousness of the ever-expanding American nation—might it not just be imperialism, plain and simple? The presumptuousness of his belief that he was America's one true mouthpiece and megaphone! The impossibility inherent in his attempt to be all things for all people! The sheer badness of some of the poetry!

And yet, rereading the diaries now, I find them so moving

that my qualms mostly evaporate. Yes, Whitman contradicts himself; yes, his actions were surely the result of a complex cocktail of motivations. But his generosity, the fact that he gave years of his life to the work of comforting those in need, seems irreducible. Think back to "The Sleepers": think of those dreams in which he feared his own passivity; think of the loneliness that runs as an undercurrent beneath his poetry's exuberance; think of his curious need to create those endless catalogues of human types, and the distance from his fellow human beings that those catalogues imply. With his work in the war hospitals, I think he bridged that distance. He translated the implicit desires of his art into social action. How many artists can make *that* claim?

In a way, Whitman's poetry achieved an impossible crossing: it ceased to be poetry altogether. His wartime experience transformed him from a poet into some other kind of creator. Both in his poems and in his diaries, we can trace his messy progress toward that crossing. Luckily for us, in those writings he laid everything bare—the good, the bad, the contradictory, the impossible. He is still waiting somewhere for us to catch up.

SIX

Inner Rooms:
Two Recent Impossibilities

Thomas Adès's The Exterminating Angel,
Chaya Czernowin's Heart Chamber

C omposers continue to attempt the impossible. Our musical moment, which is one of aesthetic ferment and unprecedented methodological polyphony, continues to yield wondrous and weird new operas—and opera-like works that resist or refuse the label—with every season. I think we're living through something like a golden age for the art form, but it can be hard to recognize creative abundance when one's in its midst. (It doesn't help that opera fans tend to be notorious nostalgists. So it might take a century or so for the richness of our moment to be widely acknowledged.) I can't think of another period in which so many new works that are so *different* from one another were bursting into the world at once. We seem almost to be living in multiple eras simultaneously.

This state of affairs is both liberating and anxiety-provoking for artists. A college-age composer in the early 2020s is unlikely to fall into the comforting illusion that their culture offers them a single well-trodden aesthetic path to follow. But given the choice between the chaos of the present and the rigid high-vs.-low, uptown-vs.-downtown divides of half a century ago, I would much rather be working now (though I would beg to exclude the year 2020 from my definition of "now").

On the American scene, the past decade has seen the emergence of important composers with widely divergent aesthetics: practically the only thing that the scalding virtuosity of Du Yun's *Angel's Bone* (2016), the liquidly engulfing voluptuousness of David Hertzberg's *The Wake World* (2017), and Missy Mazzoli's disarmingly direct *Breaking the Waves* (2016) have in common is that they all make for riveting music-theatrical experiences. Those three pieces would all be more or less at home in an opera house, but some of the strongest recent works of American music-theater live either at the very edge of opera's map or somewhere beyond it, out where there be monsters. Kate Soper's uncategorizable *Ipsa Dixit* (2016) achieves the seemingly impossible task of transforming nagging philosophical conundrums ("What is art?") into a beguiling work of performance art. Anthony Braxton continues to expand his wildly ambitious *Trillium* "opera complex," an in-progress series of thirty-six one-act works whose fantastical impossibilities practically constitute the bedrock of the project: the performing forces for *Trillium J*, for example, consist of "12 singers, 12 solo instrumentalists, dancers, Centurion guards, choir, computer music, light/image projection crew, virtual technical crew, constructed fantasy environments, and orchestra."*

Some tantalizing new works are still awaiting their leap into

---

* Braxton is aware that this *Besetzung* sounds expensive, and suggests that "as a person who has no money I would as such program 'having no money' (as a proposition) into the system model qualities' [*sic*] as an axiom for composite application."

the possible, among them Dylan Mattingly's *Stranger Love*, a six-hour anatomy of love and "a grand celebration of life itself." (The composer acknowledges on his website that this piece, in its scale and scope, "reaches for the impossible.") *Stranger Love* has so far been presented only in fragments—it's hard to convince a company to produce a six-hour opera—but the sections I've heard suggest that the whole thing would be ecstatically beautiful, the kind of music you'd want to hear outdoors, surrounded by all your friends, blasting from speakers on a starry night at a dance party on some remote mesa.

If the most exciting American operas of the past decade have largely been the work of young composers, the picture is somewhat different on the international scene, where many of the most successful operas of the 2010s have been the work of middle-aged masters, artists with decades of experience writing instrumental music, who decided to finally try their hand at opera. The English composer George Benjamin's first three operas (*Into the Little Hill* [2006], *Written on Skin* [2012], and *Lessons in Love and Violence* [2018]) manifest a dynamic, dangerous eroticism that was rarely palpable in his earlier, immaculately sophisticated instrumental music: for Benjamin, the act of writing operas seems to have unlocked some potent new force. Hans Abrahamsen, a widely beloved Danish composer, finally lent his crystalline, wintry musical gifts to opera with his setting of the Hans Christian Andersen fable *The Snow Queen* (2019). And then there is the case of the nonagenarian Hungarian master György Kurtág, whose unimpeachably wonderful adaptation of Beckett's *Endgame*—a work he had been contemplating *since the mid-1950s*—finally premiered at La Scala in 2018.

I want to take a deep dive now into two recent works that are especially dear to me: Thomas Adès's *The Exterminating Angel*

(2016) and Chaya Czernowin's *Heart Chamber* (2019). I've chosen these two simply because I feel a particular kinship with them. Of all the strange and magical operas that have hit the air over the past decade, these are the ones about which I think I have the most to say.

Thomas Adès's The Exterminating Angel

The inhabitants of the planet Tlön, in Jorge Luis Borges's story "Tlön, Uqbar, Orbis Tertius," have a radically different understanding of the universe than we earthlings do: "For the people of Tlön," Borges's imaginary historian tells us, "the world is not an amalgam of *objects* in space; it is a heterogeneous series of independent *acts*." Their languages are entirely free of nouns, and the very concept of a noun—an object with a stable, temporally continuous identity—strikes Tlönians as a physical impossibility. They have "no noun that corresponds to our word 'moon,' but there is a verb which in English would be 'to moonate' or 'to enmoon.'" The Tlönian equivalent of a statement like "The moon rose above the river" might be rendered in English as "*Upward, behind the onstreaming it mooned.*"

In the music of the English composer Thomas Adès (b. 1971), harmonies behave rather the way objects do on Tlön: they are verbs, not nouns. It rarely makes sense in his music to speak of, say, "D major" as an object that can be isolated in time; and yet a D major chord may well make itself felt as a shimmering, ever-evolving presence, part of the "onstreaming" (*upward, behind the onstreaming it D-majored*). It is this paradoxical sense of everyday musical objects defamiliarized, of nouns alchemically transformed into verbs, seemingly solid substances activated and liquefied, that has made Adès one of the most influential musicians of the early twenty-first century. For his fellow composers in particular, Planet Adès has a strong magnetic field.

Adès is both an innovator at music's cellular level—his idiosyncratic use of irrational time signatures, such as 2/6 or 5/12, might convince listeners that their hearts have developed an unsettling habit of skipping beats—and a virtuosic showman with an over-the-top, more-is-more aesthetic. This is an unusual combination. It's rare for an artist of such sheer technical mastery to also have Adès's taste for extravagance, excess, *fun*. He is willing to run antipodal aesthetic risks: at times he verges gleefully on the grotesque, while elsewhere his music manifests a disarming psychic and emotional openness. He has invented new orchestral colors, and he's taught us new ways to dance. In different ways, he is both our Berlioz and our Stravinsky.

At the core of Adès's musical psychology there lies an innocent, childlike refusal: "I have a problem—well, it's not a problem for me, but it can make life confusing talking to anyone else—which is that I don't believe at all in the official distinction between tonal and atonal music," he tells the journalist Tom Service in the first chapter of their book of conversations, *Full of Noises*. The reality of this "official distinction" was taken for granted in most discussions of classical music in the latter half of the twentieth century; indeed, the presumed tonal/atonal dichotomy became an essential organizing principle, a neat way of corralling new music into discrete schools of thought.

It was not only critics and theoreticians but also many composers who accepted this apparent opposition as a given. Philip Glass describes the situation with his usual plainspokenness in his autobiography *Words Without Music*: "In the late 1950s and early 1960s"—Glass's student years—"composers had to make a big decision, whether they were going to write twelve-tone [atonal] music or tonal music." I'm struck by Glass's presentation of the issue as black-and-white: it sounds as if, on their first day of school, would-be composers were handed a questionnaire, and had to check one of two boxes. (Glass, of course, cheerfully checked the "tonal" box, and never looked back.)

This curiously polarized way of thinking persisted into our century: as a student, I was regularly asked by musicians and non-musicians alike whether my music was "tonal or atonal." I remember feeling unnerved by the bluntness of the question: Were these the two kinds of music? If I studied at a conservatory, would I be recruited to one team or the other by some swaggering captain, as in gym class? Once I had declared my allegiance, would I have to do battle with the opposing side?

Adès refreshingly refuses the distinction, and in doing so, he assumes the stance of the child in "The Emperor's New Clothes." Sweet-talking swindlers have come to town, and they've convinced the townsfolk that there's an easy way to divide all music into two camps. Why, even the emperor is convinced! (The emperor in this story is surely Pierre Boulez.) But a child standing by the side of the road doesn't see the distinction and dares to say so. The refusal to recognize these categories implies an unwillingness to define familiar, tonal-sounding harmonies as "stable" and atonal ones as automatically "liberated." Emancipation, for Adès, lies in a third path: he freely uses chords and gestures that we might fleetingly recognize from the music of past centuries, but in his hands, they are unstable, volatile substances. They tend not toward resolution but toward evanescence and escape.

This approach also contains an implicit refusal of any purely linear idea of music history—for instance, the notion that just because a few European men felt an oppressive sense of shame about the political implications of certain post-Wagnerian harmonies after World War II, those harmonies must remain illegal for all of us. Such an idea makes no sense to Adès. (It wouldn't pass the smell test on Tlön, either.) In his eyes, the sheer availability of a millennium's worth of world music—through scores, recordings, YouTube videos—has caused a kind of flattening of the historical continuum. Within this vast repository, a composer might find material for the creation of new worlds in some pretty unexpected places. And why not, when the alternative is a narrow Oedipal struggle with the generation of one's musical parents? Adès's stance is, paradoxically, both blithely ahistorical and notable for the acuteness and thoroughness of its historical consciousness. History is not a dead weight, in his view, but rather a still-living, ever-mutating compost heap, a fertile ecosystem within which we may forage, hunt, build.

Adès's ascendancy within the insular world of new classical music parallels that of another English musical artist of the same generation, one with a much wider audience: the rock band Radiohead. Adès and the five musicians who make up Radiohead were born around the same time, in the late 1960s and early 1970s, and all six grew up in the southeast of England; both Adès and Radiohead rose to local stardom in the early 1990s, and created their first internationally acknowledged masterpieces in the middle of that decade; and the influence of each has been so widespread within their respective fields as to be, today, almost a source of embarrassment. In some circles, saying that you've been influenced by Radiohead is a bit like saying you've been influenced by the Beatles—it really ought to be taken for granted. In a similar way, Adès lurks just beneath the surface of many conversations among composers. I can't count how many times I've been chatting with a composer colleague about some unrelated topic when Adès's name will emerge unbidden, seemingly against the speaker's will. The colleague in question might list a few things they've been listening to lately, or a few artists who were on their minds when they wrote their latest piece, and then they'll pause before adding, a little grudgingly, ". . . and of course there's that Adès piece, too."

The most striking similarity between Adès and Radiohead might be the way that each artist's first international success became something of a bugbear for them: both learned the hard way how difficult it can be to erase a first impression. Radiohead first gained widespread attention through their debut single, "Creep," a gleefully grungy ballad of self-abasement whose in-your-face posture and feral walls of guitar noise created the impression—misleading, as it turned out—that the band had the aesthetic DNA of the dominant alt-rock artists of the moment, like Nirvana and the Smashing Pumpkins. "Creep" was a slow-burning sleeper hit in country after country; the song's inexorable progress culminated atop the dubious summit of MTV's *Beavis and Butt-Head*, where Butt-Head admitted that the *loud* part of "Creep," at least, was "pretty cool." Radiohead probably owes their latter-day creative freedom to the success of "Creep," but that freedom came at the cost of a decade during which the song exasperatingly followed the band around like an incubus. "Creep" has stubbornly remained perhaps Radiohead's best-known individual song, even though it's a relatively immature effort, one that bears little resemblance to the sublime soundscapes of *OK Computer*, *Kid A*, and subsequent albums. Radiohead fans have expended a lot of energy over the years convincing casual listeners that there's more to the band than this one ballad, with its lovable but limited powers of catharsis.

The equivalent of "Creep," for Adès, was the opera *Powder Her Face* (1995), a satirical portrait of Margaret Campbell, Duchess of Argyll, the British socialite who became notorious for her very public divorce proceedings in the early 1960s. The Duchess's trial made headlines for the unusually explicit evidence that the Duke marshaled to prove his wife's infidelity, including a Polaroid of the Duchess fellating an unknown "headless" man whose face was out of the frame. It's a nasty story, and *Powder Her Face* is not without nastiness of its own: though Adès and the librettist Philip Hensher embrace the Duchess as a camp icon, and though at times she attains an improbable, poignant majesty, there is something off-puttingly chilly in the way the opera's creators insist on shining a flashlight into every corner of the empty luxury suite of her soul. This is a drama that moves ineluctably toward the disintegration of its antiheroine's life, and we're surely meant to feel that she deserves what she gets. It's hard to imagine such an opera—written by two men, about a woman's humiliation—being commissioned today.

The music, however, has an irresistible, explosive energy, and by the limited standards of contemporary opera, *Powder Her Face* was a hit. Its popularity endures in part because of an instantly notorious scene in which the Duchess imperiously fellates a seemingly helpless hotel waiter. This sequence still packs a punch today, not simply because it depicts a blowjob (what's so shocking about that?), but because of how exceptionally—oh god, how to say this—*lifelike* it is. The musical mise-en-scène is uncomfortably specific. It is clearly a hot, sticky afternoon, and we're in an airless hotel room. Boredom edges indistinguishably into lust. The scene is pornographic not only in the onstage action but also in the music—even the *orchestral* writing is explicit; the instrumental parts should come with a parental advisory. The orchestra thrashes and wails, helping the Duchess sing the vowels that are (as you can imagine) difficult for her to manage, under the circumstances.

The success of *Powder Her Face* entailed certain risks for Adès, as the success of "Creep" did for Radiohead: he became, in the minds of some listeners, the guy who wrote the blowjob opera. Even in recent years, I've occasionally had to defend Adès to older colleagues who can't get past *Powder Her Face*, with its undeniably misogynistic overtones, and still think of Adès as an enfant terrible whose "cleverness" does little to cancel out his first opera's puerility. With a quarter century of hindsight, I think *Powder Her Face* is best viewed as a brilliant student piece. It's a sensational fanfare of arrival, but it's also a little mean-spirited and a little hasty in its construction. The music that Adès would write in the new millennium, on the other hand, would be baked all the way through to a glorious golden brown.

THE EXTERMINATING ANGEL

Every opera composer surely yearns, consciously or not, to find their ideal subject, the elusive story that would fit their sensibility so snugly that the distinction between what's happening onstage and what's happening in the music would—impossibly—

dissolve. The listener, encountering such a piece, might have the uncanny sense that the characters are embodiments of forces that are always present in that composer's music, even their instrumental works. These perfect marriages are exceedingly rare, but they do exist: Debussy's *Pelléas et Mélisande* is one such unicorn; Birtwistle's Orphic pieces are another. To this very short list I would add Adès's most recent opera, *The Exterminating Angel*, based on Luis Buñuel's 1962 film.

There is a Goldilocks-and-the-three-bears dynamic to the three operas Adès has composed so far: *Powder Her Face* occasionally errs in the direction of youthful, let's-see-what-we-can-get-away-with brashness, while his second opera, *The Tempest* (2004), is curiously restrained. The problems with the latter piece can largely be traced to Meredith Oakes's catastrophic libretto. Oakes adheres closely, even conservatively, to Shakespeare's dramaturgy, but she somehow manages to drain the play of every ounce of its poetic richness; Caliban's couplet "You scorn me and you strike me, / You say you do not like me" is tragically representative of the sub-Seussian doggerel that disfigures this libretto's every page. There's plenty of brilliant music in *The Tempest*, but—uniquely in Adès's output—it doesn't feel entirely *free*, since the composer can't quite shake Oakes's singsong rhythms.

If *Powder Her Face* is a little hot to the touch and *The Tempest* is lukewarm, *The Exterminating Angel* is just right. The film's plot is simple and surreal. A group of wealthy socialites arrives at the mansion of Edmundo and Lucía de Nobile for a dinner party. They have, incidentally, just been to the opera, and the evening's star soprano is among the guests. It quickly becomes clear that something is amiss: as the guests arrive, the Nobiles' servants (apart from the loyal majordomo) are hastily preparing to flee the house, mumbling excuses to their infuriated mistress on their way out. After dinner, the guests gather in the drawing room, where they unexpectedly linger for hours. When they finally decide, close to dawn, that it's surely time to go home, they find themselves incapable of leaving the room. There doesn't seem to be anything physically stopping them, but a collective mania has taken hold: no one dares to step through the doorway. As this inexplicable hostage situation stretches out over days and weeks, the guests' behavior degenerates into primal viciousness: they run out of food; a young couple commits suicide in a closet; fights break out; some people suffer hallucinations; and a few of the men finally decide that Edmundo, their host, must be sacrificed. They are liberated when a young guest, Leticia, forces everyone to retrace their steps and reenact every event from their first night of captivity. The spell is broken, and the guests finally cross the threshold, some of them weeping with relief. In the final scene, the "exterminating angel" strikes once more, this time in a church where a mass has just been offered in gratitude for the guests' apparent liberation. The priest finds himself unable to exit the sanctuary: the cycle of psychic entrapment has started all over again. The film ends with images of burgeoning violence and chaos.

It's hard to imagine a more perfect story for Adès's sensibility, for a number of reasons. There is, of course, the easy analogy between Adès's music and Buñuel's visual surrealism: a chord whose properties we thought we knew might, in Adès's work, suddenly slide off the edge of the earth, as a clock might in a Salvador Dalí painting. But this analogy, though enticing—Adès's mother, the art historian Dawn Adès, is an expert in surrealism—is also inexact: music is a temporal art, not a spatial one, and I find that Adès's mature work, for all its vividness and its power to shock, unfolds in a fundamentally organic way that has little to do with the jarring juxtapositions that often characterize surrealist visual art.

A truer basis for Adès's attraction to *Angel* is, I think, his professed sensitivity to the absurdity of many of humankind's social rituals, including the conventions of musical performance. He has said that he is prone to asking himself, even in the familiar arena of a concert hall, "What are we doing here? What are all those musicians doing?" In other words, what is the nature of the forces that propel us, as a species, to congregate in these elaborate ways? By whose will do we move from one place to another? When you stop to examine it, it certainly doesn't seem to be our own. To write an opera is to channel these mysterious social forces, albeit in a petri dish: "You get [the characters] in this situation and then: oh God, how are we going to get out of this? ... How are we going to get off stage? How are we going to get *home*?" If one becomes too aware of the strangeness of the forces that send us to a concert, or to a party, and dictate our behavior in each circumstance, one may find oneself paralyzed. *The Exterminating Angel* puts this enigmatic force under a microscope and asks what would happen if it were suddenly switched off—exterminated, that is, by some impish "angel."

Another aspect of *Angel* that seems to have attracted Adès is its sheer profligacy. Adès has a great love both for lavish musical materials—lush, extravagant orchestrations; voluptuously dense harmonic voicings—and for the thrill of setting those materials on fire and watching the whole exquisite fabric burn up in midair. He likes things fancy, and he likes them filthy (just think of the Duchess!). In his instrumental music, one will frequently encounter a well-bred orchestral instrument—an oboe, for instance—squealing in indignation at having to turn some somersault that no composer has ever asked it to perform before ("Mr. Brahms would never have made me do such a thing!"). The characters in *Angel* react with similar pique as they find themselves, in spite of their genteel manners and designer clothes, dragged ever closer to the condition of beasts.

A few years ago, an administrator at an opera house that was presenting *Angel* told me—throwing his hands up in theatrical despair—that putting this opera on night after night was "like watching money burn." *Angel* is indeed distressingly expensive to produce: the cast includes fourteen principal singers and eight secondary roles, plus a chorus and an enormous orchestra that includes a battery of offstage percussionists. I don't think my sober-minded friend intended this double meaning, but "watching money burn" isn't a bad image for the events of *Angel*'s drama. The oblivious socialites who populate the opera's cast are themselves the rarefied materials, the fresh meat, that are immolated and served up over the course of the evening. As the guests arrive in the first scene, keen-eared listeners might sense the presence of a hungry composer licking his lips, sharpening his cutlery: the ingredients are being assembled, and how tender they are! A hellish catharsis awaits. Many of Adès's pieces feel like bonfires of the vanities; this one is a bonfire of the vain.

The Exterminating Angel had a long gestation period, during which Adès took a number of detours to compose other pieces. Perhaps the most significant of these is *Totentanz* (2013), which is a tour de force even by his standards, and one of the most exhilarating musical works written so far this millennium. *Totentanz*, whose Lisztian title is the German term for a danse macabre, is scored for two singers (baritone and mezzo-soprano) and large orchestra; though it is barely thirty minutes long, it is operatic in its scope. The work's text derives from a medieval frieze in a church in Lübeck, Germany, that depicted the skeletal figure of Death "dancing" with a person from every rank of society, from the pope down to a newborn baby, with poetic dialogue between Death and his mortal interlocutors inscribed beneath the images. (The frieze was destroyed in an air raid that devastated Lübeck on the eve of Palm Sunday, 1942.) The painting's message is clear: every one of us is on Death's dance card, and no one can refuse his invitation.

In Adès's setting, the baritone is Death, while the mezzo-soprano portrays each of his human victims in turn. Death is cruelly peremptory with some characters, especially the self-important ones, while he treats others with an eerie tenderness—notably the last two, the Maiden and the Baby, the latter of whom he summons with the finespun lure of a Mahlerian lullaby. (This Death can also be venomously funny: he tells the pope, for instance, that he's going to have to take his hat off, since it won't fit in the narrow box that will be his new home.) *Totentanz*'s orchestra is a garish infernal machine full of rattles, bones, whistles, and whips, and the piece makes for an earthshaking experience; it's the only piece I've ever heard performed in New York's David Geffen Hall that managed to shatter the sound barrier of that space's notoriously dull acoustics.

Totentanz is, I think, in deep dialogue with *The Exterminating Angel*: the latter work's Angel-force and *Totentanz*'s Death-force are close cousins, two spirits that operate within the same demonic hierarchy. We might even think of the Angel as a mischievous servant-demon to Death, Puck to Death's Oberon—or, in a more specifically Adèsian analogy, Ariel to Death's Prospero. In Adès's *Tempest*, Prospero is a baritone, as *Totentanz*'s Death is;

and Ariel is a high-flying, dizzyingly acrobatic soprano. The musical behavior of Adès's Ariel is not so different from that of *Angel's* titular spirit, who is (dis)embodied not by a singer but by an instrument in the orchestra: the electronic Ondes Martenot, an "aerial" instrument if ever there was one.* Like Ariel, the Angel's daily labor entails swooping down in order to gigglingly torment a band of hapless mortals.

The mezzo-soprano Christianne Stotijn, who performed in *Totentanz's* premiere and has gone on to sing the piece with awesome mastery around the world, has aptly described the "ecstasy of panic" that overcomes some of *Totentanz's* characters, especially the ones who are attached to their worldly power and childishly cling to it, like devalued currency, even in their final moments. There is an erotic thrill to the whiteout of terror that these people experience when they realize the inescapability of the encounter, a tingle of rapture that is repeated so incessantly in *Totentanz* that it seems almost an addiction. (We might be reminded of Stravinsky's passion for a similar effect in early pieces like *The Rite of Spring*.) This same ecstasy of panic is also the source of *The Exterminating Angel's* power: the Angel has the entire cast wrapped around its ghostly finger and cheerfully toys with them before our eyes. Every motion we see onstage is the writhing of a fish on an invisible hook.

The essential similarity between the Angel and *Totentanz's* Death lies in the variability of the relationships between them and their mortal victims. The nature of each encounter depends on the victim's reaction to the presence of the supernatural being.

---

* The Ondes Martenot is an electronic keyboard instrument whose pitch may be controlled by a metal ring slid across a wire. The performer, sliding their hand back and forth, sometimes looks as though they are seated at a kind of musical Ouija board. The instrument's sound is that of a friendly, lyrical ghost; as the Ondes virtuoso Cynthia Millar said in an interview about *Angel*, the instrument "can really fly."

In general, if a character is foolish enough to thrash around in an attempt to escape, Death and the Angel are likely to be particularly nasty with them. The best thing to do—as with a frightening psychedelic trip or a skid on an icy road—is to lean into it. The characters who surrender themselves to the experience are typically treated with great solicitude.

This is exemplified by the Maiden and the Baby in *Totentanz* and the young lovers, Beatriz and Eduardo, in *Angel*, who ultimately commit suicide in a delirious joint *Liebestod*. The music for all four of these characters has an exquisite sickly sweetness that we witness, over the course of each scene, going sour and finally rotting to the core. (Curiously enough, both scenes are preceded by another character singing some variant of the phrase "Consummatum est," Jesus's last words on the Cross.) Both the Baby's music and that of the lovers in *Angel* begin as a mesmeric floating lullaby, but the misty radiance of the texture does not last: each ultimately develops a pulse, a sort of fetal heartbeat, which steadily grows into a drumbeat of annihilation. In each piece, the characters recite a mantra as the cosmic quicksand pulls them under: "My love, my refuge, my death," in *Angel*; and "tanzen . . . tanzen . . ." ("dancing, dancing") in *Totentanz*. Drumbeats bookend each bar, on the pickup and the downbeat: the inexorable pounding of nails into a coffin.

"The gates of Hell," W. H. Auden once asserted, "are always standing wide open. The lost are perfectly free to leave whenever they like, but to do so would mean admitting that the gates were open, that is to say that there was another life outside." The gates of the

Nobiles' mansion also stand wide open throughout Buñuel's film. The guests remain within not because some divine judge has ordained their imprisonment but rather because their souls are hopelessly entangled with their material wealth: they refuse to recognize that there is "another life outside." In one of the film's more repugnant moments, one character declares that the lower classes are surely less sensitive to pain than the gentry is. The working-class servants in *Angel* are in reality *more* sensitive than the wealthy guests: the servants know better than to subject themselves to this nightmare of wandering aimlessly around a drawing room, while the guests can't bring themselves to do anything else. The drawing room becomes their world because they see the world as their drawing room.

What is it that finally frees them? Adès's answer to this question differs strikingly from Buñuel's, and accordingly the climactic moment of the guests' liberation is one of the few significant points of divergence between film and opera. Buñuel's treatment of this moment reminds me of an analogous scene in *The Rake's Progress*, a work whose neat morality-tale framing might seem, on the surface, to have little to do with the antilogical world of *Angel*. Tom Rakewell, like *Angel's* socialites, is trapped in a hell of his own making, a hell in his head, and what frees him is an act of *repetition*: he has convinced himself that Anne Trulove can never love him again, that he can never return to his old life. But when, with Anne's help, he guesses that Nick Shadow has played the same card twice, he is saved. (Look at the cells that make up the word "repetition": a petition redoubled, a plea reaffirmed.) As Edward Mendelson puts it, "when Rakewell . . . accepts repetition, it proves to be, as it is in Kierkegaard, the image of eternity in the world of time."

Buñuel's cast is liberated, however provisionally, by a similar gesture. When poor Edmundo is about to sacrifice himself to his increasingly wrathful guests, the young and previously aloof Leticia suddenly cries out. She has noticed that everyone has ended up in precisely the same positions in the room they occupied on the first night of their ordeal. She insists that they reenact, as best they can recall, everything they said and did on that first evening: one guest, Blanca, plays the piano; everyone applauds; Edmundo says he wishes they had a harpsichord; and Blanca announces that she is tired. Once the guests have performed this ritual of repetition, they find that they are free: they cross the threshold and step out of the room.

We might remember at this point that the film's first scene had featured an odd, unexplained repetition: when the guests first enter the mansion, Edmundo calls for the footman to get the coats; he realizes with irritation that the footman isn't there; the guests walk upstairs—and then the entire sequence repeats itself. It feels like an editing mistake. In hindsight, however, it reveals itself as a breadcrumb dropped by Buñuel to suggest that the cast is trapped in a barren, M. C. Escher–esque temporal loop: another evening at the theater, another dinner party, another sheeplike ascent of a marble staircase. When the guests finally accept the reality of life as repetition ("the image of eternity in the world of time"), they achieve a moment of transcendent, Kierkegaardian clarity.

Though the act of surrendering to eternal recurrence is the essential liberatory gesture of both *The Rake* and *Angel*, there is an important distinction between repetition in Auden and in Buñuel. For Auden, to accept repetition is to embrace the possibility of *return*: by turning back, Tom Rakewell turns his face toward the warm light of God's love, and Anne Trulove's. To turn back is to manifest the humility that is required to seek forgiveness.

I suppose Buñuel's cast also manifests a certain kind of humility—their pride has unquestionably been beaten to a pulp—but the conclusion Buñuel draws is far darker than Auden's. To be aware of the cyclicality of existence is, for Buñuel, merely to be in on some cosmic joke: the world outside soon reveals itself, chillingly, to be simply a bigger version of the same room.

The subtle but profound difference between Buñuel's treatment of the moment of liberation and Adès's depends on the composer's decision to fuse two of the film's dinner-party guests—Silvia, the star soprano, and Leticia, the supposedly virginal "Valkyrie"—into a single character (named Leticia). In Adès, at this crucial repeated moment, the whole cast begs Leticia to sing. The first time she declines, but the second time she consents, and her song proves to be the key that opens the door out of the Angel's torture chamber. The Angel, a musical force itself, demands a musical counterspell. In Buñuel, pure repetition gets the guests out of the drawing room, but in Adès, it is Leticia's song—which is a new element, not a repetition—that makes the difference.

The text of Leticia's song is based on a haunting Zionide by the medieval Spanish Jewish poet Yehuda Halevi: "Zion, do you ask of my peace, who longs for yours?" This Hebrew-derived text is part of a rich nexus of references to Jewish poetic and musical traditions in Adès's work. Though he was not raised Jewish, he learned as an adult that his name is one of "immemorial Jewish origin," and he subsequently became fruitfully curious about this phantom heritage. (Incidentally, the Ades Synagogue, in Jerusalem, is a center for ancient Sephardic traditions of liturgical music.) Adès and Tom Service have a revealing exchange on this subject in *Full of Noises*:

> ADÈS: I'm afraid I am only at home with a certain temporariness, an instability. I should live on a boat.

SERVICE: You are conscious of the transitoriness of home?

ADÈS: Every day, the evanescence of everything, including oneself . . . I'm not Jewish, but I carry a name of immemorial Jewish origin, and that awareness of the transitoriness of place—it may not be unrelated. I always had a slight sense that I wasn't completely rooted in one place.

A few pages later, Adès quotes André Breton's line "Life is elsewhere," noting that some of his most memorable musical textures have been inspired by the idea of music as "elsewhere." The cast of *Angel*, if they hope to be liberated from their purgatorial here-and-now (where "all is stale yet all is strange," as Auden puts it in *The Rake*), must achieve the humility that's required to confess their longing for an "elsewhere." And they can only give voice to this longing in music.

When the cast implores Leticia to sing, the music traces a breathtakingly beautiful crabwise ascent that recalls a passage in Adès's orchestral piece *Tevot* (2007), whose title carries a rich double meaning. "Tevot" is the Hebrew term for bars of music, but it is also redolent of the term for Noah's ark and for the cradle that carried the infant Moses across the Nile. A bar of music is thus a vessel, a kind of raft, that might carry us from one shore to another. Elsewhere in *Angel*, one character sings an eerie little song full of ocean imagery, whose lyrics ("Over the sea, over the sea, where is the way?") are inspired by still another Hebrew-language text, a children's poem by the writer Haim Bialik.

These interconnections in Adès's oeuvre—uneasy waters, uneasy harmonies; the suffocating materiality of the present, the longing for a lost homeland; the bar, the ark, the exiled singer—are all the more potent for their subtlety. They do not advertise themselves but flow beneath the surface, in the music's bloodstream.

The suggestion that music is a quasi-Kabbalistic key, capable of opening a locked spiritual door, is a welcome note of hope in a piece that is otherwise exceedingly bleak. My only qualm about *Angel*, which is not a criticism so much as a content warning, is that, in addition to being exhilarating, it is also exhausting. My nerves feel pretty raw just studying the score; I can't imagine what it's like to perform. Adès's music is so explosive, and so densely packed with musical nourishment, that I find I often prefer to experience it in smaller doses—a twenty- or thirty-minute symphonic or chamber piece, for example, rather than the multi-course banquet of an opera.

Adès has expressed some ambivalence about certain works by the composer György Ligeti, whose music he fundamentally admires, for its unalloyed grimness of outlook: "Why are we here, dealing with this," he wonders, "if it's all just a black joke?" *The Exterminating Angel* toys with a similarly dark worldview; Ligeti's one opera is called *Le Grand Macabre* (1978), and surely *Angel* is Adès's own *grand macabre*. But I think the opera's powers of catharsis far outweigh the violence it does to the listener's nervous system (and the finances of any theater that dares to present it). Like the Angel with which he wrestles, Adès's spell is mighty hard to resist.

Chaya Czernowin's Heart Chamber

When I am required to account for my love of opera to someone who's unfamiliar with the art form, I often feel—even in the throes of advocacy—like a crazy person. I'll be speaking passionately about opera's capacity to manifest otherwise-incommunicable inner experiences, its ability to layer *multiple* inner experiences simultaneously, its moments of intimate revelation—and then I'll notice that my interlocutor's eyebrows are raised in undisguised skepticism. They will tell me that they have, in fact, been to an opera; more often than not, the production will have been by Franco Zeffirelli. I realize with a twinge what my conversation partner's experience of the art form must have been: I can picture all too clearly the mascara-plastered soprano, vibrato wide as a freeway, shrieking her way through *Turandot* (1926) as candy-colored confetti falls on the gargantuan, serpent-gilded columns of the ice princess's palace. What exactly, my interlocutor asks me innocently, do I find so *intimate* about this kind of spectacle?

The truth is I've only ever had a few experiences, whether as a composer, a conductor, or a listener, that have even come close to realizing my dream of what opera can be. High on that list is my first encounter with the Israeli-born composer Chaya Czernowin's opera *Heart Chamber*, which I heard in its premiere production at Berlin's Deutsche Oper in 2019.

Czernowin (b. 1957) aptly describes *Heart Chamber* as "a grand opera of the smallest physical and psychic changes that push two strangers towards or away from each other." This radical fusion of the intimate and the epic is one of the piece's signal achievements: Czernowin's concept of opera is founded on a refreshing trust in the enormous dramatic potential of interior experiences so fleeting and so private that few composers would dare make them a central focus. By putting such experiences under her potent musical microscope, she has opened up fertile new terrain for the art form.

There are only two characters in *Heart Chamber*, and there are essentially no external events, only seismic inner ones. Most of the hallmarks of grand opera are missing: if you turn to opera *exclusively* for murder, adultery, incest, and apocalypse, you should look elsewhere. But this opera's interior events are magnified to feel as huge within the acoustic "chamber" of an opera house as they do within the "heart chamber" of the human body. To experience *Heart Chamber* is to summon the precarious sensation of being in love; this piece embodies that heightened state when one seemingly chilly glance from the person you love can be a catastrophe. This is opera at once expanded and boiled down to its essence. In a vital sense, it's more operatic than *La bohème*.

Early in Czernowin's career, it might have seemed unlikely that she would write operas at all. Czernowin emerged as a powerful voice in the European avant-garde during the last decade of the twentieth century, near the end of a period in which a predilection for opera would have struck many experimental-minded musicians as somehow suspect. The very term "opera" sounded, to some composers, every bit as antiquated as a more specific formal designation like "symphony." As a result, some prominent European composers, such as Pierre Boulez, went their whole careers without writing a major work for the stage. Others, like Luigi Nono, insisted on calling their music-theater works anything *but* operas. Opera as such was presumed dead.

The next generation of European avant-gardists inherited this knee-jerk aversion to the medium, and in their youth, many of them proclaimed their distaste for it. But a few major artists, including Czernowin and the Finnish composer Kaija Saariaho (b. 1952), found themselves increasingly attracted to opera as they reached artistic maturity. Both Czernowin's music and Saariaho's manifest a sensual curiosity, a desire to explore outer limits of experience: in different ways, the work of both artists inhabits climate systems where conditions are so extreme that the borders between forms of experience—tactile, psychological, spiritual—are liable to break down. And while abstract instrumental music is the ideal vehicle for some forms of sensory exploration, opera opens up new avenues of inquiry by allowing the composer to speak through specific human subjects—characters with names, faces, life histories.

Instrumental music always implies an insoluble question: *Who is speaking?* (Another way of asking this is, *To whom is this happening?*) I feel in my gut that Mahler's music, for instance, is experienced in the first person, while the voice that speaks through Sibelius's symphonies is a nonhuman one, a voice both vaster and more elemental. But it's maddeningly hard to isolate musical evidence that would prove the veracity of either idea.*

---

* One clue, I think, is the presence or absence of the onstage/offstage distinction. Mahler is fond of putting brass players and percussionists offstage to create a faraway (*lontano*) effect, and the existence of an "offstage" space implies that some protagonist is listening

Opera makes this question concrete and offers a kind of answer: we can see the human beings *to whom the music is happening*.

To put a human subject onstage is, after all, to acknowledge the possibility of communicable subjective experience. And for many postmodern musical thinkers, this was an inadmissible acknowledgment. It made a lot of late-twentieth-century avant-gardists squeamish to contemplate putting real, living-and-breathing human beings onstage in all their messiness. This is a shame, because some of the techniques the European avant-garde was developing at the time—especially their experiments with raw noise and their willingness to go to sonic extremes—are nothing if not operatic.

For such techniques to yield successful operas, what was required was composers who possessed both technical mastery and the courage to be vulnerable, to run the risk of maybe—God forbid!—revealing something of themselves through compassion with their characters. Czernowin and Saariaho have been among the trailblazers in this area. They have shown, and continue to show, that there is no contradiction between forward-looking musical techniques and explorations of individual experience. And the most volatile experience one could explore, of course, is love.

Heart Chamber, an elemental, unflinching enactment of the psychic trials by fire undergone by a woman and a man over the course of their relationship, is as perfect a fit for Czernowin's sensibility

---

from a fixed point "onstage." No such distinction exists in Sibelius's symphonies; the idea of something being heard from "offstage" does not compute in his musical universe.

as *The Exterminating Angel* is for Adès's. Czernowin's earlier theatrical works, like Adès's, also go to opposite extremes that are, in
Heart Chamber, fruitfully combined. Czernowin's first substantial
music-theater work, *Pnima . . . ins innere* (2000), features just two
characters: an old man, who is a Holocaust survivor, and a young
boy, presumably his grandson. (Onstage, they are portrayed by
actors, who are silent throughout; they are given voice by offstage
singers.) When she wrote *Pnima*, Czernowin still espoused the
anti-opera stance that prevailed in avant-garde circles—in fact,
she referred to the piece as an "anti-opera." In a recent interview
with the composer Clara Iannotta, Czernowin explains that "at
that time I was very attached to the progressive, and I even said to
people that I hated opera—which was not completely accurate."

Czernowin's resistance to the term "opera" had worn off by
the time she wrote *Infinite now* (2017), a 150-minute work that
combines aspects of Erich Maria Remarque's classic war novel *All
Quiet on the Western Front* with the contemporary Chinese writer
Can Xue's story "Homecoming," in which a woman visits a house
that she thinks she knows, only to discover that the house is seemingly built on top of an abyss, and it is now impossible to leave.
(Though Czernowin's music has little in common with Adès's, it
is striking that *Infinite now*, which had its premiere within a year
of *The Exterminating Angel*'s, also features a character inexplicably
trapped within a house's surreal inner world.)

Infinite now is epic in its scope: the piece explores both communal wartime experiences—death and dehumanization as well
as unlikely acts of tenderness and generosity—and the dizzyingly
unstable psychological landscape of Can Xue's narrator. This material is so rich, and so varied, that Czernowin decided that "opera" really was the only term for it: the condition of "infinite now"
is, in the composer's words, "the place where you are given all the

means in abundance, a kind of euphoric abundance of everything you could be, in a way, a stage for all your ideas . . . And for me, that is really connected to the experience of an opera."

One of the keys to *Heart Chamber*'s power is its fusion of key aspects of *Pnima* and *Infinite now*: like the former piece, there are only two characters in *Heart Chamber*, and the opera is an excavation of their relationship, of all that is unspeakable or inaccessible between them. But though it shares *Pnima*'s interpersonal intimacy, *Heart Chamber* is as lushly epic in its musical realization as *Infinite now*—possibly more so.

Heart Chamber's narrative frame is skeletal and clear. A woman meets a man in a chance encounter, and they feel an intense connection. We hear their separate expressions of loneliness. The woman gathers her courage, calls the man, and invites him to go for a walk. They fall in love. There are moments of overwhelming joy; there are painful miscommunications. We witness a crisis, a reconciliation, a deeper crisis, a deeper coming-together.

Czernowin wrote *Heart Chamber*'s English-language text herself—always a risky decision for a composer to make, and doubly risky for one writing in a language other than her mother tongue. But *Heart Chamber*'s libretto is a wonder, and the fact that it is written in its author's second language is, I think, critical to its success. I doubt whether a native English speaker could have accessed the raw poetic register that Czernowin inhabits throughout the piece, a register that is inseparable from the poignant sense of effort that attends these characters' utterances to each other.

Anyone who speaks a second language—especially if one

speaks that language well, but not perfectly—is probably familiar with the sensation of reverting to an earlier stage of life, or even becoming a slightly different person, in the act of speaking that language. My Italian is pretty fluent, for example, but I've noticed an unguarded, teenage quality to my utterances in Italian that is not present when I speak English (at least I hope not). I am capable of saying things in Italian that I would be embarrassed to say in English, but which are no less true—they might even be *more* true—for their directness. The act of speaking in a new tongue strips me of my verbal defenses, my ability to spread a smoke screen of jokes, cultural references, double meanings. In Italian, I have no choice but to express myself directly.

This emotional candor, which is in evidence throughout *Heart Chamber*'s libretto, is beautifully suited both to opera in general and to this piece in particular. Czernowin's aim is to explore the very edge of what two people in a relationship are capable of communicating to each other, as well as the limits of what they are capable of *feeling*, what the heart can contain within its "chamber"; the piece is both an investigation of limits and a transgression of them. As a result, one of its prevailing emotions is frustration: frustration that the burning core of love that each character feels cannot simply communicate itself to the other, but instead gets tangled up in the self's outer layers, the crust and the magma of each character's insecurities and anxieties. Both characters are plagued by a painful awareness that the words they speak are *not enough*—a struggle that one can feel in the very fierceness with which Czernowin wields the blunt instrument of her English.

For the heart, any language is a second language. And in this piece, the pressure of the heart's frustration—its sadness that it must express itself in language at all—opens up a space for music.

Czernowin's libretto is notably score-like in its construction. The opera's two characters are each portrayed by two onstage singers—the woman by a soprano and a contralto, and the man by a baritone and a countertenor—as well as by pre-recorded alto and tenor parts and an offstage chorus of sixteen voices. In the printed libretto, the singers' lines are stacked vertically, their words scattered across the page like text magnets on a refrigerator. Czernowin instructs us to "read the text as you read a score"; that is, we should read left to right, but we should read all text down the vertical axis simultaneously. More even than most libretti, this one is a diagram, a spatial blueprint for its musicalization, and this diagrammatic quality extends even to individual words and phrases, which often seem to be protoimages of musical events. Certain dreamlike passages could be descriptions of the activity of composition: the woman imagines peeling and scraping away at moss that grows from underneath bathroom tiles; the man imagines a tree breaking through the floor of his house, then seeing numberless ants forming "a moving vista: a net of tunnels, hanging palaces." (The latter is not a bad image for the seething richness of Czernowin's music.)

The pairs of singers who portray each character often sing simultaneous, overlapping lines, which creates the sense that we are hearing two layers of each character's consciousness at once. It's tempting to define these layers as "conscious" and "subconscious," but that would be reductive; there are more than two layers at play here, and they shift throughout the piece. Of the two singers who portray the woman ("She"), the soprano is more often the upper layer of consciousness, the voice of speech or consciously articulated thought, while the contralto is usually the voice of a deeper, more instinctive layer. In the case of "He," the baritone typically takes the role of the more conscious layer, while the countertenor voices the more unconscious one. For both "She" and "He," the voice type that functions as the more "conscious" layer—the one that each character projects into the social world—is also the one that is more closely associated with conventional ideas of that character's gender: the feminine-sounding soprano, the suavely masculine baritone. In each case, the "inner" voice balances this energy with qualities conventionally associated with the opposite gender: the complementary androgynies of the throatily masculine contralto and the ethereal, angelic-demonic countertenor.

When the woman first calls the man, we hear both the man's (baritonal) speaking voice, which is cautious to the point of skepticism ("A walk? But where?"), and a subconscious (countertenor) voice, which is lovably unrestrained ("yes, yes . . . yes . . . I will come"). Later, when the relationship hits a crisis, each character's two voices embody the sayable and the unsayable, respectively. "I did not mean to," the baritone says carefully in one fraught moment, while the countertenor articulates what he is actually noticing: "when your nostrils move slightly I know you feel exposed." When the crisis deepens, the baritone woundedly pleads with his lover ("what? you can't just suddenly turn away like that") while the countertenor mutters the man's unutterable, panic-stricken need to escape ("get away get away get away get away").

The libretto does contain a couple of irredeemable clunkers that a native English speaker would have been unlikely to write ("My bathroom is long and endless," "Will you be like a father, but a good father?"). On the whole, however, Czernowin's supercharged, nakedly emotional poetry is disarmingly beautiful—and given the complexity of the piece's music, its bluntness is also a practical necessity.

In discussing Czernowin's music, let me begin by saying that I love notes. Really I do. Notes, those gleaming, adorably oblong little dewdrops of ink! Notes are my bread and butter. Where would we be without notes?

That's how I usually feel, anyway. But Chaya Czernowin's music makes me wonder if notes are perhaps hopelessly crude, outdated instruments.

Let me explain. Czernowin often makes use of both acoustic and electronically produced sounds. When she writes for acoustic instruments, she generally requires the performers to master various "extended techniques": that is, techniques that go beyond or against an instrument's conventional playing technique, and that can produce sounds very different from those typically associated with the instrument. The extended techniques that Czernowin uses are capable of summoning multiple musical universes, and no blanket description of what they sound like could possibly be accurate. But they can be defined in the negative: they typically produce *anything but notes*. Czernowin might require a kind of body-to-instrument contact so full of friction that it yields a shower of sonic sparks; or she might ask the performer to breathe into their instrument so that it speaks with a gossamer, ghostlike whisper. Her musical camera is zoomed in to a microscopic world full of infinitesimal details, and as a result, her sounds almost never crystallize into notes.

It's rare to encounter a composer whose work challenges one's own so fundamentally, at the level of music's essential materials, but Czernowin's work—and also the music of her ferociously gifted former student Ash Fure—does just that. Her music makes me feel that I am working with cells, whereas she's working with atoms and subatomic particles.

Come to think of it, it's comforting to articulate the difference that way. After all, there is surely a place in the world for both biologists and particle physicists, isn't there?

Heart Chamber opens with an effortful meeting of two sound-producing bodies that usually live at opposite ends of the registral spectrum—one very low, one very high. The first sound we hear is an amplified double bass, which plays an extended, wandering solo that shows off a wide array of high-friction performance techniques: circular bow strokes, flesh pizzicato, slow bow with extreme pressure. The bass eventually reaches the tenuous perch of a high C-natural, which is sustained with tremulous, jittery vibrato. A female voice enters on the same pitch, in the same octave; the singer is asked to "try to melt into the double bass color." We might think of this unlikely meeting point as a musical image of the charged encounter that is the opera's essential dramatic event.

This is an audacious way to begin an opera, first of all because it sets an imposingly high standard for sonic inventiveness—I can't think of another opera in which a female singer is asked to fuse her sound with that of a double bass. And the idea of opening a "grand opera" with a bass solo is itself a bold gesture. The double bass is not a glamorous solo instrument. As jazz aficionados know, bass solos have long been fodder for jokes among musicians, because—let's face it—they are often a huge bummer.

You can't hear what pitches they're playing down there anyway! Who wouldn't rather hear a sax solo, or a drum solo, or really any other kind of solo at all?

Czernowin subtly toys with this trope. Yes, the bass is probably the orchestral instrument that would sound the feeblest if it were forced to play an unamplified solo from an orchestra pit. But it is also the one that, in its very construction, most closely resembles the adult human body: bassists, lugging their instruments around a city's streets and subways, often seem to be toting a body bag on wheels. Czernowin electronically amplifies her solo bass to such a degree that we hear—we *feel*—every touch of the player's bow and fingers against the strings. She shines a light on the primal moment of contact between human and instrument, which is after all the fundamental drama of music-making. *Heart Chamber* announces from its first moments that it will inhabit a usually inaccessible world within the human body, and that it will accordingly require, from the listener, a radical shift in perspective.

There's a helpful analogy in another of Czernowin's works, the cello-and-orchestra piece *Guardian* (2017), which Czernowin has taken pains to emphasize is *not* a cello concerto. It is, rather, written for a kind of macro-cello, "as if the cello is so huge and inside it there sits an orchestra . . . It is like one voice that contains the whole orchestra. The cello is the hard skin of the orchestra which is the soft flesh." In *Heart Chamber*, too, we first meet the "hard skin" of the double bass, and then the whole orchestral picture—the flesh and blood, the body's inner rhythms and rivers—begins to be colored in.

And those colors! Practically everywhere throughout *Heart Chamber*, Czernowin refuses the prefabricated orchestral materials that, like a set of Crayola colored pencils, serve most composers' purposes just fine. She prefers, instead, to manufacture her own pigments—a process in which the performers must be willing co-conspirators. Her idiosyncratic graphic language is full of visual renderings of the shapes that the performers will trace on their instruments, as well as exquisitely specific verbal directions: "On the bass drum," reads one instruction, "write with the hard tip of a feather or a similar object: a quite sharp tip but with some flexibility." Below these words, a squiggly line dips and ascends, like a cardiogram showing the fluctuations of an unsteady heart. This elemental inventiveness yields a breathtaking array of textures, which include pre-recorded "choirs" of scattering marbles, plucked combs, a hum of bees, delicate "storms" of clicking percussion sounds, and the whir of dry leaves; the ticking of an antique clock amplified to a head-splitting violence; wind and brass players whispering the word "strange" into their mouthpieces; the sound of rice being poured into a bowl; an electric guitar scratched with a rough sponge; the sound of many hands rubbing rhythmically together; and high waves of guitar sound that wail and wander like whale song.

Most of these effects depend on electronic sound enhancement, and I think if enough people heard *Heart Chamber*, the question of whether opera is automatically cheapened or endangered by the use of electronically produced sound would be settled once and for all. The amplification of the singers allows for "close-up" vocal effects whose subtlety would otherwise be lost in a big theater: whispers, inward breaths, and surely opera's first-ever extended solo for vocal fry—the creaky, unglamorous vocal register more readily associated with the Kardashians than with Maria Callas. At one point, the chorus whispers the word "failed," with slight downward sliding gestures, to create what Czernowin calls "a porous wall" made entirely of that word, a haunting, soft-textured cloud of failure. Elsewhere, the whispered word "you" is deliciously twisted, through an aspiration at its beginning, into a kind of laser-gun sound, a sound I remember making as a kid in *Star Wars* playground games.

These effects are, importantly, not incompatible with operatic tone production. At the performance I heard, part of what made the soprano Patrizia Ciofi's portrayal so captivating was the way she toggled, moment-to-moment, between a luminous, expertly produced cantabile tone and the raw sounds that Czernowin's more extreme vocal effects require. Ciofi attacked every one of the score's all-but-impossible tasks with equal gusto. We composers tend to regard artists like Ciofi, who seem both up for anything and capable of anything, with awestruck gratitude that verges on disbelief.

Of the operas discussed in this book, the only one to which *Heart Chamber* bears any meaningful resemblance is Birtwistle's *The Mask of Orpheus*, whose soundscapes, though produced by very different means, resemble Czernowin's in their sensuous complexity. The two pieces also have certain unusual features in common: libretti that are practically musical scores in their own right; individual characters who are each depicted by two onstage singers; even the presence of an electronic "aura of bees."

But the basic difference between Birtwistle's and Czernowin's operas highlights what makes Czernowin's work special. Birtwistle gives epic scope to an epic story; Czernowin makes interior events feel equally epic. In an extraordinary passage near the beginning of *Heart Chamber*'s second act, the composer discharges wave after wave of snarling low brass sound, punctuated at first by timpani and bass drum and later accumulating other sounds (distorted guitar, pounding piano) to become a solid wall of noise. It would seem that nothing especially violent has occurred in the drama to precipitate this catastrophe: we've just witnessed the couple's first phone call, and they've agreed to go for a walk. But the possibility of happiness, tantalizing and fragile, has evidently unleashed a kind of inner hell for each character. The white noise of panic overwhelms the body's control center. A surging river of chemicals floods the brain. If you have ever experienced the mood swings that accompany the sensation of being helplessly, dangerously in love, you are likely to find this section both frightening and all too plausible.

The hyper-refinement of Czernowin's sound world gives rise to an unusual problem: on the infrequent occasions that she makes use of conventionally produced sounds, those sounds can seem unpleasantly coarse. Sometimes this contrast in texture is startling and effective: midway through *Infinite now*, a sudden surge of pre-recorded synthetic strings (taken from a BBC broadcast) makes for a welcome palate cleanser. But elsewhere, these conventionally produced sounds feel clumsy when compared to the extreme rarefaction of their surroundings. At the performance of *Heart Chamber* I heard, for example, I found that when the baritone soloist sang in the register that is typical for his voice type, the effect was sometimes "operatic" in the bad sense: bland, emotionally unspecific, self-serious. But surely it's an achievement in itself that Czernowin is capable of retuning our ears so thoroughly that a familiar sound suddenly seems unacceptably gauche! The main effect of these minuscule lapses, for me, was to remind me of the breathtaking inventiveness of the other ninety-nine percent of the score.

Heart Chamber ends with the spoken words "I love you." All throughout this painstaking account of a love affair, we have not yet heard this phrase. And yet it surely lay at the core of everything we *have* heard—all the piece's storms, crises, collisions. By daring to end with this most naked, most vulnerable of statements ("clear, true," the composer writes in her direction to the singer), Czernowin creates the sense that this phrase is *Heart Chamber*'s final excavation, and its most hard-won. The opera boils down to "I love you." In this, as in so much else, *Heart Chamber* is a liberation.

Finding Eurydice

urydice, the opera I recently finished writing with the playwright Sarah Ruhl, was a labor of love. I mean that in more ways than one. The piece is itself an anatomy of love and the Herculean labors that it asks of us, and I started work on it at the same time that I fell in love myself: I sketched the opera's first scene in the same week, at the end of 2015, that I met my husband, Clay. I'm usually skeptical of close life-to-art correspondences, but I do think that the music of *Eurydice*'s first act—most of which I wrote in Nova Scotia, during the first extended trip Clay and I took together—has a sense of innocence that's unusual in my music, and that surely owes something to the unselfconscious joy I was feeling at the time.

I've just put the last touches on the revised version of the opera's score. After *Eurydice*'s premiere in Los Angeles, I made a few minor edits in anticipation of future production at New York's Metropolitan Opera. The singers already have their music; the full score and orchestral parts are now being shipped to the Met's library. *Eurydice* is finally out of my hands.

It's unwise, when one's in the midst of a musical endeavor, to ever look back—just ask Orpheus. But now that there's a modicum of distance between *Eurydice*'s life and my own, I want to reflect on the long, tortuous journey of its creation.

EURYDICE'S PRE-GENESIS

From 2012 to 2014, I worked as a part-time pianist and assistant conductor on the Met's music staff, and as a freelancer at opera houses around the world. I was also a grad student at Juilliard at the time, studying for a master's degree in composition. To do both at once proved impossible—impossible in the bad sense. It was a train wreck. Every day during the periods when I was working on a Met production, I was required to be in two places at once. The fact that the two institutions were separated only by the asphalt moat of West Sixty-Fifth Street did little to make the situation workable.

My goal was to put myself through a double trial by fire. On one side of Sixty-Fifth Street, at Juilliard, I wanted to whip my still-sloppy composition technique into shape with the help of my teacher, the composer Robert Beaser, and the school's legendary ear-training guru, Mary Anthony Cox. Across the street, in the bowels of the Met, I was looking to hone my craft as a conductor and pianist. (As my boss Craig Rutenberg put it in an email I still cherish, "there's nothing like getting your hands sticky and gooey by being at the bowl of pasta dough before it becomes spaghetti.") The Met job both forced me to master challenging scores at the piano—my assignments included Thomas Adès's

The Tempest and Shostakovich's *The Nose* (1930)—and afforded me the opportunity to work with, and observe, an astounding array of artists in many disciplines: the visual artist and director William Kentridge; the choreographer Crystal Pite; conductors including Valery Gergiev and Adès himself; singers like Renée Fleming, Simon Keenlyside, and Peter Mattei.

I wouldn't want to relive the crucible of those two years—I doubt my nervous system could handle it. But I'm grateful that I put myself through it, because this impossible situation led to an unlikely opportunity.

Word must have gotten around the Met that the new kid on the music staff was also a composer, and the company's dramaturg and director of new works, Paul Cremo, came to hear a student recital that featured some of my music. Next thing I knew, I'd been invited to meet with Peter Gelb, the Met's general manager, as well as Cremo, Sarah Billinghurst (the company's beloved second-in-command), and André Bishop, the artistic director of Lincoln Center Theater. The Met and Lincoln Center Theater had just formed a partnership for the development and incubation of new works. Would I be interested, they asked, in writing an opera?

This was, needless to say, a thrilling invitation for a twenty-three-year-old composer to receive. But it was also a temporarily paralyzing one.

Young composers are accustomed to working within clearly defined, sometimes-stifling parameters. You've got seven instruments, now write a ten-minute piece. Or you've got a big orchestra, but you can write only a *three*-minute piece. Around the time I started this dialogue with the Met team, one project I was working on—my chamber opera *Second Nature* (2015), commissioned by the Lyric Opera of Chicago—came with comically specific requirements: the piece had to be under an hour long and suitable for audiences as young as second graders; the "orchestra" could consist of no more than three musicians; and the opera would premiere at Chicago's Lincoln Park Zoo, where there was no guarantee that the performances wouldn't be interrupted by squawking toucans or trumpeting elephants. In the end, I had a blast writing *Second Nature*, not in spite of these restrictions but *because* of them. There were so many decisions I didn't have to make!

The Met project posed the opposite challenge. There was no guarantee they'd actually produce the opera I wrote (that would depend on a successful "workshop" performance), but when it came to the piece's scale—the practical considerations that usually, for better or worse, give a new work its shape—the invitation was wide-open. I was welcome to dream big, to imagine making full use of the company's peerless orchestra, chorus, and theatrical apparatus. It felt like being invited to paint a mural on the side of the Flatiron Building, or to redesign Mount Rushmore. What kind of piece would feel *right* on such a huge canvas?

To my consternation, I felt thoroughly stuck. I explored, tested, and abandoned idea after idea. This one felt too much like a spoken play; that one felt pretentious; that other one depended on an overcommitted collaborator who was unlikely to deliver a full libretto.

Nearly two years after the Met's initial invitation, I still hadn't so much as decided on a subject. I felt like a failure, an ingrate. How the hell had I been so slow to act on a once-in-a-lifetime opportunity? I was sure that any day I'd get a call telling me I'd missed my chance, and that there were plenty of *other* young composers who would be glad to, you know, *do something*.

And then, in the spring of 2015, right around the time my opera *Crossing* had its premiere in Boston, my body and psyche let me know in no uncertain terms that I needed to press "pause," to slow down and catch my breath—*immediately*.

From the outside, things probably looked like they were going okay for me, but I knew I was at serious risk of burnout. The previous three years, since I'd graduated from college, had been exhilarating, but I can't say they'd been entirely happy. In my mistrustful amazement at the fact that I was actually making a living as a musician, and mainly as a *composer*—a prospect that had always seemed far-fetched, and still had a mirage-like quality—I had worked myself to the bone. I'd written one full-scale opera and one chamber opera, plus a ton of orchestral and chamber music. Though I paid rent in New York, I was traveling constantly, and found it hard to sustain even my closest friendships, never mind a romantic relationship. For the first time in my adult life, I felt a gnawing loneliness and an unsettling sense that I couldn't quite *see* myself: I had immersed myself so deeply in my scores that I felt at risk of disappearing into them, melting unnoticed into the river of notes.

The week of *Crossing*'s premiere, in May 2015, I happened upon a searing essay of self-revelation that my colleague Nico Muhly had published on his website. Nico is an artist of slippery, silver-tongued virtuosity in his scores and his social media feeds alike—he's often extremely funny—so I sat up straight when I realized this essay was dead serious, an unflinching reckoning with feelings of psychic and emotional burnout that had finally grown too strong for him to ignore. It's a beautiful and very raw piece of writing, and its relevance extends far beyond the field of classical music: future historians in search of a clear-eyed account of the warp-speed mercilessness of the mid-2010s gig economy should look no further.

With disarming candor, Nico describes his fixation on the pure lubricity of productiveness, the way that he found himself striving for the gig economy's unattainable, sleepless sublime. To my ears, some passages sounded more like professional advice from an Uber executive than the diary of a creative musician: "When people text me, I text them right back. I write back to emails quickly and try to stay connected to everybody . . . I write back to professional out-of-office emails with bitter, scathing essays about why it is that they can't manage to make their iPhones work in whatever sad holiday destination (Alicante, usually) they've chosen instead of performing professional immolation on the fires of productivity."

I read this essay at a falafel restaurant a block from Boston's Shubert Theatre, just a couple of hours before I conducted *Crossing*'s dress rehearsal. Reader, it scared the living shit out of me. I didn't want to admit it, but much of what Nico said felt bruisingly familiar. The polluted atmosphere he was describing was one that every American freelancer was forced to breathe. The unsustainable pace, the expectation of being perpetually and inextricably *connected*, the pressure to *produce*. How could anyone do deep or thoughtful work in these conditions? Such a culture might well produce a huge *quantity* of music, but would it be vital music, nourishing music, music that had been given time to bake all the way through?

The section of the essay that disturbed me most was Nico's description of his opera *Two Boys* (2011), a noirish tale of teenage loneliness, fraudulent online identities, and desperate attempts to connect via chat rooms in the "Wild West" days of the early-aughts internet. After seeing the opera staged, Nico came to feel that the piece was "a giant, expensive act of displacement and disengagement": he implied that his need for perpetual connection—and the exhaustion that it engendered—had leaked into his music, and maybe even determined his opera's subject and its aesthetic DNA.

I thought uneasily of my own opera, which I was going to share with thousands of people that same week. Sitting alone in that sterile, mostly empty chain restaurant, watching my colleagues—dancers, orchestra members, the tech crew—pass by outside on their way to the stage door, I wondered what exactly it was that I was about to reveal to the world. What was *Crossing*, anyway, other than an embarrassingly obvious self-portrait, an unconscious revelation of my own psychic Achilles' heel? And my idiosyncratic take on Walt Whitman—this chameleonic, connection-seeking wanderer, the guy who needs to convince everybody he's *totally okay*, that he's a radiant force of positivity and musicality, even as he flees from anything resembling real life—who was he if not me?

I knew then that I needed to take a break, slow *way* down, and really think about—or not even think about, but *feel my way toward*—what both my life and my music needed to be.

That summer, after wrapping up *Crossing*'s first run of performances, I stepped off the treadmill of work and gave myself the kind of psychic space I hadn't had since I was a teenager. I chased a couple of love affairs on a couple of continents. I road-tripped with friends in Europe and the American Southwest, and the latter journey led to a clarifying, purgative psychedelic experience on a backpacking trip in the wilderness of New Mexico.

Somewhere along the way, in those months of emotional regeneration, the new opera's idea came to me unbidden. Of course: I had to return to my old friend Orpheus.

FROM *THE ORPHIC MOMENT* TO *EURYDICE*

In the previous year, 2014, I had written a short "dramatic cantata" called *The Orphic Moment* that seems, in hindsight, almost like a study for *Eurydice*. Scored for countertenor, solo violin, and chamber ensemble, *The Orphic Moment* is a musical dilation of the final few milliseconds before Orpheus's backward look. It's a dark piece, one that gives voice to my personal reading of the myth: Orpheus, being the ultimate narcissistic aesthete, turns around not because of a momentary impulse but because he knows *loss* is the best possible nourishment for music.

I'm not typically the fastest-working of composers, but I sketched all seventeen minutes of *The Orphic Moment* in one weekend of furious work in Chicago, in the midst of an especially bitter midwinter "polar vortex." (There's no better incentive to getting work done than the feeling that even a quick trip outside might result in frostbite.) Writing *The Orphic Moment* was the kind of experience that, for me anyway, is all too rare: the piece emerged almost fully formed, a wrapped gift from the universe. It felt like a sign that I wasn't finished with this subject, that Orpheus and I had more to say to each other.

My original idea for the opera that became *Eurydice* was to expand the grim world of *The Orphic Moment* into an evening-length piece. But I ultimately soured on this idea. One reason was that it felt depressing to write yet another piece that does little but wallow in a male artist's narcissism for two and a half hours. The more important factor, though, was that I was introduced to Sarah Ruhl.

The suggestion that I connect with Sarah came from two trusted sources. One was André Bishop, who was a longtime colleague of hers. When I told André I was tempted to try my hand at an Orpheus adaptation, practically the next words out of his mouth were "Sarah Ruhl." The other source was my sister, Christine, who knows the world of contemporary theater far better than I do. She had been urging me to check out Sarah's work for years. I asked her if she thought André's suggestion was a good one, and she looked at me like I was crazy for even having to ask.

SARAH RUHL'S MAGICAL REALISM

I started to read Sarah's plays, and found myself repeatedly moved to tears in a way that was unfamiliar and a little distressing. I've always been susceptible to intense *musical* experiences, but if a piece of music is likely to overwhelm me, I can usually sense that possibility a mile off: the ground seems to shift beneath my feet, a wave takes shape and starts to crest. That's not how Sarah's plays operate with me. The emotion in her plays does not build—it blindsides. The devastating moments often seem to materialize out of nowhere, like cloudbursts. Reading her plays, I would feel perfectly calm one second, and the next I'd notice my eyes were wet and I was suffering some kind of severe ice-cream headache.

Sarah sees the world with a gaze so clear, so penetratingly innocent, that she remakes what she sees. She takes nothing for granted. Like Thomas Adès, she's gutsy enough to assume the role of the kid in "The Emperor's New Clothes": she refuses rules that many of her peers have accepted as grim, inescapable realities. In one of her essays on theater, she skewers the hideously transactional language that has infected the creative process of many a new play: "The language of 'investing in the character' is the language of capitalism," Sarah reminds us, and the act of "*tracking the main character's journey* . . . makes us into bloodhounds." She also posits the uncomfortably plausible idea that Aristotelian dramatic structure is based on "the structure of the male orgasm," and quotes one of her (male) students describing one of his own plays thus: "First it starts out, then it speeds up, and it's going and it's going, and then bam, it's over." Yikes. Too real.

The more I read of Sarah's work, the more qualities I noticed that seemed ready-made for opera. For one thing, she prefers poetry to prose: her plays might *seem* to be written in prose, but their true fabric, secretly, is poetry. In this, she strikes me as something of a unicorn among contemporary American playwrights (at least the ones I've encountered), many of whom prefer to write in a register that's about as lyrical as the dialogue on *Seinfeld*.

Sarah also prefers text to subtext. She regards the postmodern fixation on subtext—the idea that, in a play, what a character is *really* saying can't possibly be what they *say* they say—with quizzical mistrust. "If you're acting in a play of mine," she writes in one essay, "please, don't think one thing and then say another thing. Think the thing you are saying."

These two aesthetic preferences—poetry over prose, text over subtext—are linked: "Did the rise of subtext correspond to the rise of prose on stage over and above poetry on stage?" she wonders. Poetry, like music, is capable of obliterating subtext with sheer *presence*: "How to indicate subtext when singing a song from

The Tempest? One speaks or sings, 'Full fathom five thy father lies,' and one thinks something different? Impossible." This last statement might remind us of the ethos of another stellar librettist, our old friend W. H. Auden, who insisted that "music is immediate actuality and neither potentiality nor passivity can live in its presence." (I bet Sarah and Auden would have gotten along famously.)

Yet another quality that makes Sarah's work opera-ready: she is a surrealist, or perhaps a magical realist. It's perfectly reasonable, in a Sarah Ruhl play, for a character to grow so depressed that she turns into an almond, or for a man to drag an enormous yew tree across North America in hopes of saving his dying lover with medicine made from its bark. Fantastical occurrences like these have led some commentators to describe her plays as "whimsical" or "quirky." She rightly despises both adjectives, because they imply that the moments of obvious, *visible* magic are random or unwarranted, rather than a natural consequence of the subtle warping of space-time that is actually present *throughout* each play. In much of her work, Sarah quietly refuses the rigid distinction between interior experience and exterior action. With this in mind, transforming into an almond is really not such an unlikely consequence of depression.

And then there's the improbable beauty of Sarah's stage directions, which often seem to be self-contained micro-poems, personalized messages to the reader or performer. Sarah italicizes her stage directions, but she does not enclose them within the embarrassment of parentheses. I never noticed, till I read Sarah's plays, that the sequestering of stage directions into parentheses can disfigure a text: doing so tends to imply that it's regrettable that these directions have to be included at all, that they ought to be hurried through or swept under the rug. Sarah's, by contrast, tend to look more like this:

The Father creates a room out of string for Eurydice.
He makes four walls and a door out of string.
Time passes.
It takes time to build a room out of string.

A passage like this—with the generous indication "Time passes. It takes time . . ."—is practically an invitation for a spacious orchestral interlude. In fact, Sarah's plays are regularly dotted with these "orchestral" sequences. They're like parks within the city map of a play's text, green open spaces where music might grow and breathe. What more could a composer ask for?

Sarah's play *Eurydice* (2004) retells the Orpheus and Eurydice myth through the eyes of its heroine; we spend most of the play down in the underworld with Eurydice rather than with Orpheus in the world above. Sarah also adds to the mix an invented character, Eurydice's father, who is modeled on her own. (The Father is arguably the play's most important character after Eurydice herself—he upstages even Orpheus.) The play is as much a meditation on the fragility of memory as it is an exploration of the usual Orphic themes of love and art: the amnesic waters of the River of Forgetfulness hover in the background, threatening to erase everything we see before us. Like the room that the Father builds for Eurydice out of string, there is a poignant tenuousness to the drama, a sense that everything we've come to love could, at any moment, be washed away before our eyes.

My first instinct, after I'd read *Eurydice*, was to fuse Sarah's characterization of Eurydice with my own post–*Orphic Moment* conception of Orpheus. But the more I tried, the more I realized the two were incompatible. My slightly sadistic Orpheus didn't want to play nicely with Sarah's openhearted Eurydice; they had nothing to say to each other. So I had to make a choice: Would I continue to inhabit my own grimly musky Orphic world, or would I fully engage with Sarah's radically different reading of the myth?

Well, you know the answer. After *Crossing*, which I'd come to feel ran the risk of being an unconsciously solipsistic psychodrama, I wanted to expand my music's range by engaging with another artist's work. In the end, I chose *Eurydice* precisely because it's *not* my version of the myth, because it inhabits a universe that I couldn't have dreamed up myself. I didn't want Wagnerian sameness; I wanted Stravinsky-and-Auden tension and transformation. Sarah's *Eurydice* was mythic yet personal, grand yet intimate, theatrically savvy but also patient and wise. It felt magical, in a sometimes-goofy, *Alice in Wonderland* way, but its magic did not dilute its emotional verisimilitude. It traced a winding, looping, recursive shape; it refused to sweatily strive for the expected climaxes ("it's going and it's going, and then bam, it's over"). All this felt to me like a bracing breath of fresh air.

I also felt there was room to expand on the play through music. Some of its theatrical effects—the raining elevator that carries the newly dead down to the underworld; the construction of the "string room"—would surely be even more potent with the added horsepower of an orchestra. And I wagered that music might fruitfully complicate a couple of its characters, especially Orpheus. It seemed to me that *Eurydice* had the potential to expand to opera's larger-than-life scale without losing its identity—a bit like Alice herself, when she steps into her "wonderland."

ADAPTING *EURYDICE*

I was already deep into the composition of *Eurydice* when I noticed something important: *Eurydice* is not, at its core, an Orpheus and Eurydice piece. It's an entirely different story within which the Orpheus and Eurydice myth is embedded. Yes, the myth's crucial events do occur: Orpheus goes down to the underworld, he makes the fatal mistake of looking back, etc. But these events feel almost incidental to Eurydice's journey.

At the beginning of the opera, Orpheus and Eurydice are a young couple ("a little too young and a little too in love," in Sarah's description). Orpheus impetuously proposes, and Eurydice—a little unsure of herself—says yes. At their wedding, Eurydice finds she can't stop thinking about her father, who has recently died. She steps out of the party for a drink of water, and encounters a mysterious man who claims that he has a letter for her from her father. At first Eurydice doesn't believe him, but before long, she convinces herself that of *course* her father would try to send her a message from the afterlife on her wedding day. She leaves the party and follows the man to his penthouse apartment, where he attempts to hypnotize and seduce her. (The man, it turns out, is Hades, Lord of the Underworld.) Eurydice tries to escape, and falls to her death down the thousands of stairs that lead from Hades's penthouse into the land of the dead.

Down in the underworld, Eurydice passes through the River of Forgetfulness and loses her memory. In this blank, disoriented state, she encounters her deceased father, who patiently helps her to recover her sense of herself. Meanwhile, up above, Orpheus resolves to come find her. He descends, and successfully moves the Stones—three obnoxious, Greek chorus–like guardians of the underworld—to tears with his music. Hades explains the rules of Eurydice's liberation: she may follow Orpheus back to the world of the living, but he must not look back to make sure she's behind him.

As Eurydice walks behind Orpheus, she starts to doubt whether it's really him in front of her. In a moment of panic, she calls his name. Orpheus turns and looks at her. (Eurydice is not only the drama's center of gravity; she is also culpable for Orpheus's backward look.) The lovers are pulled apart as if by a magnetic force. Eurydice returns to the underworld.

Meanwhile, Eurydice's father, distraught at her departure, decides to dip himself in the River of Forgetfulness—an action that, for an already-dead person, is tantamount to suicide. By the time Eurydice returns, her father has obliterated his memory. Eurydice, left alone, decides to do the same. She writes Orpheus a last letter and dips herself in the river. In the drama's final moments, we see Orpheus descending again, this time in the elevator that carries the souls of the dead. (Maybe he has killed himself, or maybe decades have passed in an instant, and he has simply died of old age.) He sees Eurydice and is overjoyed, but as he walks toward her, he is rained on by the waters of forgetfulness. He forgets everything. He picks up Eurydice's letter, but cannot read it.

The last scene is a Shakespearean piling-up of bodies: it feels, with its multiple missed connections, more like *Romeo and Juliet* than Orpheus and Eurydice. And there's no equivalent in the original myth for the play's middle act, which consists mostly of *waiting*: Eurydice slowly relearning her identity in the underworld, Orpheus wasting away up above. There's a special glow to this act, a warmth, a patience: *it takes time to build a room out of string*. In a world in which plays often face pressure to perpetually crackle with nervous energy lest they lose the attention of a distractible audience, I relish the way that this long sequence slows the passage of time and pauses to reflect.

My job in adapting *Eurydice* was to ensure that the play's characters would both survive the journey from speech into song and be transformed in the process. Since every character posed their own unique challenge, let's take a look at each one.

EURYDICE

Eurydice is the core of the drama, and the only character who evolves: the Father is dead, and his geniality has assumed its Platonic eternal form; Hades is an immutably banal force of darkness; and poor Orpheus, a simple singer-songwriter type, isn't really capable of growing up. Eurydice, on the other hand, undergoes a dizzyingly nonlinear psychological journey.

When we first meet her, she's a kid, an exceedingly smart and very self-conscious teenager or college student, someone who's prone to overthinking every situation. Eurydice is as closely aligned with language as Orpheus is with music, and she manifests all the uncertainties that tend to accompany a language-centric worldview: she often gets flummoxed when she's required to give an unambiguous answer or take decisive action. Wrapped in her own thoughts, she strikes us, at first, as sweet, guileless, a little awkward.

But at her wedding, Eurydice gives voice to something deeper: a raw, unhealed grief at the loss of her father, a still-open wound that makes her susceptible to Hades's advances. At the beginning of Act Two, after she has died and passed through the River of Forgetfulness, she is unrecognizable. She has been reduced to a terrified tabula rasa; she has no idea who she is or what has happened to her. When she encounters her father, Eurydice reacts with a jittery defensiveness, almost like a dementia patient: she's under the impression that she has just arrived at a hotel in some unknown city, and her father is the incompetent bellhop who's to blame for everything going wrong.

As Eurydice's memories ripen in her, she passes through multiple life phases before our eyes. When her father teaches her new words, we witness her preadolescent curiosity, the special teacher-student bond that can form between a dad and a super-smart nine- or ten-year-old. When Eurydice finally remembers Orpheus, she seems to enter a new adolescence, to experience the first flush of longing all over again.

It's all downhill from here: in the final act, when Orpheus arrives, Eurydice panics—she's not sure if she wants to follow him. She precipitates Orpheus's backward look by calling his name: as usual with Eurydice, language itself is to blame. After Orpheus looks back, Eurydice suffers a second death and returns briefly to her tabula rasa state, which turns to real desolation only when she discovers that her father is also newly lost to her. In the opera's final scene, however, Eurydice evinces a deep, hard-won serenity: her last action is to write a generous, loving letter to Orpheus's future wife.

That's a pretty formidable range of affects for one character! If I was to have any chance of doing justice to Eurydice's nuances, I would have to treat each of her psychological states as its own "voice." This would inevitably make a daunting ask of the singer. It has become a truism in the opera world that the role of Violetta, in Verdi's *La traviata*, demands (impossibly) a different type of voice for each of the opera's three acts. Without in any way comparing myself to Verdi, I'm afraid I may have written a not-dissimilar challenge into Eurydice's music. This is a soprano role that requires a number of almost self-contradictory qualities: beauty of tone; agility; speechlike directness; tensile, steely strength. Her music in the opera's first act is mostly lyrical and sweet, but once she arrives in the underworld she vacillates between distracted, birdlike fleetness and expressions of something wilder and more desperate. These latter outbursts call for a sound with a dramatic edge.

What makes the role particularly tricky is that these sections often follow one another with no notice—it's like flipping a switch, both in the psyche and in the voice. No wonder that a couple of very lovely lyric sopranos, who were under consideration for the part, looked through the music and said no thanks, that's not for me. This role requires a singer who is willing to take some chances. (Thankfully, both Danielle de Niese, who sang the world premiere in LA, and Erin Morley, who will sing the role in New York, are adventurous souls.)

Sarah told me that Rainer Maria Rilke's poem "Orpheus. Eurydice. Hermes" was on her mind when she was writing the play; it struck her as one of the few pieces of Orphic art by a male artist that considers Eurydice's subjective experience:

> She was deep within herself, like a woman heavy
> with child, and did not see the man in front
> or the path ascending steeply into life.
> Deep within herself. Being dead
> filled her beyond fulfillment. Like a fruit
> suffused with its own mystery and sweetness,
> she was filled with her vast death, which was so new,
> she could not understand that it had happened.

She had come into a new virginity
and was untouchable . . .

(trans. Stephen Mitchell)

The mystical warmth of Rilke's poem—the sense of something ripening from within—was an important clue, for me, to the atmosphere of the opera's second act, which culminates in Eurydice's aria "Orpheus never liked words . . . This is what it is to love an artist." This aria is really the fulcrum of the whole opera. It is in this moment that we know Eurydice has fully returned to herself, because she has remembered what it was to be in love. It's a moment of total sensory openness, and it eventually verges into erotic ecstasy. The memory of love becomes, for a moment, overwhelmingly present.

Eurydice compares being in love with Orpheus to being lit by the moon's beautiful but cold light: when you're with Orpheus, "the moon is always rising above your house." I sculpted each of Eurydice's first phrases so that they reach upward, like limited, mortal attempts to trace the moonrise. At a certain point, a shadow passes over the harmony, and the moon seems to change direction, to start setting. Eurydice's lines now tend helplessly downward: "But he is always going away from you," she sings.

After Eurydice has traced this sad shape—upward-reaching, downward-sliding—she remembers a single moment of happiness. "Words can mean anything," Orpheus had said to her. "Show me your body—it only means one thing." Eurydice repeats these last words in a smiling, mumbling sort of way ("it only means one thing, it only means one thing"), as if she and Orpheus are both a little drunk, a little sleepy, fumblingly undressing each other. The phrasing here was inspired by a moment I love in Joni Mitchell's song "All I Want," a tipsy, deliriously sexy repeated line—"wanna make you feel free, wanna make you feel free." If I could make one recommendation to sopranos who sing this aria, it would be to make it as Joni-esque as possible.

I remember that when I was composing this music, I could see the long climactic section coming from a long way off; I could sense the way that this huge wave was going to slowly, inexorably crash ashore. I remember thinking, Am I really going to do this? Am I really going to write music this open, this vulnerable? But by then it was too late: I'd already heard what the music wanted to be. If I'd stopped to think, I might not have dared.

ORPHEUS AND HIS DOUBLE

Of the characters in the original play, Orpheus was the only one I felt the need to fundamentally rethink. We musicians are notoriously sensitive to imprecise deployments of musical language (just try using the phrase "build to a crescendo" around a musician), and the play's Orpheus is prone to a certain kind of generalized musical rhapsody: the way he announces "Symphony for twelve instruments" before conducting the music that he hears in his head, or his search for a magical "note" that will transport him to the underworld. I don't think a musician could have written these lines, which—unlike the rest of the play—struck me as a tad too cute.

How to give our Orpheus the dark, Dionysian sense of mystery that I knew the character was capable of? It occurred to me that just as Eurydice is torn between her love for Orpheus and her attachment to her father, Orpheus is torn between his love for Eurydice and for music. One of the flaws of Orpheus and Eurydice's relationship is that Eurydice never quite believes that Orpheus is showing her *all* of himself. There is something inaccessible about him, some presence she can't quite see, like the "third who walks always beside you" in Eliot's *The Waste Land*.*

I decided to give this hidden facet of Orpheus a body and a voice. Orpheus in his mortal guise is a pretty normal guy, and I made him a baritone (which is surely the "regular guy" of operatic voice types). Orpheus's Double, on the other hand—an embodiment of his musical, magical side—is a countertenor.† In some sections of the opera, the baritone-Orpheus sings by himself. But whenever he goes into one of his frequent musical trances, the baritone is bathed in a halo of countertenor sound.

Orpheus's Double poses a certain dramaturgical challenge—what does he look like, anyway?—but I hope it's one that stage directors will relish, since it's wide-open to interpretation. The only thing I'm sure of is that Eurydice cannot see the Double, though she sometimes senses his presence. I can imagine a wide range of theatrical solutions: the Double might sometimes be invisible, singing from the orchestra pit or offstage; he might look exactly like Orpheus, and be onstage the whole time; or he might be a totally different kind of being, an Ariel-like spirit floating somewhere over Orpheus's head.

THE FATHER

Eurydice's father is a big, generous spirit, and most of his lines translated seamlessly to song. But there's one important excep-

---

* "Who is the third who walks always beside you? / When I count, there are only you and I together / But when I look ahead up the white road / There is always another one walking beside you / . . . I do not know whether a man or a woman."

† Chaya Czernowin also represents a single character with a baritone and a countertenor in *Heart Chamber*. Evidently she and I had the idea around the same time: *Heart Chamber* and *Eurydice* premiered within three months of each other.

tion, one scene that did *not* readily lend itself to music. Just before the Father dips himself in the River of Forgetfulness, he prepares for this irreversible step by recalling the directions to his child-hood home in Iowa. He narrates, in detail, an imagined return to his psyche's primal scene: take Tri-state South 294 to Route 88 West, then follow the back roads, look for the house with a good climbing tree in the yard, then get out of your car, take off your shoes, and walk down the hill toward the Mississippi River, where "catfish are sleeping in the mud." It's one of the play's most haunting moments, a quintessentially Ruhlian mingling of the quotidian and the metaphysical.

In my first draft of the opera, I set these lines to a lyrical, slow-as-molasses melody that unfolded above a meditative, "om"-like drone in the orchestra. I wanted to create the sense that the Fa-ther was following the liquid line of his own sound deep into his consciousness, into the waters of memory.

It didn't work. When we tried this scene out in a workshop, it sounded awful; the whole aria felt melodramatic and artificially inflated. I realized the problem was that the Father was singing at all. Throughout this scene, he's supposed to be stripping away his social self, returning to a childlike ur-state. The very act of *singing*—an act of self-magnification, of projecting oneself out into the vast space of the auditorium—was all wrong for this moment.

Somehow, Sarah, Mary Zimmerman (the production's direc-tor), and I all reached the same conclusion independent of one another: the Father should speak this whole sequence rather than sing it. I rewrote the scene with the Father speaking over a gentle, watery texture in the orchestra—tuned gongs, bowed vibraphone—and a softly humming chorus. It was a big improve-ment. After the premiere in Los Angeles, a number of people told me this was their favorite scene in the opera. (I wasn't quite sure how to feel about the fact that people's favorite scene was also the one in which there is almost no singing.)

HADES

Operatic villains tend in general to have low voices, and operatic *devil* figures, from Berlioz to Boito to Stravinsky, are almost inevitably snarling, sneering basses or baritones. This also applies specifically to the Hades/Pluto role in Orphic operas: he is a sonorous bass in Monteverdi, Peri, Caccini, Rossi, and Charpentier's versions of the myth.

The Hades of *Eurydice* is certainly demonic, but he has very different DNA from his diabolical cousins. This Hades is an absurd figure, a shapeshifter who first takes the guise of a sleazy middle-aged businessman and later becomes a ten-foot-tall giant. (In Mary Zimmerman's production, our Hades, the spectacular Barry Banks, has to sing his vocally arduous final scene on stilts.) Everything he says is a little bit . . . *off*. His attempts at small talk begin with the line "Hello. Are you a homeless person?" He is an apparition out of Lewis Carroll, a creature who lives on the border between the comic and the terrifying.

How to musicalize such a character? Surely Hades had to be some kind of extreme voice type, but he possesses none of the gravitas that we typically associate with the Lord of the Underworld. So I decided he should live at the opposite extreme: he had to be a tenor, an *extremely high* tenor. I wanted to create the sense that when Hades visits the human world, he sounds a bit like he's just inhaled a gulp of helium, but he has no idea how ridiculous he sounds. For him, this tone of voice is normal. For everyone else, it's pretty freaky.

Of course, Hades doesn't hang out at the giddy top of his range all night. The whole point is that he can turn on a dime and become quite scary. The first sign of this comes in his first scene. He has just met Eurydice outside her wedding, and she—slightly weirded out by him—has turned to leave. Hades, however, has a plan: he pretends to serendipitously find a letter from her father lying on the ground. Until this moment, the orchestra has been playing a muffled version of the music from the wedding party, heard from afar: a muted but insistent pulse in the bass, violins chattering like party guests. When Hades snaps his fingers to get Eurydice's attention, the whole orchestra "snaps" with him. This moment should be a jolt: the earth should seem to shake, the lights flicker. I want the listener to feel in their bones that Hades is actually the puppet master of everything we see.

There's another jarring contrast in the following scene, when Hades leads Eurydice to his penthouse apartment. At first, he's impossible to take seriously: he puts on terrible mood music, leaves, and returns wearing a ratty bathrobe. But when he finally grabs Eurydice's hand, the mood changes, and Hades becomes a kind of snake charmer: his aria, "Orpheus's fingers are weak and long," is one long act of hypnotism, full of teasing curlicues around a droning D-natural. When he returns to the high notes that are his home turf, there is a new violence to them.

A Conversation with Sarah Ruhl

The composer-librettist relationship tends to be a pretty fraught one: John Adams has said that such collaborations are arguably, "next to double murder-suicide, . . . the most painful thing two people can do together." So I feel extra lucky that Sarah and I forged a friendship in the course of creating *Eurydice*. Whenever I found myself at a creative impasse, I knew that a phone call to Sarah was likely to leave me feeling refreshed. I think you'll feel the same way. Let's give her a call.

MATT: In one of our first conversations about adapting *Eurydice*, I remember that you brought up some of the funny moments in the play; I think we were talking through how various scenes might translate to music. I recall that you asked, though maybe not in these exact words, "Can opera be funny?"

I remember wanting to laugh and cry when you asked that, first of all out of sheer gratitude that I was working with you, because the answer to your question was of course *yes*, opera desperately needs joy and levity and absurdity in its tool kit.

But I remember also thinking that opera has really failed at some basic task if someone as deeply versed in the theater as

Sarah Ruhl is wondering if opera is, by its very nature, incapable of being funny. That struck me as a very depressing failure on the part of opera-makers. I decided in that moment that no matter what else we achieved in *Eurydice*, we should make sure that there were a few laugh-out-loud funny moments—moments where the audience would not sort of chuckle knowingly, as opera audiences often do, but where they would actually be at risk of peeing themselves.

This is a roundabout way of asking what your impression of opera was when we first started working on *Eurydice*, since you hadn't written a libretto before, and whether that impression changed at all through the process of workshopping the piece and bringing it to life.

SARAH: Yes, I do remember that. I had never seen a funny opera. And I certainly had not seen a funny contemporary opera. I had an idea that maybe some Mozart operas were meant to be funny. But I had no deep experience of laughing at an opera. And for me—laughing is a portal to grief, and the comic and the tragic exist side by side in my plays, and certainly in *Eurydice*. When I heard your first scene, I knew immediately that you were able to find humor in the way that you rhythmicized language. One example: when Orpheus asks Hades if he liked his music and you wrote a musical line that I am not sure I can describe but you can describe much better, something like, "No—o!" With the "No" starting very low and going up. And that was funny. And I cannot tell you why, but it was a bit of a musical joke, partly because of the way it imitated human speech. There were also musical jokes in the blending of genres—in the ridiculous rock and roll song that cycled through the wedding music. I was so grateful that I was able to belly laugh at rehearsals.

MATT: I think we got some belly laughs from our audiences in Los Angeles, too—and not always in the places I expected. I had no idea, for example, that people would find it funny when Orpheus switches into Latin for his plea at the gates of Hell ("Felix, qui potuit boni"), but it got this huge wave of laughter at every performance. I remember on opening night I was so startled by this sudden gale of sound behind me—I was in the pit conducting— that I think I might have actually turned around in surprise, as if to ask the audience what was so funny. (Which is very rude, of course, turning around to stare at the audience. A real breach of opera-conductor etiquette.)

SARAH (*laughing*): Yes, that's right. And I never knew that you almost turned around in surprise. Nor did I know that it was a breach of etiquette to look at the audience.

MATT: It usually feels like an intrusion to me when a conductor turns and looks at the audience, since they tend to look sort of dictatorial—like a teacher turning around at the blackboard to scold the class.

Anyway, that moment at the gates isn't necessarily comic in itself, but admittedly we did sort of invite laughter by adding a line for one of the Stones: Orpheus is standing outside the gates, the Stones say he won't be allowed in, and then Big Stone (who is not the brightest bulb) announces imposingly that the only way Orpheus might succeed is if he sings in a "dead language."

SARAH: Yes, exactly.

MATT: The reason we added this line is itself pretty funny. It seemed perfectly natural to both of us that Orpheus would switch into a dead language for this critical moment—it's like he's casting a spell, so there needs to be a sense of magic to it. You don't want to *understand*, you just want it to be this overwhelming sensory experience. In *The Lord of the Rings*, if Gandalf spoke his spells in English, it wouldn't sound magical at all, it would just sound silly.

SARAH: I think it was also a moment of reaching for the sublime; that since Orpheus was a poet and a musician, and he sang music beautiful enough to make stones cry, the poetry of what he sings should be almost beyond the reach of mortals—not quotidian— that there should be a slight opacity to the words so that we ease completely into the music. We chose Latin because it sounds so beautiful sung, and because the Boethius poem about Orpheus, which is quoted at that moment, is quite beautiful.

MATT: But in a workshop of the opera, we got a lot of pushback from some of our colleagues, who said that the Latin didn't make sense to them. We expended a lot of energy insisting that it's not supposed to make *sense*, it's supposed to be a *spell*.

And then I remember you added that line for Big Stone ("You have to sing in a dead language") in a sort of exasperation, as a way of convincing our colleagues to keep this Latin bit that we both loved. It was a way of saying, "Sorry, we *have* to keep the Latin, the Stones say so." And it turns out that this inside joke translated to the piece itself, communicated itself to the audience.

SARAH: Yes, it was a joke, and an explanation, and also, I suppose, in league with the moment when Eurydice can't speak in the language of the dead to the audience. There is an untranslatability of experience: "Try speaking in the language of stones," the stone gatekeepers say to her when she tries to wake up her father.

MATT: Another moment where the audience reaction amazed me is the moment when Eurydice calls Orpheus's name, and he looks back. Every single night, there was this enormous gasp behind me in the auditorium; sometimes people literally yelled, "Oh, no!"

This is bizarre, right? The piece is called *Eurydice*; most people in the audience surely knew that Orpheus was going to look back. And yet it causes this visceral response every single time. Why do you think that is?

SARAH: I love that moment. And it happened in the stage play version too. I always felt it meant we were doing our jobs right. That the myth has an inevitability that we forget for a while, and then we are surprised back into the moment of emotion, the moment of loss. That moment has captured the imagination of so many poets and musicians. We all wonder what is inside that gasp. The surprise of sudden loss that is beyond understanding. And that, unfortunately, is not only part of mythology, but part of what it is to be human.

MATT: Speaking of loss: the adaptation of a play into an opera entails metamorphosis, and with that comes loss. In a way, the play has to pass through its own River of Forgetfulness en route to becoming an opera. It becomes a blank slate before it's rebuilt anew. The rules are different in music's "underworld."

SARAH: I love that thought. That switching genre amounts to swimming in the River of Forgetfulness.

MATT: But *Eurydice* required waaay less transformation than many plays do. This is mostly because the play's often quite spare; it's not like adapting, say, a Shakespeare play, where you end up having to excise eighty percent of the text to keep the opera from being eight hours long.

SARAH: Thank God! I did think of the translation of play into opera as a kind of distillation. I once had a poetry teacher who was quite mathematical about "reductions." He would have us do a word count of a poem and then he'd say: "Reduce this poem by twenty percent." And, lucky for me, I love distillation and I love cutting as a practice. A kind of linguistic Zen-weeding. And then of course there is the comfort of the play being out in the world, so anything we had to cut for the opera remains in play form.

MATT: A couple of things in the play that ended up on the opera's cutting-room floor were Hades in the guise of a snotty kid on a tricycle, as well as a lot of the specific anecdotes that the Father retells *Eurydice* as she regains her memory. We also added new things: the vows that the couple speaks, which you originally wrote for the poet Max Ritvo's wedding; the presence of Orpheus's Double; the Latin; and so on.

SARAH: True. I don't miss Hades on his tricycle. And while I was sad to lose those specific anecdotes, there is something about them that is very much in the idiom of spoken word. Which makes sense; some of those stories that the Father tells in the play, I recorded on a tape recorder with my father talking. And my father did not speak in operatic cadence. Also, there's something about the opera form that resists digression, I think; whereas in a play you can sit in a story within a story for a while, the form of opera seems to want to press forward, with the momentum of the music.

And I did love being able to honor Max Ritvo by the addition of the blessing which I gave at his wedding. And I was able to tell him, while he was alive, that there would be a whisper of him in the Eurydice opera, and it pleased him greatly.

MATT: Now that we've finished the opera, how do you feel about those transformations? The process felt remarkably painless to me—the proof of that is that we're still on speaking terms, unlike many composer-librettist duos!—

SARAH: Is that right? Do composers and librettists come to blows?

MATT: —but I remember being very conscious along the way that the material we were working with was very close to your heart, since it derives from events in your life. It was refreshing to me how willing you were to try new things with it.

SARAH: It's true. That play sits very close under my skin. It helped that I've had twenty or so years to process the grief that gave birth to the play. It also helped that I've seen many, many productions of the play, and the repetition makes me feel that the play belongs more and more to other people—the collaborators, the audience—and less to me. Putting the play in a different form creates more space—to transform, to breathe.

MATT: One of the few moments in the play that gave us a lot of trouble was a very important section right at the drama's center: the extended sequence in which Eurydice slowly relearns her identity, with her father's help. He teaches Eurydice new words and tells her stories about their family, while Orpheus, up in the land of the living, makes various unsuccessful attempts to reach her.

In the play, there's a lot of cinematic jumping back and forth between the underworld and the overworld—a technique that works beautifully in a play, because the surrounding atmosphere is made of silence. But I realized it wouldn't work in our opera, because the underworld and the overworld had two distinct musical atmospheres. To jump back and forth between them again and again in a single scene would have felt a little bit hysterical, which was definitely not the mood we were going for.

SARAH: Right. And I think it took me a while to wrap my mind around that difference in form.

MATT: Weirdly, the solution was to *layer* the two worlds, to make the two scenes happen simultaneously: Orpheus pines for Eurydice at the same time as the Father, in a lovably geeky and very dad-like way, enthusiastically expands Eurydice's vocabulary with new words ("ostracize," "defunct").

SARAH: Yes, and I've come to love the way that sequence was built.

MATT: I remember that you were understandably skeptical about the wisdom of layering these two scenes—your concern was, if we layer them, won't we just *not understand anything at all*? I didn't have a very good answer: I think I basically said, "Probably not," but I also said that the big layered ensemble is one of my favorite tools in the operatic arsenal, and can we have one, Sarah, please, pleeeeeease can we have one? That was the gist of my argument, I think.

SARAH: It also makes me think about the relationship between prose and poetry, and how that difference slides into opera-land . . .

Let me try to parse. Poems *stop time*. In general, in plays and operas, one must move forward in time. But occasionally, in a play, one wants to stop time, with a poem of sorts, which seems to me quite like an aria. The section "This is what it is to love an artist" was originally a poem (I wrote it before I wrote *Eurydice*, then snuck it into the play), it became a soliloquy, and it now exists as an aria. (An exquisitely beautiful one, I might add—complimenting the composer. When I first heard it sung I thought my head would pop off, so transcendent did I feel.) Whereas the *stories* that the Father tells to Eurydice in the underworld are prose; anecdotes. They neither stop time nor move time forward. They circle time; which makes sense in the underworld, which is fairly static. But stasis is tricky in an opera (I would distinguish between stasis and stopping time—which is like catching your breath and having a moment of transcendence). I think Orpheus's heroic forward motion—*I want, I want, I must find her, I will find her!*—layered with the easy back-and-forth storytelling between the Father and Eurydice, works. Orpheus's forward motion almost pierces a language field that is deliberately more plainspoken and prosaic.

MATT: I never thought of it that way, but it's true—there's a tension *within the texture* between Eurydice / the Father's joy in the present, and Orpheus's lack of satisfaction, his need to push forward. Layering these two things made a really lush musical atmosphere possible, even if you lose a word here or there. Plus, I think the listener *can* understand what Eurydice and the Father are saying—I intentionally put their lines in the foreground and treated Orpheus / Orpheus's Double's lines more as a background musical texture.

SARAH: Yes, and losing a word here or there to higher purpose always interests me. The other thing that fascinates me about plays, and I think it's also true of operas, is that as a playwright or librettist you are in a profound linguistic paradox. The language is *everything*, and the language is *nothing*. The language creates the container for an experience that should be entirely beyond language.

MATT: Throughout this book, I've been exploring opera's inner workings—the invisible gravitational forces that are at play in the art form, the hidden laws that may help a given piece catch fire and burst into glorious life, while another seemingly worthy subject might fizzle. For example, one principle I've noticed is that in opera, all speech is dream speech, whether you want it to be or not. Everything that's sung has a slightly surreal, dreamlike quality. If you embrace this quality, the opera gods will smile on you. If you resist it, they're likely to get annoyed and play some pretty nasty tricks on you.

SARAH: Dream speech! All speech is dream speech! I love that! (It makes me think for a moment about John Berryman's *Dream Songs*.) It also reminds me of my favorite ars poetica from an eight-year-old I taught in Queens for a Poetry in the Schools project. I asked them to write a poem about what a poem is, and this young boy Patrick wrote: "Sing while you think / a poem is not so hard / if you sing while you think." I think that is like dream speech. Thinking and singing at the same time—that seems to be a requirement for opera.

MATT: You'd think so, though some singers definitely prefer singing *without* thinking . . .

I'm curious, now that you've been through a four-year operatic incubation process, if you've noticed these sorts of gravitational laws at work—and if so, what have you noticed?

SARAH: Let's see . . . gravitational laws . . . Distillation is one. Distill, distill, distill. And repetition: repeat, repeat, repeat. Maybe making vodka or wine is not so different from making opera. Though I've never made spirits, I imagine there is distillation and repetition involved. And this makes sense for a Dionysian form—we are making distillations for the spirit world.

MATT: Spirit spirits. I love it. On a related note, what other subjects do you think would make for good operas?

SARAH: I think mythic subjects are good—you and I talked about the Norse myths—some Shakespeare that has yet to be done. I *don't* want to see an opera about Trump, although the last two weeks have felt somewhat operatic. [*Note: we had this conversation in mid-January 2021.*] Students sometimes ask me what themes I return to again and again and I always say love and death. What else is there? My children think that is very boring and that I should make some inroads into new terrain. But I think the same holds for the opera world—love and death. And that's why Trump would make for a bad opera. There is no love in him.

EIGHT

Music as Forgiveness

Mozart's Le nozze di Figaro

A ny good rule needs an exception, right? The impossibility that is opera's lifeblood—the unattainability of its attempt to gather every artistic medium and every human sense into a single unified experience—both shapes and warps practically every opera ever written, but if any one work is capable of evading or surmounting this foundational impossibility, for me it's Mozart's *Le nozze di Figaro* (*The Marriage of Figaro*). *Figaro* would likely be my desert-island pick if I had to choose a single favorite work of art, period—and that includes books, movies, plays, and paintings as well as music. In this three-hour transfiguration of Beaumarchais's politically charged comedy, Mozart and the librettist Lorenzo da Ponte achieve an aerial view of the human soul, a portrait of everything that's irresistible and brilliant and sexy about human beings, and also the things that make us so infuriating to one another. The opera's secret ingredient is love.

Mozart loves his characters, even when they're at their lowest, and so we end up loving them too.

Figaro also has the unique ability to make me forget, as I experience it either as a conductor or a listener, that I'm hearing an opera at all. This is abnormal. In opera, artifice typically reigns supreme; usually this is part of its fun. When I perform or listen to Verdi or Wagner, I never forget that I'm experiencing a capital-O Opera, nor am I supposed to. The same is true, I think, of Mozart's other operas: as I experience *Don Giovanni* (1787) or *Die Zauberflöte* (1791), I never quite forget that I've been transported to a fantastical imaginary world.

But *Figaro* is a different beast. It is so close to reality that, in its uncannier moments, its artifice can't be perceived. Its music seems somehow to bypass my ears and enter my heart and psyche unmediated. The sensation of being immersed in *Figaro* is no different, for me, from the feeling of gratitude for being alive.

I'm hardly alone in my baffled amazement. "It is totally beyond me how anyone could create anything so perfect," no less an authority than Johannes Brahms once said of *Figaro*. "Nothing like it was ever done again, not even by Beethoven." The pianist Mitsuko Uchida chose *Figaro* as the work she would want as the soundtrack to her life: "It has everything that's central to people's lives . . . Only birth and death are missing."

And *Figaro* is the only opera I've ever conducted that, over the course of a given production, reliably provokes daily expressions of amazement from the cast, even from singers who've performed the piece dozens of times. It can be grueling to rehearse a single piece for a month or more; by the time the cast moves from the rehearsal room to the stage, it's not uncommon for everyone involved to be a bit tired of the opera at hand. But with *Figaro*, in my experience, hardly a rehearsal day goes by that someone or other doesn't pause, shake their head, and say, "This is just the greatest fucking thing ever, isn't it?"

In some ways, *Figaro* is responsible for my being a musician, and it's certainly responsible for my work in the field of opera. When I was eight years old or so, I loved classical music but couldn't stand opera, which I'd heard only bits of on Saturday-afternoon radio broadcasts. Operatic singing struck me as jarring and unpleasant. I was even a little embarrassed on the singers' behalf: they seemed to have no idea how silly they sounded.

For whatever reason, maybe because I was enthusiastic about Mozart and was playing some of his easier piano music at the time, my parents bought me a VHS tape of *Figaro*—Peter Hall's production, recorded at Glyndebourne in 1973. I realize now that this performance featured a dream cast of leading ladies: a young Kiri Te Kanawa as the Countess, an even younger Frederica von Stade as Cherubino, the Romanian soprano Ileana Cotrubaș as Susanna.

This video had a huge impact on me. It gave me the sense that I suddenly had direct access to formerly unknown adult emotions. I felt a visceral connection to Mozart's characters, a sympathy for them in my gut and my throat, in spite of their confusing grown-up problems. I didn't grasp the nuances of *Figaro*'s plot, but something communicated itself to me nonetheless. In the opera's ensemble scenes, Mozart has a way of layering his characters' psychic states such that we experience *the sum total of the spiritual energy in the room*. In these scenes, no emotion or intention can be hidden; every secret feeling is brought to light. All the guilt and desire and insecurities and loathing and love accumulate and cause the musical air molecules to vibrate furiously. I think what moved me, in these ensembles, was the sheer self-contradictory mass of them, the sense that I was in the presence of a complex, tightly wound ball of emotions whose strands I could never untangle. It's precisely because Mozart leaves nothing out and shows each person in all their messy contradictoriness that it's impossible to condemn his characters, no matter how awful they are to one another. The music is itself an act of forgiveness.

Figaro affected me in less lofty ways, too. One thing I love about Mozart is the inextricability, in his music, of the spiritual and the sensual, and *Figaro*, in addition to constituting a thorough spiritual education, is also very sexy. As an almost-adolescent listener, the dangerous, painfully prolonged erotic games in the opera's second act made me feel queasy. What on earth was I looking at? The androgynous Cherubino—the character is a teenage boy, but he's sung by an adult mezzo-soprano—is stripped of his pageboy outfit by two women, Susanna and the Countess, so that they can dress "him" up as a woman. (Cherubino is in big trouble, and they're trying to disguise him as a woman so he can avoid being sent to the army.)

It sure looks as if Cherubino and the Countess might end up having sex—or maybe the two of them and Susanna are on the verge of a threesome. I reasoned, as a nine-year-old, that the extreme erotic tension between these women was okay because Cherubino was "really" a boy—but then, I also tried to reason away my crush on von Stade's Cherubino by insisting to myself that Cherubino was "really" a girl. What did "reality" mean here anyway?

Whatever I was looking at, it was mighty queer. I had no idea music could embody such transcendently transgressive sensations, these fleeting surges of warmth, of uncontainable desire for *something* or other. I'd just begun to experience such sensations myself, and they made me feel very guilty. What did it mean that Mozart, that most angelic-sounding of composers, also evidently felt such things?

(In hindsight, I'm proud to claim von Stade's Cherubino as my first queer icon. She inhabited the role so completely that to this day, my mental image of Cherubino is von Stade and no one else. When I studied with the great Italian conductor Riccardo Muti, I was tickled to learn that he too had a special place in his heart for von Stade's page boy: "She *was* Cherubino," he said, speaking of von Stade with a combination of awe and affection that was highly unusual for him.)

I want to conclude this book with a close reading of the last few minutes of *Figaro*—a sequence that many before me have highlighted as one of the wonders of the operatic world. For Theodor Adorno, *Figaro*'s finale was "one of those [moments] for whose sake the entire . . . form might have been invented." The Icelandic artist Ragnar Kjartansson's aptly named performance piece *Bliss* (2011) consists of an excerpt from the finale of *Figaro* performed on loop for twelve hours. And I've turned to these few minutes of music many times in my own life, both in times of difficulty and in moments of joy.

I wouldn't dare to claim I can "explain" what makes these few minutes so magical. But maybe I can offer some clues.

Figaro is a long and complex work of theater, one that's riddled with numerous interleaving subplots, but to appreciate its finale, you only need to understand the narrative's basic through-line. Count Almaviva, a Spanish nobleman, has been lusting after Susanna, his wife's chambermaid, who is about to be married to his own manservant, Figaro. The Count has recently enacted an official abolition of the feudal droit du seigneur, the legendary right of the master of an estate to sleep with his female servants on their wedding nights. He knows that this enlightened gesture has earned him significant social capital among his servants, but he wants to sleep with Susanna anyway. He figures he just has to be a little sneakier about it than prior generations did.

But the Count underestimates the strength of Susanna's friendship with his wife: Susanna tells the Countess everything, and they join forces with Figaro to expose the Count's hypocrisy. At her wedding dinner, Susanna slips the Count a note inviting him to a nighttime rendezvous in the garden. But when night falls, Susanna and the Countess trade outfits; unbeknownst to him, the Count ends up wooing his own wife.

Across the garden, Figaro and Susanna, the latter of whom is dressed as the Countess, pretend to be overcome by passion for each other. The Count overhears them—just as they intended— and believes that Figaro has seduced his wife. Enraged, he yells bloody murder; the whole population of the estate comes running. But just as the Count prepares to punish his wife's wrongdoing, his actual wife steps out behind him. He realizes he has been tricked. Everyone stands dumbstruck, waiting to see how he'll react.

It's worth noting how fraught this moment would have looked to a European audience in 1786. A nobleman has been outsmarted and publicly humiliated by his servants and his wife. Surely the Count's father or grandfather would have fired Figaro and Susanna on the spot, or sent them off to prison, or worse.

But the question of how a man was to respond to such a situation was a borderline issue at the time, not so different from the question of how certain companies were supposed to react when their CEOs were accused of sexual harassment in the fall of 2017. We all know what *used* to happen, and we all know what the right thing to do is—so what'll it be?

The whole cast waits, breathless. All eyes are on the Count.

He falls to his knees. "Contessa, perdono," he sings. "Countess, forgive me."

Mozart sets these words to an ascending major sixth, starting from the dominant. It is a gesture of supplication, an aspiring upward from a point of abasement. The Count's first "Contessa, perdono" concludes by relaxing downward from the tonic, G, down a half step to F-sharp.

He pauses. He realizes that he doesn't sound quite sorry enough.

He repeats himself: "perdono, perdono." This time, he stretches his first syllable upward across the interval of a seventh, a slightly wider reach, the sense of entreaty intensified. His last "perdono" finishes with the twinge of a precarious upward appoggiatura from A-sharp to B-natural.

It is a pleading, childlike gesture, one that barely dares to hope. The Count sounds anything but authoritative. His "forgive me" is not a command, as it easily could have been: we might remember that back in Act Two, the Count had grudgingly asked the Countess to excuse him for having gotten needlessly angry, and *that* apology had been much less earnest. This final "perdono," by contrast, is almost a prayer.

The Countess pauses. When she begins to sing, her phrasing is almost identical to the Count's; they are married, after all, and they speak in the same aristocratic cadences. But compare the placement of each of the Count's pitches with each of the Countess's. Whereas the Count starts on the dominant and yearns upward with a plaintive major sixth, the Countess begins on G, the tonic, and reaches beneficently up a perfect fifth.

This gesture bespeaks a profound serenity and poise: she is entirely in control. "Più docile io sono," she sings, "e dico di sì." "I am gentler" (a moment before, when the Count thought he'd caught her in the act, he had loudly refused to forgive her), "and I will say yes."

The first time the Countess sings the words "e dico di sì," she doesn't sound especially convincing. Mozart places the word "sì" on a gentle slide from D down to C, the fifth scale degree down to the fourth, a gesture that could easily be read as a weary sigh of resignation.

She knows it doesn't sound quite right. It's not easy to forgive. Just as the Count had realized, after his first "perdono," that he needed to try again, the Countess realizes that her first "yes" wasn't quite generous enough. She repeats herself—"e dico di sì"—this time coming gently to rest on the tonic. No more hesitations, no drawn-out appoggiaturas, just: *yes*.

The violins sing a descending arpeggiated figure that—how to put it—is a blessing, light breaking through clouds. The whole cast gives voice to their hushed wonder at the reconciliation they have just witnessed. Now, they say, we will all be happy.

So why, the listener might wonder, are they singing the saddest music ever written?

The double gesture of the Count's humility and the Countess's forgiveness causes an overwhelming release of energy: it is as if the cast has been transformed into a huge pipe organ. But what is this energy that's suddenly released? Why is this moment so heartbreaking? What are they really saying?

Look closely at the words they sing. "Ah, tutti contenti / Saremo così." An idiomatic English translation would be "Ah, we will all / Be happy like this." But an awkward, word-for-word translation reveals something else: "Ah, all happy / We will be like this."

We will be like this. The separability of that last line makes all the difference. Mozart sets this text as a slow, inexorable chorale, and he repeats the words again and again until repetition uncovers a meaning that's in direct opposition to the literal one.

Saremo, saremo così. We will be, will be like this.

They know. The whole cast knows that what they've witnessed is a beautiful illusion. They know the Count won't change, and neither will the Countess, and nor will any of them. Life will stay complicated. They'll still marry one person and fall in love with another; they'll still get jealous, and misunderstand one another, and hurt one another without meaning to. And maybe, once or twice in a lifetime, they'll be granted a moment of utter clarity. A sense that it's all beautiful, even if it's not beautiful *for them.* An aerial view of their own souls. For whatever that's worth.

What could be left to say or do?

Once this heart-scouring chorale has floated home to G major, the strings slowly trace a descending line that gradually outlines a dominant seventh chord: G–E–C-sharp–A.

I can't describe this passage any other way than to say that, in the afterglow of the chorale, it feels like someone is choked up, and when the strings descend from G down to a fleeting E minor, a tear finally breaks free and runs down their cheek. (The Count and Countess usually embrace at this point.) But this naked emotion lasts only an instant. That C-sharp, containing as it does the possibility of modulation out of G major into D major, has a gleam in its eye, a welcome hint of Mozartean mischief. Together with the high E that the flute plays above it, the C-sharp seems to be asking, "Are we finally ready to have some fun?"

Yes indeed. The music bursts open into a hard-won *allegro assai*. After this exhausting, all-illuminating excavation of the human heart, everyone desperately needs to let off some steam.

This moment is challenging for conductors, and the reason has everything to do with the characters' psychological state. In fast quarter notes, the whole cast sings the words "corriam tutti": "let's all run" (that is, to get drunk and forget themselves as quickly as they can). Beneath them, the strings and bassoons play a light-speed line of running eighth notes in D major. It is very nearly a recapitulation of the opera's famous overture.

The singers inevitably rush here. It's a law of gravity. In no performance *ever* have the singers not felt inclined to push forward at this moment. After all, their part is much easier than the orchestra's, and both the music and the words ("let's run let's run let's run!") encourage them in that direction. The poor orchestra, meanwhile, is down in the pit breaking a sweat just trying to stay together. Even on some rather well-known studio recordings of the opera, singers and orchestra come egregiously unstuck here.

You know what? I think the singers are right. These characters are trying to outrun reality itself. Damn right that they should speed up. It's the conductor's job, and the orchestra's, to keep up with them. The end of *Figaro* should go up in smoke. Having examined the heart's every crevice, having exposed every weakness, every selfish or shameful desire, and *still* insisting that love conquers all, there's nothing left to do but light the fireworks.

Works Referenced

PREFACE

Ulrich, Thomas. "Lucifer and Morality in Stockhausen's Opera Cycle *Licht*." *Perspectives of New Music*, vol. 50, no. 1–2, 2012. https://www.jstor.org/stable /10.7757/persnewmusi.50.1-2.0313.

1. A FIELD GUIDE TO THE IMPOSSIBLE

Adams, John, and Peter Sellars. *Doctor Atomic* (Vocal Score). New York: Boosey & Hawkes / Hendon Music, 2005 (pp. 227–28).

Auden, W. H. *The Complete Works of W. H. Auden, Prose: 1963–1968*. Edited by Edward Mendelson. Princeton, NJ: Princeton University Press, 2015 (p. 386).

von Rhein, John. "Horne of Plenty." *Chicago Tribune*, January 26, 1992. https:// www.chicagotribune.com/news/ct-xpm-1992-01-26-9201080314-story.html.

Wakin, Daniel J., and Michael Cooper. "Jessye Norman, Regal American Soprano, Is Dead at 74." *New York Times*, September 30, 2019. https://www .nytimes.com/2019/09/30/obituaries/jessye-norman-dead.html.

2. PRIMAL LOSS

Adlington, Robert. *The Music of Harrison Birtwistle*. New York: Cambridge University Press, 2000 (pp. 19–20).

Apollodorus. *The Library of Greek Mythology*. Translated by Robin Hard. New York: Oxford University Press, 1997.

Berlin, Isaiah. *The Hedgehog and the Fox: An Essay on Tolstoy's View of History*. 2nd ed. Princeton, NJ: Princeton University Press, 2013 (p. 1).

Birtwistle, Harrison, and Fiona Maddocks. *Harrison Birtwistle: Wild Tracks—A Conversation Diary with Fiona Maddocks*. London: Faber & Faber, 2014 (p. 46).

Birtwistle, Harrison, and Peter Zinovieff. *The Mask of Orpheus*. London: Universal Edition, 1986.

Charpentier, Marc-Antoine. *La descente d'Orphée aux enfers*. Edited by John S. Powell. http://www.personal.utulsa.edu/~john-powell/LaDescenteDorphee AuxEnfers/ (p. 64).

Critchley, Simon. *Things Merely Are: Philosophy in the Poetry of Wallace Stevens*. New York: Routledge, 2005 (p. 32).

Cross, Jonathan. *Harrison Birtwistle: The Mask of Orpheus*. New York: Routledge, 2009 (pp. 59, 115, 149, 152, 153).

"French Music Notes." *New York Times*, February 16, 1930. https://www
.nytimes.com/1930/02/16/archives/french-music-notes.html.

Gardiner, John Eliot. "John Eliot Gardiner: Britten to Beirut in the Back of a
Taxi—My Night with Bernstein." *Guardian*, August 4, 2019. https://www
.theguardian.com/music/2019/aug/04/john-eliot-gardiner-west-side-story
-leonard-bernstein.

Gardner, Thomas. "An Interview with Jorie Graham." In *Regions of Unlikeness:
Explaining Contemporary Poetry*, 214–37. Lincoln: University of Nebraska
Press, 1999. Interview reprinted on Jorie Graham's website (https://www
.joriegraham.com/gardner_interview_1999).

Hewett, Ivan. "Harrison Birtwistle: 'I Know How Stravinsky Felt.'" *Telegraph*,
June 4, 2011. https://www.telegraph.co.uk/culture/music/classicalmusic
/8552911/Harrison-Birtwistle-I-know-how-Stravinsky-felt.html.

Hill, John Walter. "Florence: Musical Spectacle and Drama, 1570–1650." In *The
Early Baroque Era: From the Late 16th Century to the 1660s*, edited by Curtis
Price, 121–45. Englewood Cliffs, NJ: Prentice Hall, 1994 (p. 128).

Hitchcock, H. Wiley. *Marc-Antoine Charpentier*. New York: Oxford University
Press, 1990 (p. 5).

Molleson, Kate. "An Opera, a Dram, and a Quip with Sir Harrison Birtwistle." *Herald* (Glasgow), January 10, 2017. https://www.heraldscotland
.com/life_style/arts_ents/15014398.opera-dram-quip-sir-harrison-birt
wistle/.

Muhly, Nico. "Think Fast." The website of Nico Muhly, July 1, 2014. https://
nicomuhly.com/news/2014/think-fast/.

Robinson, Tom. "A Knight Errant at the Ivors." *Guardian*, May 26, 2006. https://
www.theguardian.com/commentisfree/2006/may/26/post116.

"Six of the Best: BBC Proms World Premieres." *BBC Music Magazine*, July 12,
2018. https://www.classical-music.com/features/articles/six-best-bbc-proms
-world-premieres/.

3. THE FIREWOOD AND THE FIRE

Auden, W. H. *Collected Poems*. Edited by Edward Mendelson. New York: Modern
Library (Random House), 2007 (pp. 157–58).

Auden, W. H. *The Complete Works of W. H. Auden: Prose, Vol. 3: 1949–1955*. Edited by Edward Mendelson. London: Faber & Faber, 2008 ("direct experience
of his own body" and "tensions and rhythms," p. 297; "self-determined history"
and "A succession . . . act of choice," p. 250; "an imitation of human wilfulness"
and "monomaniac[s]," p. 252; "cannot present . . . active *and* passive," "too interesting . . . translatable into music," and "maniacal busybody," p. 252; "Every
high C accurately struck . . . fate or chance," p. 302; "No good opera plot . . .

when they are feeling sensible," "not one sensible ... remark," and "very difficult
... Wagner managed it," p. 253; "a situation ... are not in" and "the pleasure ...
frivolous," p. 298; "The verses ... letter to the composer," "moment of glory,"
"the moment ... certain melody," "they must efface ... what happens to them,"
"sung syllables," and "in song ... syllables are not," p. 301).

Auden, W. H. *The Complete Works of W. H. Auden: Prose, Vol. 6: 1969–1973*. Edited by Edward Mendelson. Princeton, NJ: Princeton University Press, 2015 ("dramatically essential ... to the spoken" and "they do," p. 663).

Auden, W. H. *The Dyer's Hand and Other Essays*. New York: Vintage International, 1989 (p. 471).

Auden, W. H., and Chester Kallman. *The Complete Works of W. H. Auden: Libretti and Other Dramatic Writings: 1939–1973*. Edited by Edward Mendelson. Princeton, NJ: Princeton University Press, 1998 ("it is the librettist's job to satisfy the composer ..." and "I need hardly say ... greatest honor of my life," p. 579; "The hero, of course, will represent Pride ..." and "He ought to be anointed with a chamber pot ... Piss is the only proper chrism," p. 579; "perverse sexuality," p. xxiii; "point out little flaws ... in their place," p. 626; "a man to whom the anticipation ... disappointing" and "elated ... remembrance of the recent past," p. 617; "but then ... *very* good girl," p. 628; "Two librettists ... complete personality," p. 575; "the censor-critic ... this corporate personality," p. xxi; "the day that Baba ... stand up straight," p. 626; "is exclusively acted *upon*," p. 627; "[Anne] has become ... even rather like her," p. 627; "Presumably what he is supposed ... renounce Love," p. 623).

Boulez, Pierre, and John Cage. *The Boulez–Cage Correspondence*. Edited by Jean-Jacques Nattiez. Translated by Robert Samuels. New York: Cambridge University Press, 1993 (p. 118).

Darvas, János. "5-Igor e Cocteau." *Igor Stravinsky: Composer*, accessed Jan. 22, 2021. https://www.youtube.com/watch?v=ARLnH0BOwSY&list=PL3DC6D7 CC42C1AC68&index=5.

Downes, Olin. "'Rake's Progress' Has U.S. Premiere." *New York Times*, February 15, 1953. https://www.nytimes.com/1953/02/15/archives/-rakes-progress -has-u-s-premiere-stravinsky-opera-with-audenkallman.html.

Griffiths, Paul. *Igor Stravinsky: The Rake's Progress*. New York: Cambridge University Press, 1982 ("treasured every word ... very few of them," p. 19; "*not* a Musical Drama ... definitely separated numbers," p. 10; "a Choreographic Divertissement ... ," p. 10; "between the two acts, there should be a choric parabasis," p. 12).

Mendelson, Edward. *Later Auden*. New York: Farrar, Straus and Giroux, 1999 ("Vision of Eros," p. 31).

Taubman, Howard. "'Rake's Progress' Creates Furor." *New York Times*, September 23, 1951. https://www.nytimes.com/1951/09/23/archives/rakes-progress -creates-furor-new-opera-by-stravinsky-has-its.html.

4. VERDI'S SHAKESPEARE OPERAS

Boito, Arrigo, and Giuseppe Verdi. *The Verdi-Boito Correspondence*. Edited by Marcello Conati and Mario Medici. Translated by William Weaver. Chicago: University of Chicago Press, 1994 (pp. xxvi–xxviii, xxxiii, lvi).

Boito, Arrigo, and Giuseppe Verdi. *Verdi's* Falstaff *in Letters and Contemporary Reviews*. Edited and translated by Hans Busch. Bloomington: Indiana University Press, 1997 (pp. 3–7).

Budden, Julian. *The Operas of Verdi, Vol. 1: From* Oberto *to* Rigoletto. 2nd ed. New York: Oxford University Press, 1992 (p. 270).

Conati, Marcello, ed. *Encounters with Verdi*. Translated by Richard Stokes. Ithaca, NY: Cornell University Press, 1984 (p. 201).

Noseda, Gianandrea, and Richard Wigmore. "Verdi's *Macbeth*: A Complete Guide." *Gramophone*, October 4, 2016. https://www.gramophone.co.uk /features/article/verdi-s-macbeth-a-complete-guide.

Stoppard, Tom. *Arcadia*. New York: Faber and Faber, 2008 (p. 52).

5. WALT WHITMAN'S IMPOSSIBLE OPTIMISM

Dizikes, John. *Opera in America: A Cultural History*. New Haven, CT: Yale University Press, 1993 (pp. 184, 186).

James, William. *The Varieties of Religious Experience*. New York: Simon & Schuster, 2004 (pp. 64–66).

Whitman, Walt. *Leaves of Grass: First and "Death-bed" Editions*. New York: Barnes & Noble Classics, 2004 (pp. 56–57, 111–12, 115, 560–69).

Whitman, Walt. *Specimen Days & Collect*. New York: Dover Publications, 1995 (pp. 24, 26, 37, 52, 59, 63, 69–70, 74, 78, 80).

Whitman, Walt, to Lewis K. Brown, 8–9 November 1863. The Walt Whitman Archive. https://whitman-prod.unl.edu/biography/correspondence/tei/loc .00802.html#loc.00802_n2.

6. INNER ROOMS: TWO RECENT IMPOSSIBILITIES

Adès, Thomas. *The Exterminating Angel*. Metropolitan Opera. Performed November 18, 2017. Warner Classics, 2019. DVD.

Adès, Thomas. *The Tempest*. Metropolitan Opera. Performed November 10, 2012. Deutsche Grammophon, 2013. DVD.

Adès, Thomas, and Tom Service. *Thomas Adès: Full of Noises: Conversations with Tom Service*. New York: Farrar, Straus and Giroux, 2012 (pp. 3, 12–13, 66–67, 140).

Arseni, Christian. "Interview with Thomas Adès and Tom Cairns About the World Premiere of *The Exterminating Angel*." *Seen and Heard International*, July 28, 2016. https://seenandheard-international.com/2016/07/new-interview-with -thomas-ades-and-tom-cairns-about-the-operas-world-premiere/.

Auden, W. H. *The Complete Works of W. H. Auden: Prose, Vol. 2: 1939–1948.* Edited by Edward Mendelson. Princeton, NJ: Princeton University Press, 2002 (p. 428).

Borges, Jorge Luis. *Collected Fictions.* Translated by Andrew Hurley. New York: Penguin Classics, 1998 (pp. 72–73).

Can Xue. *The Embroidered Shoes.* Translated by Ronald R. Janssen and Jian Zhang. New York: Henry Holt, 1997.

Catton, Pia. "Thomas Adès's Death Comes, with a Whistle." *Wall Street Journal*, March 10, 2015. https://www.wsj.com/articles/thomas-adess-death -comes-with-a-whistle-1426031127.

Czernowin, Chaya. *Heart Chamber* (libretto). Program book printed by the Deutsche Oper Berlin, 2019.

Glass, Philip. *Words Without Music.* New York: Liveright, 2015 (p. 66).

Iannotta, Clara. "The Smallest Island of Strangeness: An Interview with Chaya Czernowin." *VAN Magazine*, March 30, 2017. https://van-us.atavist.com /chaya-czernowin.

Mattingly, Dylan. *Stranger Love: An Opera in Three Acts.* https://www.stranger .love.

Mendelson, Edward. *Later Auden.* New York: Farrar, Straus and Giroux, 1999 (p. 271).

Veselý, Ondrej. "Chaya Czernowin with Ondrej Veselý." *Brooklyn Rail*, March 2020. https://brooklynrail.org/2020/03/music/Chaya-Czernowin-with -Ondrej-Vesel.

Young, Katherine. "Anthony Braxton's *Trillium* Opera Complex." *Sound American.* http://archive.soundamerican.org/sa_archive/sa16/sa16-the-trillium -operas.html.

7. FINDING *EURYDICE*

Eliot, T. S. *The Complete Poems and Plays, 1909–1950.* New York: Harcourt Brace, 1980 (p. 48).

Hajdu, David. "Music Lessons." *New York Times*, October 24, 2008. https:// www.nytimes.com/2008/10/26/books/review/Hajdu-t.html.

Muhly, Nico. "Thoughts on Being Well." The website of Nico Muhly, May 27, 2015. http://nicomuhly.com/news/2015/thoughts-on-being-well/.

Rilke, Rainer Maria. *The Selected Poetry of Rainer Maria Rilke.* Edited and translated by Stephen Mitchell. New York: Vintage Books, 1989 (pp. 51–53).

Ruhl, Sarah. *The Clean House and Other Plays.* New York: Theatre Communications Group, 2006 (pp. 367, 402–403).

Ruhl, Sarah. *100 Essays I Don't Have Time to Write: On Umbrellas and Sword Fights, Parades and Dogs, Fire Alarms, Children, and Theater.* New York: Farrar, Straus and Giroux, 2014 (pp. 16, 27–28, 46, 66).

8. MUSIC AS FORGIVENESS

Adorno, Theodor W. *Quasi una Fantasia: Essays on Modern Music*. Translated by Rodney Livingstone. New York: Verso, 1998 (p. 60).

Barnett, Laura. "Portrait of the Artist: Mitsuko Uchida, Pianist." *Guardian*, March 13, 2012. https://www.theguardian.com/culture/2012/mar/13/mitsuko-uchida-pianist.

Harris, Robert. *What to Listen for in Mozart*. New York: Simon & Schuster, 2002 (p. 141).

Recommended Recordings

Since I imagine some readers will find it helpful to listen along as they read, I'd like to share my favorite recordings of the operas that are discussed in the greatest detail.

Only one recording is available of certain recent works; this is true of Adès's *The Exterminating Angel*, Birtwistle's *The Mask of Orpheus*, and Czernowin's *Heart Chamber*. My operas *Crossing* and *Eurydice* have not yet been recorded, though recordings of both should become available in the next couple of years.

When it comes to older works that have been recorded dozens or scores of times, I've picked two contrasting recordings. For all three of Verdi's Shakespeare operas, I've picked one studio recording that has relatively clear sound quality, followed by one especially exciting (but inevitably scratchier-sounding) live recording.

2. PRIMAL LOSS

Claudio Monteverdi, *L'Orfeo*

Jordi Savall (conductor); Furio Zanasi, Sara Mingardo, Montserrat Figueras et al.; Le Concert des Nations; La Capella Reial de Catalunya. Alia Vox, 2002, compact disc.

Nikolaus Harnoncourt (conductor); Lajos Kozma, Cathy Berberian, Rotraud Hansmann et al.; Concentus Musicus Wien; Capella Antiqua München. Warner Classics International, 1969, compact disc.

Marc-Antoine Charpentier, *La descente d'Orphée aux enfers*

Sébastien Daucé (conductor); Robert Getchell et al.; Ensemble Correspondances. Harmonia Mundi, 2017, compact disc.

Harrison Birtwistle, *The Mask of Orpheus*

Andrew Davis (conductor); Jon Garrison, Alan Opie, Juliet Booth, Marie Angel et al.; BBC Symphony Orchestra; BBC Singers. NMC Recordings, 1997, compact disc.

3. THE FIREWOOD AND THE FIRE

Igor Stravinsky, *The Rake's Progress*

John Eliot Gardiner (conductor); Ian Bostridge, Deborah York, Bryn Terfel, Anne Sofie von Otter et al.; London Symphony Orchestra; Monteverdi Choir. Deutsche Grammophon, 1999, compact disc.

4. VERDI'S SHAKESPEARE OPERAS

Giuseppe Verdi, *Macbeth*

Thomas Schippers (conductor); Birgit Nilsson, Giuseppe Taddei, Bruno Prevedi et al.; Orchestra and Chorus of the Accademia di Santa Cecilia, Rome. Polygram Records, 1964, compact disc.

Victor de Sabata (conductor); Maria Callas, Enzo Mascherini, Italo Tajo et al.; Orchestra and Chorus of Teatro alla Scala, Milan. EMI Classics, 1952, compact disc.

Giuseppe Verdi, *Otello*

Tullio Serafin (conductor); Jon Vickers, Leonie Rysanek, Tito Gobbi et al.; Rome Opera Orchestra and Chorus. RCA Victor Living Stereo, 1960, compact disc.

Carlos Kleiber (conductor); Plácido Domingo, Mirella Freni, Piero Cappuccilli et al.; Orchestra and Chorus of Teatro alla Scala, Milan. Music & Arts Program, 1976, compact disc.

Giuseppe Verdi, *Falstaff*

Herbert von Karajan (conductor); Tito Gobbi, Elisabeth Schwarz-kopf, Anna Moffo, Fedora Barbieri et al.; Philharmonia Orchestra and Chorus. Warner Classics, 1956, compact disc.

Arturo Toscanini (conductor); Mariano Stabile, Mita Vasari, Dino Borgioli et al.; Vienna Philharmonic Orchestra; Chorus of the Vienna State Opera. Mangora Classical, 1937, compact disc.

6. INNER ROOMS: TWO RECENT IMPOSSIBILITIES

Thomas Adès, *The Exterminating Angel*

Thomas Adès (conductor); Tom Cairns (director); Amanda Echa-laz, Audrey Luna, Alice Coote, Iestyn Davies, Rod Gilfry et al.; Metropolitan Opera Orchestra and Chorus. Warner Classics, 2019, DVD.

Chaya Czernowin, *Heart Chamber*

Johannes Kalitzke (conductor); Claus Guth (director); Patrizia Ciofi, Dietrich Henschel, Noa Frenkel, Terry Wey; Ensemble Nikel; SWR Experimentalstudio; Orchestra of the Deutsche Oper Berlin. Naxos, 2021, DVD.

8. MUSIC AS FORGIVENESS

W. A. Mozart, *Le nozze di Figaro*

Georg Solti (conductor); Kiri Te Kanawa, Lucia Popp, Frederica von Stade, Samuel Ramey, Thomas Allen et al.; London Philharmonic Orchestra. London/Decca, 1982, compact disc.

John Eliot Gardiner (conductor); Bryn Terfel, Rod Gilfry, Alison Hagley, Hillevi Martinpelto et al.; English Baroque Soloists; Monteverdi Choir. Archiv Produktion, 1994, compact disc.

Acknowledgments

I want to thank my friends and family, especially Victoria Crutch-field, Alec Treuhaft, Zack Winokur, Patricia O'Connor, and my parents, Carol and Don Aucoin (both of whom are extraordinarily perceptive editors), for reading drafts of this book's manuscript along the way, and for sharing ideas that made it richer and stronger. I'm also grateful to Lucy Caplan, Stephen Stubbs, Will Crutchfield, Timothy Redmond, John S. Powell, Tim Carter, Reuben Stern, Bob Holland, Damien Kennedy, and Craig Rutenberg for clarifying specific points, and to Sarah Ruhl for generously agreeing to let our collaboration spill into these pages.

Jonathan Galassi is the wisest and most patient of editors, and I feel inexpressibly lucky that he lavished such care on this book. I'm grateful to my agent, Jeff Posternak, for his efforts on behalf of this project since its inception.

I can't imagine having undertaken this project without the support of my husband, Clay, who was there every step of the way and who contributed to it in ways he might not even know.

Some sections of the chapter on Verdi's Shakespeare operas were previously published in *The New York Review of Books* and *The Yale Review*. Part of the chapter "Inner Rooms: Two Recent

Impossibilities" was also published in *The New York Review of Books*.

Early versions of the chapter "Walt Whitman's Impossible Optimism" were originally delivered as lectures at Harvard University and Stony Brook University. I tried out many of the ideas in "The Firewood and the Fire: Words, Music, and Stravinsky's *The Rake's Progress*" in a conversation with the pianist Kirill Gerstein, broadcast as part of his lecture series "Kirill Gerstein Invites," hosted by Berlin's Hochschule für Musik Hanns Eisler.

I am also grateful to the MacArthur Foundation.

Permissions Acknowledgments